Living Aboard Your RV

Second Edition

A Guide to the Fulltime Life on Wheels

Janet Groene and Gordon Groene

Ragged Mountain Press
Camden, Maine

Published by Ragged Mountain Press, a division of McGraw-Hill, Inc.

1 0   9   8

Library of Congress Cataloging-in-Publication Data
Groene, Janet.
  Living aboard your RV : a guide to the fulltime life on wheels /
Janet Groene and Gordon Groene.
     p. cm.
  Includes index.
ISBN 0-87742-340-7
  1. Recreational vehicle living. I. Groene, Gordon. II. Title.
TX1110.G76 1993
643'.2--dc20   92-46578

Questions regarding the content of this book should be
addressed to:
Ragged Mountain Press
P.O. Box 220
Camden, ME 04843

Questions regarding the ordering of this book should be
addressed to:
McGraw-Hill, Inc.
Customer Service Department
P.O. Box 547
Blacklick, OH 43004
Retail customers: 1-800-822-8158
Bookstores: 1-800-722-4726

A portion of the profits from the sale of each Ragged Mountain
Press book is donated to an environmental cause.

Living Aboard Your RV is printed on 60-pound Renew Opaque
Vellum, an acid-free paper that contains 50 percent recycled
waste paper (preconsumer) and 10 percent postconsumer
waste paper.

Text design by Patrice M. Rossi.
Edited by Jim Babb, Dorathy Chocensky, and Pamela Benner.
Production by Molly Mulhern.
Printed by Fairfield Graphics, Fairfield, PA.

CONTENTS

••••

PREFACE

••••

The RV revolution is truly one of the wonders of our time. It grew out of the dream of traveling without leaving "home" and into the reality of today's fine-quality, fully equipped, and eminently roadable recreational vehicles.

People choose to travel in many ways and to live in many kinds of domiciles. However, it has always been difficult to combine nonstop travel with a real home. In the past, people who wanted to do both could hitch a prairie schooner to a team and shout, "Westward, ho!" For the wealthy there were private rail cars complete with kitchen and bath. No longer practical today, they have been replaced by the modern RV.

To those people who decry RVs as a desecration of the "camping" spirit, we suggest that RV fulltiming is not a replacement for tenting or backpacking. It is a replacement for house and garage, garden and grass, tool shed and cellar. The RV is a home as well as a base from which all other pursuits, careers, and activities—including primitive camping—can proceed.

As you consider fulltiming as a way of life, we wish you safe miles, a soft bunk, and a chance to brighten the many corners you'll encounter along the way.

Janet Groene
Gordon Groene

CHAPTER ONE

Song of the Open Road

We woke up to a thin, cold dawn and the pounding of a patrolman's fist on our camper door.

"Move along," he said, not unkindly. "I've let you sleep since two o'clock this morning, but it's six now and time you hit the road."

No, we weren't homeless alcoholics, sleeping off a cheap drunk under a tent of yesterday's newspapers. We were young, able, self-sufficient adventurers who had stopped late last night in a highway rest plaza, and we had overslept the two-hour limit.

Our visit from that policeman was just another in a long series of reminders that, in shedding our old style of life and adopting a new role as fulltime wanderers, we had lost a lifelong mantle of respectability. Our new life baffled some people, amused others, and enraged more than a few.

What had we gotten ourselves into?

What It's Got; What It's Not

Close your eyes and picture the free, roving life on wheels. Immediately you imagine a cozy, self-contained camper beside a rushing, trout-packed brook. You have no deadlines, no lawn to mow, no leaves to rake, no committees, no neighbors to be stuck with year after year. You fantasize about a life you perceive to have no ties, no traps, no taxes. The fulltime RV life is all you hope for and much, much more. But it's also a break with treasured possessions, with status, with symbols, with your Place In Life.

Can you handle it?

The RV itself is a red flag in the faces of politicians in some cities, where special laws have been passed against RVs simply because they *are* RVs. Fort Lauderdale won't let you park an RV at the beach, even if it fits in a car-size parking place. Other communities have laws prohibiting RVs from staying within the city limits overnight, and a few don't want you in town *anytime*.

We have on occasion been hassled, threatened, vandalized, and humiliated.

It isn't our aim to talk you out of following our mud flaps, but we do want to prick your dream balloon enough to bring you back to treetop level. In knowing there will be bitter with the better, you'll be better armed to make necessary adjustments in yourself, in your dealings with society, and in your relationships with family and spouse.

In the Beginning

For us, it all began back in Danville, Illinois, where Gordon was a professional pilot for a large corporation. He liked the company and the job, and he valued his professional relationship with his co-workers. We both liked friendly little Danville, which was large enough to have good shopping and a nice mix of people, yet small enough that I could do most of my shopping by bicycle. We were only ten minutes from the airport, church, or a night on the town, and an hour from big-city theater and concerts.

Still, we began to toy with the idea of early retirement. One of our friends had died of a heart attack at forty-one, another of leukemia at thirty-eight. What if time ran out before the traditional retirement age of sixty-five?

The Ties That Bind

At this point, you're probably wondering how we could even think of dropping off the edge of the world with all the family obligations one usually has at that stage in life. First it's the children, then grandchildren, then the care of your elderly parents—an unending treadmill of obligations. However, people differ in how they handle such "obligations."

We met some young parents who became fulltime travelers not *despite* their children but *because* of their children—either because they wanted to spend precious years traveling and learning together while the kids were young, or because they were determined to get their children out of an environment they perceived as too materialistic, too violent, or otherwise not up to the standards they wanted for their families.

Mail-order schooling, once just an oddball way of educating kids whose parents were missionaries or who traveled with the circus, is being used today by thousands of parents at home and on the go. Most feel that they can provide a better education than the schools can, citing such public-school problems as weapons, drugs, and overcrowded classrooms. With "home" schooling now available, affordable, and common, children can travel full time and still get a first-class education.

One of the largest and most popular home-school systems for kindergarten through eighth grade is the Calvert School, 105 Tuscany Rd., Baltimore, Maryland 21210; phone (301) 243-6030, FAX (301) 366-0674. We've met many children who have had some or all of their early schooling through Calvert, and there wasn't a failure in the bunch.

Home-study courses for kindergarten through grade 12 as well as teacher training and parent sensitivity courses are available from Oak Meadow, Box 712, Blacksburg, Virginia 24063. Additional learning resources are available from Learning at Home, Box 270, Honaunau, Hawaii 96726 and Holt Associates, 2269 Massachusetts Ave., Cambridge, Massachusetts 02140. Mail-order high school is available through the American School, 850 E. 58th St., Chicago, Illinois 60637.

You might also check with your school district, which may offer schooling by mail at least for a short term. Try your church, too. Some denominations, such as the Seventh Day Adventists, provide mail-order schooling. Others, including the Lutheran Church–Missouri Synod, offer Sunday school by mail.

It's true that many people prefer to stay put until their children are grown. Others feel they must stay with elderly parents, a shut-in sibling, or a family business or farm. One of today's most common dilemmas is that of the "sandwich" generation, in which middle-aged people are saddled with the care of their aged parents just when their own children get divorced and move back home with *their* children.

We've heard just about all the reasons why you can't go. They range from very good ones to mere cop-outs. The truth is that you probably can take to the road if you and your spouse or companion(s) or family make the effort to work it out. And if you think you can't go because you don't *have* a spouse or family to travel with, think again. Legions of singles, both men and women—widowed, divorced, never married, available, and unavailable—are out there fulltiming and having the time of their lives.

Hundreds of case histories show that you *can* do it—alone or together, as a couple or with a group—as long as everyone is on the same wavelength.

"But," you say, "I'm handicapped." Fulltiming is not only possible for you, it's the *best* choice for many types of disabilities. For one thing, it is the only lifestyle that allows the physically challenged of any age to harvest their share of camping, fishing, and sightseeing in our state and national parks.

Financial problems? Fulltiming can cost pearls or peanuts, and we'll tell you how.

Career not portable? We've met fulltimers in a long list of professions, from publishing to plant care, catering to wood carving.

For the next few hundred pages, we'll focus on the who, why, when, where, and how of this very possible dream.

What Kind of Fulltiming Life for You?

RV living is not one lifestyle, but many. Much of your happiness and success in fulltiming depends on finding just the right niche for yourself. For many people, the camping itself is the whole nine yards.

They delight in camping clubs, camp meetings, RV shows, camping rallies, group caravans, and campground get-togethers.

At the opposite end of the spectrum are those who camp to get away from it all. They avoid destination campgrounds and memberships because they don't want to clump with other campers. They may be good neighbors, always willing to pitch in on a project or lend a hand with a repair problem, but they don't want to group up—either because they prefer to keep to themselves entirely, or because they have a very full life quite separate from the camping scene.

Fulltimers come from all income and age brackets. Some are financially independent retirees; some work at professions that require them to live several months in each spot. Others live in an RV because it provides a movable home while they pursue some special interest, such as sports car racing, fishing tournaments, surfing, lecturing, archaeology, working carnivals or rodeos, or creating and selling artwork or crafts.

Some fulltimers move on relentlessly, never content to stay in one spot for long and always excited about what they'll find around the next bend. Some camp in one campground each summer, and spend every winter in another. Still others buy a campsite and rarely leave it.

For ourselves, the motorhome makes a comfortable home and office when we're on assignment as a travel-writer team, but we've never attended an RV rally or participated in an RV caravan.

For some of us, the RV is merely the vehicle (pardon the pun) that serves a particular lifestyle. To you, the RV alone may provide the life you're seeking. We're all part of the camping family, so *vive le difference*!

Exploding Some Myths

Before you get too far into your planning, we may as well hit you with some hard realities, the kinds of things you don't read about in the ads.

Myth: By living in an RV full time, you can live on almost nothing.

Reality: Fuel, oil, tires, insurance, and turnpike fees cost more all the time. Campgrounds are rarely free; it's not uncommon now to pay thirty-five dollars per night. You can't outrun the insatiable tax collector either. You'll pay taxes on almost everything you use or buy on the go: sales taxes when you buy the vehicle, yearly license fees, property taxes (because they are reflected in campground rates), and federal income taxes.

Myth: Wanderers have no responsibilities, no cares, no problems.

Reality: You'll have most of the same problems you've always had—staying on a diet, cooking and cleaning, making ends meet, doing the Christmas shopping, touching up the gray, grooming the poodle—plus many new ones, such as finding acceptable campsites, staying alive on the highway, and getting along with your mate in less space than a German shepherd is allotted at the dog pound. You'll be living in a very complex shebang that includes living quarters, sewer, waterworks, engine, and chassis, all of which you'll have to manage yourself.

Myth: It'll be like a second honeymoon, just the two of you on an endless highway of travel delights.

Reality: After a couple of weeks in close quarters, you may start thinking about divorce, if not murder.

Myth: No more winter.

Reality: It is possible to follow the seasons, but crowds and high prices do so too. On the other hand, if you stay in a cold climate in winter, heating costs will be high and comforts elusive. Each of us must find his or her own affordable, practical, geographic comfort zone.

Myth: Wide-open spaces.

Reality: Only in RV ads is one camper given exclusive rights to the entire Grand Canyon. In most campgrounds you'll be closer to your neighbors than you ever were back home.

Myth: Personal problems will melt away once you're on the road.

Reality: Troubles are an unseen trailer that follows all of us everywhere. If you're in a bad marriage, are in debt over your head, or are addicted to harmful substances or habits, fulltiming won't change you. Look at the RV life as an avenue to new adventures and successes, not as an escape. It isn't one.

We thrived on fulltime travel for ten happy years. If there is a secret to our success, it's that we not only expected difficulties, we welcomed new challenges. In exchange for the hardships of fulltime travel we formed priceless friendships with folks in many states and nations, and we were freed from former careers to develop an entirely new life in travel writing. Best of all, all those miles of roaming allowed us to live in many parts of the country and take a leisurely assessment of them before deciding where to put down roots.

To change lifestyles, no matter how flexible we consider ourselves, is a tough assignment. The rest of this book is our effort to help you through the roadblocks, breakdowns, detours, and potholes ahead.

2

Get Ready

Exactly how can you begin preparing, right now, for a fulltiming life that may be months or even years away? First, get your priorities straight. Sit down with your dependents and decide what really matters to you. Then take the following approach to making your dream a reality.

Test the Waters

If your goal really is to live aboard your RV, stop fantasizing and try the real thing. Rent or borrow a suitable rig and take off for as long as possible. A trial run may sound expensive, but it's a bargain compared to what it will cost to quit your job, sell everything you own, take off in an RV, and then find out you hate the new life and want to recapture the old one. (We met one couple who took off with great zest and fanfare. They flitted across the country visiting all their friends and partying with old army buddies, and then ran out of things to do and people to visit. Somehow, they never came to terms with fulltiming as an ongoing way of life.)

Stay away for at least three weeks—more if possible. During this time you'll encounter some of the realities of the fulltimer's life: rainy days when you're shut in until you could scream, mechanical breakdowns, finding campgrounds, putting up with campground neighbors, using coin laundries, getting mail and keeping in touch with loved ones, trying to cash personal checks in places where you're not known, walking the dog, living in very limited space, and filling your days with meaningful activities. (Believe it or not, some people find it boring not to have a job and a schedule.)

At the end of this time, you'll also have a good idea what expenses you'll encounter over the long term as you slip into this new lifestyle: camp fees, pay phones, fuel costs, changes in food and entertainment costs, and probably some unpleasant surprises such as an unexpected repair or replacement.

Even so, this is only a hint of true fulltiming. During this rehearsal you'll still have a home to retreat to if things get too rough. You'll still have an address, an identity, perhaps a job waiting for you, and lots more elbow room aboard than you'll have when you're carrying everything you own. Still, it's enough of a preview to tell you, before you quit your job and sell the house, if fulltiming is what you expected it would be.

Get Control of Your Health

Among today's biggest killers are obesity and the abuse of drugs, including tobacco and alcohol. These are problems that can be treated. If you get help now, while you're still planning your RV getaway, you'll have time to succeed at a 12-step program or some other treatment.

We often think about a close friend we'll call Harry, who worked for two years toward his fulltiming dream. When it came true, he was going to quit smoking. He was outfitting his RV when he was diagnosed with lung cancer. Six months later, he was dead.

Another major killer and crippler, highway accidents, becomes far less a threat if you use a seat belt for *every* trip, *every* time. As of August 1992, traffic fatalities in Florida were 1,415 compared to 1,530 for the same period in 1991, thanks to increasing compliance with the state's six-year-old seat belt law. Of those who were killed, seventy-five to eighty percent were not wearing seat belts, according to the Florida Highway Patrol.

Similarly, when boating, wear a life vest. Of all boating deaths, ninety percent are caused by drowning; eighty percent of those victims were not wearing flotation gear.

Live for Tomorrow, but Don't Sacrifice Today

From the moment we decided we wanted to change our lifestyle, we began shopping with resale in mind. Although we didn't have to give up a spacious home, good cars, occasional vacations—the good life in general—we weighed every purchase not only for its present value but for its resale potential. We could have afforded a higher mortgage in a swankier section of town, but we chose instead a big, old, five-bedroom house in a stable neighborhood near good schools, knowing it would sell readily to a large family.

Our car was an expensive German make famous for holding its value. Gordon groomed it meticulously, washed off the salt after every winter trip, kept it garaged, and generally treated it royally. It gave us endless hours of fun and good service, and sold for the plum it was.

Our furniture was in solid woods, not veneers, in traditional styles that never lose their popularity. Many pieces were antiques that we refinished ourselves. Our appliances were good brand names. When the time came to sell out, everything brought top dollar.

That money was only part of our nest egg, but we met one family from Vermont who bankrolled an entire two-year trip for themselves and their two small daughters with money they got by renovating an old house and its antique furnishings.

Get Your Financial Picture in Order

It's easier said than done, but *get out of debt*. Start by hiding your credit cards. Don't borrow another cent for anything but a real emergency. Start mopping up all the little obligations: credit cards, time payments, petty loans. Keep your eye on the real goal, which is full-timing, and impulse purchases will lose some of their luster.

Do financial planning for today and for a long line of tomorrows. One couple didn't cut loose from "real life" until they had established trust funds to pay their children's college tuition. Another couple persuaded their elderly parents to sell a home they could no longer maintain properly, and go into a life-care community where they would have companionship and help while their children were on the road.

Such planning usually benefits from professional help. There are all kinds of planners, and the letters that follow their names can provide some clues to their backgrounds: an APFS is an Accredited Personal Financial Specialist (a CPA who has done further study); a CFP is a Certified Financial Planner; a CPA is a Certified Public Accountant (be sure to find one who has additional training in financial planning); and an MFS, or Master of Financial Science, has a master's degree in investment planning. Financial advisors may have other credentials, but often they apply to specialties such as pensions or insurance. And some designations are meaningless letters, indicating only that the person has paid dues to a professional association.

We went to a fee-only financial planner—one who doesn't also sell stocks, insurance, or other financial products—to get unbiased advice. For a list of fee-only planners in your area, write the National Association of Personal Financial Advisors, 1130 Lake Cook Rd. #105, Buffalo Grove, Illinois 60089. Request their brochure, "Financial Planner Interview," which lists all the things you need to know before hiring a planner. NAPFA recommends interviewing at least two individuals from different firms before making a choice.

While you may want to consult an attorney as well as a CFP, especially where taxes or inheritance are concerned, keep in mind that lawyers are usually not qualified to give investment advice. Don't rely on one as your sole financial consultant.

Some planners don't want to bother with people whose net worth is less than $250,000 to $500,000, although none of those we interviewed had any such limits. In fact, none even asked our net worth. CFPs charge $75 to $150 per hour, so this service doesn't come cheap. However, you're buying a strategy that can get you started on the right track for the rest of your life.

Free advice is available too. You can solicit complete work-ups from individuals who sell insurance or precious metals or mutual funds. The result will no doubt be skewed, because investments outside their fields bring these advisors no commissions, but a certain pattern will probably emerge after you've consulted three or four.

If you're in debt over your head, nonprofit credit-repair advisors will work with you. Check with your local volunteer bureau or community service agencies and in the Yellow Pages under Credit and Debt Counseling.

If you're willing to reveal every penny of your assets, expenditures, and debts, to be published for all the world to see, there's one more way to get professional financial planning advice, absolutely free. Some large newspapers and many magazines, including *Money*, do regular features in which they outline a family's financial position and have it analyzed by two or three experts who tell them, and the reading audience, how to reach their goals. If you're not concerned about privacy, volunteer for such treatment.

Don't Burn Your Bridges

We've all dreamed about walking into the boss' office someday and saying, "Take this job and shove it." Unless you're retiring permanently, however, keep in mind that someday you may want to go back to the same company, for a recommendation or a reference if not for a job.

If possible, take a leave of absence. You can always resign later, but you've left the door open in case circumstances change. Keep as many ties as possible. For example, you may be able to keep your group health insurance for a stated period after you leave, or leave your pension plan in place for investment and tax advantages. If your company has a good human resources department, consult it about your options.

Other ways to keep doors open: make your first trip a modest one, so you aren't in Alaska or Baja if you find fulltiming isn't for you. And set milestones at which to reevaluate your plans, so you won't feel you've made an irrevocable break with your past life. For instance, you and your mate might agree to a serious rethinking after, say, two years. Or when you reach a certain age. Or when your savings get down to so many dollars.

Take It Slow

The RV of your dreams may beckon you to the showroom, but don't buy that rig too early unless you can also enjoy it, maintain it, and afford it. Timing is very difficult. If you purchase the RV too early and can't sell your home, double payments could break your back. If your home sells too quickly, you could make too rash a decision on an RV.

Also, most of us want to do a lot of customizing in a new RV, and it's handy to have the home workshop and tools available for most of the work. Lots of things have to dovetail, so don't act in haste.

Don't Let Possessions Run Your Life

Many people have told us they'd love to go fulltiming but can't part with their library, or Hummel collection, or billiard table. Your fulltiming life can't get off the ground until you can jettison all the pounds of impedimenta that clutter your life. When you're living in tight quarters, tempers can flare over whose straw is breaking the camel's back.

Develop Interests and Hobbies

Shifting into the fulltiming life may still be more of a jolt than you think. Travel alone may not be enough to fill your days. At times, you may be weathered in, or holed up for repairs, or simply too much over budget to fill the fuel tank as often as you'd like.

The travel life can lead to countless hobbies: ham radio, gravestone rubbing, postcard collecting, square dancing, photography, letter writing. Hobbies give you purpose and identity, something to do on rainy days, and social focus when you're in areas where you don't know anyone.

Network

Join national camping clubs, retiree groups, professional organizations, and hobby groups. By networking, you can keep current on the job picture in your field, or get the latest information on treatment for your handicap, or find out where the season's best jazz festivals will be held, or what steps to take to further your favorite political cause.

It may be difficult to connect after you take off, so join before you go.

Compute Your Launch Value

When you stand ready on the launch pad of your fulltiming life, what will your net worth be? The closer you are to leaving, the more accurate your figures will be, but here are some tips on adding up your net worth as of today.

Keep in mind that we are talking *net worth*, not monthly income, which is another matter. For example, Social Security is not listed. It may have a value to you, but only month by month, depending on your age and your lifetime earnings. Since it has no lump-sum value for the purposes of a net-worth statement, it doesn't figure in this ledger.

Get out a pad and pencil and start a list. The object is to come up with a figure that tells you what you would have in hand today if you liquidated everything. In the process, you will gain an overview of how independent you are right now.

Ready Cash

In this column, list liquid assets plus other assets that are fairly well assured. These include bank accounts, money market funds, CDs, cash on hand, and monies that you are fairly certain to collect soon (such as a maturing insurance policy or an IRS refund).

Add in any sums you intend to have on hand on your upcoming takeoff date, if it's close at hand, such as a retirement bonus or lump-sum settlement, IRA or Keogh, vested interest in a profit-sharing or other retirement plan, insurance settlement, or maturing bonds or other investment.

Today's Value

In this column, you can list only the value of these items *today*, because they could be worth much more or less tomorrow. Include stocks, mutual funds, trusts, and tangible deposits such as silver bars or gold bullion. Add in the cash value of your life-insurance policy—

not the loan value, but today's cash-in or rollover value.

If you have a business partner, get a professional appraisal of what your share is worth on today's market. Add in the current market value of your car, boat, home (its fair market value, not your equity), and furnishings, and the garage-sale value of items you could liquidate easily.

The total will probably be impressive if yours is a typical household complete with appliances, yard care equipment, shop tools, electronics, sporting goods, and so on. If you don't have an inventory of these items, do one immediately. Even if you don't sell out and go, you'll need it to collect your insurance if your home burns down or is robbed.

Now add in the present worth of valuables including jewelry, Oriental rugs, guns, sterling silver and china, antiques, art, furs, and collectibles of all kinds. Again, if you have no idea of their value, have them appraised and inventoried immediately. You'll need a professional appraisal to sell them at the best price. Or, if you plan to keep them, you'll need an appraisal before insuring them to take with you or to leave behind in storage.

The Debt Ledger

This is the tough part. Just when you thought you were riding high, you start listing your obligations. They include the balance due on your home mortgage, unpaid taxes, the unpaid balance on the cars and RV, the *full balance due* (not the monthly payment) on all credit cards, and the balance due on any other loans.

Don't forget any lump-sum expenditures that are coming up, such as a balloon payment, maturing of an auto lease, annual real estate taxes, college tuition, or insurance premiums.

If you have any debts to your broker, such as a margin account, list them too. If you have debts in partnership with someone else, don't forget them. If, for example, you have co-signed a note with one of your children, or have made bail for someone, you'll have that hanging over you until it is paid off or resolved. No matter how well intentioned you or the other party is, something could go awry.

You're now ready to subtract the little number from the big one to find out if you're ahead of the game, and how far. By looking over the figures, you'll be better equipped to decide whether to sell the house or keep it, to use your available funds to pay off the RV or to keep making payments, or to sell the Oriental rugs and keep the coin collection.

You can start making decisions about what assets to roll over, which to sell now (consider the tax consequences), and which to switch into assets that will contribute more income, more security, or more growth potential.

When you're on the road full time, it will be harder (and a lot less fun; you'll have better things to do) to shift your funds constantly to squeeze another ¼ percent interest out of a CD, or to keep abreast of the stock market. The time to strategize is *now*. And that process begins with knowing just where, on the great fiduciary treadmill of life, you are trotting at this moment.

Keep reassessing your goals, your changes and chances, your pleasures, your future. Keep learning, searching, growing. Go. Do. Enjoy.

CHAPTER THREE

Fulltimer Case Histories

It's always useful to read about how others have handled fulltiming. Here are some case histories of fulltimers who were kind enough to share their stories and secrets with us. Once on the road, you'll hear dozens of absorbing, inspiring stories from others who have paved the way before you. In fact, yarn swapping around the campfire—especially yarns about where you came from and how you got into fulltiming—is one of the best things about life on the go.

RV travelers are among the finest folks anywhere. To become one of them, especially full time, is a privilege and a joy. We hope you'll be lucky enough to run across people like these.

Jerry and Eileen O'Neill

After camping with their five children, the O'Neills knew they liked the informality of that lifestyle. Three years before Jerry was to retire, they began plotting their Great Getaway. Their house on Long Island sold in October 1986; they bought a nearly new thirty-two-foot Winnebago Elandan in November; and by 6 P.M. on December 20, they had hit the road, ready for their January retirement. The last we heard, they were still fulltiming and living the life of Riley.

Costs? Jerry says, "Like most Americans, we live up to every penny we make," so they spend their $28,500 retirement income for all it's worth. Recently turned sixty-two, Jerry has added another $9,600 in Social Security, but Eileen is still only fifty-one, so the couple have some years to go before they are financially secure.

Proceeds from the house paid for the motorhome, finished paying for the five kids' college educations, and were invested in a duplex which is, at this point, a break-even situation. Among their expenses: $1,200 a year to insure their RV and car; life insurance at $275 per year; and $110 monthly on phone bills. They've also built a retirement cottage in the foothills of the Catskills, in anticipation of the time when they must give up fulltiming.

Helme and Tedi Calfee

With their fourteen-month-old daughter, Mettie, the Calfees began fulltiming in the spring of 1992 after two years spent planning, liquidating Helme's business, and consolidating. They went fulltiming not *despite* having a child, but largely *because* of her.

"Day care (for children) doesn't make sense to me," says Helme. "All that effort is put into creating a child, and then during their most formative years they are turned over to someone else to raise. I understand that eighty percent of all learning is done in the first three years of life. If this is correct, then we do not want someone else teaching our child the basics of humanity."

The Calfees bought an older GMC motorhome and set out to see if three people could live in a 200-square-foot domicile. Calfee says that they managed, "by unloading everything that we could not carry with us," to get the payload aboard their rolling home down to about 1,500 pounds, which he finds "a most economical way to live." He says, happily, "Our passion is travel and the unknown."

David and Frankie Guilne

"What made us fulltimers?" says Frankie. "Grass cutting and home maintenance." After David retired, the couple traveled extensively but had to keep coming home to take care of the house and yard. The more they worked at it, the more they hated it. So one day they put the house on the market, and suddenly they were on the road full time.

Frankie couldn't bear to part with a lifetime's belongings, so many of their things were parcelled out to the kids or put in storage. "Our original plan was to fulltime it for a year, then buy another house on the lake or beach," Frankie says. But after one year, they decided to try another year, then another. They've been at it now since 1985.

One of the low points came when David had a heart attack and ended up in an intensive care unit, leaving Frankie to live alone in the RV. "It took me three hours to do a thirty-minute job," she says in describing the first time she had to do the hooking and unhooking. Her stories, though, are heartwarming. The hospital invited her to stay in its own mini RV lot, which had full hookups. Men appeared out of nowhere to help her hook up, and to get the car off the dolly she was towing. "I love them to this day," she says.

The happy ending for the Guinles is that David had bypass surgery, recovered fully, and went back on the road. "We have never looked back," says his wife.

Among their best investments, the couple cite membership in Coast to Coast Resorts (see Chapter 15 for details). They use member campgrounds almost exclusively, except in state or national parks or when they are in areas that have no CTC resorts, so their camping costs average only about fifty dollars monthly. They have a debit card with their broker, and get most of their cash through a nationwide ATM card. Their biggest expense, reports Frankie, is gasoline, because they stay on the go, a week here and a week there. (About twice a year they get "home" to Memphis to see the family, doctors, and dentists.) Their RV gets 7.3 miles per gallon; the little car they tow for sightseeing and errands gets 40 mpg.

Among their biggest problems they list getting quality repairs for the RV and car; finding dentists and doctors on the road; carrying too many clothes and shoes; and using public telephones.

The couple eat out at least four times a week, usually at lunchtime. Frankie likes crockpot cooking and quick recipes. "When I cook in the RV, it's those good Southern dishes we can't get in restaurants: garlic-cheese grits soufflé, beans and cornbread, and gumbo," she says. Mail is forwarded via Federal Express. "It's expensive, but worth it," they say.

"My biggest advice to fulltimers is to make sure the wife can drive (the RV) and do every chore that needs to be done. I know many women who refuse to drive. Take it from one who has been there, it may save your life or your spouse's," says Frankie.

John and Barbara Taylor

Part-time campers, the Taylors began easing into fulltiming in 1978 with a slide-in camper mounted on the frame of a cargo van. One RV led to a larger one. By 1992 they'd been fulltiming for five years and "enjoying every minute" in their thirty-three-foot motorhome, towing a small truck.

As a Certified AKC Licensed Field Trial Judge, John accepts assignments judging beagle field trials all over the country. Discovering that house payments would be little more than what they were paying to store their household goods, they bought a home in the Davis Mountains of Texas. Costs, they report, are $1,800 to $2,000 monthly including both the travel and about five months a year in their house. They, too, consider their Coast to Coast membership one of their best investments.

The Taylors work for part of each year, partly for extra funds and partly to "add spice" to their lives, John says. They advise doing something different from the field you were in before retirement. "There's comfort in knowing you have only to do whatever it is for a few months, and then continue on your way," they report.

They've been lucky with repairs. John is faithful about having the motorhome serviced on schedule, and they try to use factory-authorized repair locations for the RV's components. They're both in good health, and they get their medications by mail through the American Association of Retired Persons (AARP) pharmacy at discount prices. For their few medical emergencies they have used twenty-four-hour walk-in clinics.

Mail hasn't been a problem; they know it will be slow, and they plan accordingly. The Taylors keep track of all their bills so they know at once if one goes astray, and they prepay whenever possible.

The Van Keurens

An ex-fulltimer, Frances Van Keuren rhapsodizes about once again having a telephone, a postal box, a porch, a small yard, and a full-size sink and stove. When fulltiming, the Van Keurens didn't get a cellular telephone because their daughter, who lived in Maine, was not in a cellular corridor. They, too, found that pay phones were a pain. "Use whatever service is available, and pay," Frances advises. She found that it just wasn't worth it to jump through hoops trying to get through to her chosen carrier.

As fulltimers, the Van Keurens' luxury was eating out four or five times a week. For cooking in the RV, Frances favored pastas, hot or in salads, green salads, and whole grains.

Kathleen and Marilyn Janke

This is one of our favorite fulltimer case histories because the Jankes are the only mother–daughter fulltimer team we met. And what a dynamic duo they make!

Marilyn Janke was a Chicago-area tax appraiser for eleven years; her daughter Kathleen, living in her own apartment in another Chicago suburb, was reaching burnout in her high-pressure career in police work. Her five children raised and her house too big, the widowed Marilyn phoned Kathy and suggested, "Why don't we go into business for ourselves?" Kathy's immediate reply: "I'll give notice at work tomorrow."

Marilyn, who was still in her fifties, and Kathy, just turned thirty, began making plans. They wanted to see more of the country before settling down. Marilyn sold her house, Kathy gave up her apartment, both women put their furniture in storage, and they took off in their new twenty-seven-foot Fleetwood Jamboree motorhome.

Kathy is bright and bubbly; Marilyn is the serene, unflappable, practical mother. They left shivery Chicago in January, headed south toward Florida, and followed the coast into Texas, following what Kathy calls "perpetual springtime." For the next seventeen months, they visited every national park in the United States, every province in Canada, and a few areas of Mexico.

How did the family take the news that the two were hitting the road? "My mother thought we were crazy," admits Marilyn. "But the only word for our friends' reaction is sheer joy," remembers Kathy. "They knew it was the chance of a lifetime."

Adjusting to the new lifestyle was easier than either had hoped. Kathy did most of the driving, especially after Marilyn broke a foot in Oregon. Marilyn made a good navigator, planner, detail person.

Kathy, an amateur artist like her father, brought her art equipment and cameras. Both women brought motor scooters. They also packed a sewing machine, an inflatable canoe, a typewriter, and "tons" of reading material.

They loved the RV lifestyle so much, they decided to buy a campground, Little River Village, on the edge of Great Smoky Mountains National Park at Townsend, Tennessee. Working twenty-hour days, seven days a week, they waded in. "I like cleaning," enthuses Kathy, "so I started in on the dust and dirt while Mom learned to run the cash register. The day after we arrived, school was out and the crowds arrived. We've been going gangbusters ever since."

Today, Little River Village is a famous destination, even among non-campers, for mile-high deli sandwiches, salads, juicy broasted chicken, and forty flavors of creamy, homemade fudge. Locals and savvy travelers alike stop here for take-away foods on their way into the park.

In addition to creating their Chicago-style deli, the pair expanded and improved the campground, manage a staff of twenty-five and more, and take winter vacations all over the world.

They both are proud of what they've learned and accomplished. "If something breaks, I have to fix it or pay to have it fixed," Kathy says. "I'm not afraid to take things apart and, sure enough, I'm often able to find the problem and put things back together. There isn't anything I can't do with PVC pipe now, and I'm catching on about all sorts of electrics, mechanics, and carpentry."

"She spends the money and I hang onto it," laughs Marilyn as she describes how well they work together. Kathy works up new ways to make money, does the hiring and firing, schedules projects and improvements, and does much of the hands-on repair work. Marilyn keeps the books, orders merchandise, and handles the day-by-day planning.

"I learned more in the past two years than in the twenty years before that," says Marilyn, smiling placidly. What the Janke women did was daring and unconventional, but for this mother–daughter duo, life took a detour that led them into and out of fulltiming to find new careers, and the satisfaction of getting paid for doing what they like best.

E.C. and L.L. Davis

Like many early retirees, the Davises became "fed up" with jobs that had changed with the times and just weren't "fun" anymore.

They fulltimed for two years in a truck-cum-camper before they bought a motorhome and became a one-vehicle family. "Our insurance costs went from $512 for the truck and camper to $360 for the motorhome, with better coverage," they wrote.

Newlyweds at ages sixty-two and fifty-two, they have six children and three grandchildren between them, and they find that gifts for all the birthdays really add up. Still, they're able to save money while living on their combined pensions of about $1,800 monthly, and will be able to save more in two years when an additional $302 a month kicks in from another pension. Also, his pension from the Air Force includes both COLAs and medical/dental insurance, so they have few worries about inflation or the cost of treating an illness.

Campsite fees amount to very little thanks to campground memberships they bought at highly discounted resale prices, and to the many nights they spend in boondocks campsites without hookups. To keep their battery fully charged while in the boonies, they have a solar panel that gives them eighty-eight watts of juice in full sun.

"Problems? We haven't had any," they write.

"We left to get away from strange persons, but they are out here too," they admit. "Fortunately, some of our closest friends have been found since we began fulltiming. Everyone has a story to tell, and all are interesting."

Jim Revel

Jim Revel wrote us from El Paso, Texas, with thoughtful advice, bright observations, and a wonderfully upbeat story he calls, "Confessions of a Rookie Fulltimer: My First Year on the Road in the Old Soldier's Home on Wheels."

After twenty-five years of military service, Revel retired at the age of forty-seven, not realizing that he would soon lose his wife to lupus. Unable to face life alone in a big house, he donated the furniture to charity, rented the house, studied floor plans of several coaches, and ordered a brand new thirty-three-foot Itasca by phone. Six weeks later, he was up to his neck in fulltiming.

Now both older and wiser, he has invaluable advice for would-be fulltimers. Military life had put Revel in a lot of large vehicles but "nothing prepared me for the agonizing thrill of driving a thirty-three-foot, 16,000-pound vehicle," he says. "The unexpected influence of wind currents on the steering was shocking." He invested $316 in a stabilization system called Steer Safe, which he recommends.

Five pounds of reference material came with his rig, and he pored over it. "When all else fails, read the operator's manual," he advises. When he found one manual missing—the one for the dash radio—he called Winnebago, which sent it promptly. Without it, he couldn't set the clock radio.

In the driver's area of the cockpit alone, he has twenty-nine controls plus a rear-view TV monitor, cellular phone, and CB radio. "The operator's manual effectively explained the proper function of each," he says.

"There is no substitute for experience when it comes to operating a motorhome," Revel says. He had minor problems at first, most of them corrected by the dealer. One of his own additions was a Plexiglas shield on the wall next to the stovetop, which allows him to wipe off spatters easily.

On the road, he had anti-rock shocks installed, added an awning, and toured the factory where his RV was made—a visit he recommends to everyone. After 10,000 miles he decided he needed to tow a car, and did extensive research into his options. "Four wheels down is the most cost effective," he finds, but the dolly method is the most practical, as well as the one most complained about by RV owners. More research is definitely needed, he says.

Costs? He figures about $215 per thousand miles for gas alone, at $1.29 per gallon. He spends $235 per month for long-term parking, $350 per month when on the go. Payments on the RV, food, telephone, and laundry add up to just over $1,700 monthly, not including maintenance, propane, storage, and medical expenses.

Among his suggestions to motorcoach builders: Add more wardrobe and bathroom space, bigger air conditioners, a curtain behind the driver for night driving, and water purification as standard equipment. Add leveling jacks to all Class A motorhomes; offer telephone jacks as an option.

His advice to prospective fulltimers: Minimum size of the live-aboard RV should be thirty-six feet (we manage in twenty-one feet); stick to back roads to find the real America; keep the galley area carpet-free; try winter camping for special opportunities and challenges; and don't get an awning without a metal cover or it will unroll in highway winds.

"After a year on the road, fulltiming is not the dream I envisioned,"

Revel admits. "The decision to keep my house emerges as the best of the year." (We agree, not because we believe that fulltimers should keep their homes—we didn't, and we're glad—but because Revel had been newly widowed. He was wise not to burn all his bridges at once.)

"Freedom is not free," he concludes. "Fulltiming demands a high price in dollars and emotional expense . . . periods of highs, followed by lows, fueled by boredom and idleness." However, there is a happy ending—Revel has found a new traveling companion.

CHAPTER FOUR

The Cost of RV Living

We are asked surprisingly often how much it costs to "get by" when one lives in an RV. We usually counter with another question: "How much does it cost to live in a house?" Immediately, people realize the complexity of the question, and the impossibility of giving pat, bottom-line answers.

The full cost of RV life can't be gauged in advance, any more than you can tell, right now, what it will cost to live for the next few years on a farm or in a co-op apartment. You can't predict whether you'll have a medical disaster, a sudden demand for gum surgery, or a family emergency that throws all your plans into a cocked hat. Nor can you measure the cost of missed career opportunities, or of income lost because you chose early retirement.

Other fulltimers can tell you what they spend, but their figures may have little meaning for you if your needs or standards are different. We know people who are happy if they have a few dollars in their jeans, and others who wouldn't consider fulltiming until they had $100,000 in the bank. You can live in a modest RV or a rolling mansion, eat hamburger or high on the hog, save your pennies or play the ponies. We all have our own definitions of luxury and rock-bottom necessity, emergency and economy, splurge and sensible.

What You Spend Now

To project *your* actual fulltiming costs, first determine your current living expenses. Make a list of weekly, monthly, and yearly expenditures. It won't be easy, but you need to know where your money goes now, and what will change when you go fulltiming.

List everything on your worksheet, including those expenses that are sure to stop after you start fulltiming. Work from the top of your head, thinking it through day by day. Then use credit card bills, check stubs, receipts, and other records to fine-tune the list as accurately as possible.

Weekly: List here everything you buy by the week, such as groceries, bus fare, church donations, lunches, lottery tickets, newspapers, magazines, fuel, Friday night bowling, or Sunday dinner in a restaurant.

Monthly: This list should include time payments of all kinds, credit card bills, utilities, rent or mortgage, child support, and so on.

Yearly: These expenses include insurance, annual medical checkup, maintenance contracts, dental care, eyeglasses, subscriptions, dues, and Christmas and birthday gifts.

Continuing Costs

When your list is finished, highlight those expenses that are unlikely to change when you go fulltiming: life and health insurance, clothing and linens, magazines and newspapers, church contributions, care of an aged parent, medicines and eyeglasses, family gift occasions, dentistry, veterinary care, time payments (cemetery lots, credit card debt, college loans), greens fees, club dues, alimony and child support, and food, for example.

Add five percent to your food bill—you'll be buying in smaller, less economical quantities, you'll probably eat out more often, and as a stranger in town, you may not always shop at the most economical supermarkets. If your food bill is now unusually low because you do a lot of gardening and home canning, add ten percent or more to your projections.

You'll still have utility costs. Electricity is extra at some campgrounds and included in fees at others. In long-term site rentals, you may have your own meter. Telephone charges may be higher than before, especially if you have a cellular phone. You'll be buying your own propane and paying for dump station use. Water is the only (usually) free utility in the roaming life.

It's true that many of your current expenses—mortgage payments, home insurance and maintenance, the second car, lunches at work, commuting, and business clothes—will cease once you're on the road. However, if you're financing the RV, payments can be as much as or more than house payments. If you tow a car or boat with your RV, or use a car or truck to tow a travel trailer, you'll continue to have expenses for a second vehicle.

New Expenses

With a few phone calls, you can come up with a lot of projected answers, even if your plans are still hypothetical. Call a bank and ask what monthly payments would be on an $80,000 RV for five years or a $100,000 RV for ten years. Get a quote from your insurance agent on all the policies you'll need for an RV, its contents, and its tow vehicles. Get quotes from a couple of mail forwarding services. Check into monthly costs for having a cellular phone, an answering service, a pager.

Now list other new costs you'll be adding: coin laundries at eight to ten dollars per week, management fees if you intend to rent out your house, the cost of furniture storage, legal fees if someone is managing your business or affairs back home, and the special expenses associated with life aboard.

Energy and Fuel

Figure out how many gallons your generator burns per hour, then multiply that by how many hours per day you'll be running it—say, twelve—to project that cost. Assume about ten dollars a month for propane, and fine-tune the figures after you've fulltimed for a while. If you travel in cold climates and run a gas furnace, your costs will be much higher.

Work out several travel scenarios. For example, if you drive 10,000 miles a year in an RV that gets 8 miles per gallon, and buy fuel at $1.20

per gallon, simple math tells you that your fuel costs will be $1,500 a year. Add costs for oil and other fluids; the driver's manual will tell you how many quarts are needed, every how many miles.

"Rent"

Campground fees can vary from almost nothing to as high as $40 or more per night. Many fulltimers bless the day they bought a membership in one of the nationwide camping resort chains. Initial investment is $5,000 or more, but it's a lifetime deal that entitles you to camp in any member campground for as little as one dollar a night.

Before investing in any resort membership or condo campsite, read the contract very carefully and be sure the deal is for you—financially, geographically, and socially.

Campground discounts go with membership in almost any of the camping clubs (see Chapter 15). KOA has its own membership discount card. Senior citizens' discounts are also available for camping in state and national parks. Ask as you go.

We suggest that you wing it for the first year, until you have a better idea of what kinds of campgrounds best suit your fulltimer lifestyle. You may find that you need the luxury and security of a full-facility camping resort; or, you may find yourself seeking out the most remote, primitive campsites, far from the nearest neighbors and free of charge. For now, minimize nightly costs by taking weekly or monthly rates, staying in free or very inexpensive state and county parks, parking here and there with friends and relatives, or working by the season in a campground that gives you a free site in exchange for doing chores.

Maintenance and Repairs

These are a huge and frightening question mark. If you're lucky enough not to have accidents or catastrophic failures, and can do all your work yourself, maintenance will cost very little. If you have to pay for every little service, and your RV proves to be a lemon, your savings will melt away in mere months.

We recommend keeping a reserve equal to five to ten percent of the value of the vehicle each year. As the RV ages and its needs accelerate, you'll need these reserves for major replacements: upholstery, generator overhauls, engine and transmission work, and so on. If these reserves aren't used, the account continues to grow towards the day when you need really major repairs or a newer or larger RV. During some years you'll draw on the account hardly at all. Nevertheless, continue adding to it at a steady rate because, inexorably, time will take its toll.

Entertainment and Admissions

This category is pure guesswork, and the sky is the limit. A couple of days at Disney World or a few days' ski lift tickets can cost $200 per couple or more.

Even if you're a careful spender, the travel life demands certain expenses: museums, attractions, theme parks, restaurants, guided tours, guidebooks, maps, and the like. Presumably, the reason you're traveling is to see and do things, and some of the best things in life, such as a whitewater trip down the New River, or a helicopter tour of the Grand Canyon, aren't free.

As much as we'd like to give you slick answers, nobody can tell you how far your dollars will go, literally or figuratively. Fulltime life-on-the-go is as unpredictable, as cheap, and as expensive as your life has always been, but infinitely more rewarding than the things money can buy. When you're living out your dreams, experiencing the joy of travel, you're creating a bank account's worth of memories that no one can ever take away from you.

What Retirees Spend

Here is how the average retired couple spends their money, according to the Bureau of Labor Statistics:

Food: 29.3%
Housing (RV, campsite): 33.6%*
Transportation: 8.9%*
Clothing: 4.7%
Personal care: 2.9%
Medical care: 9.8%
Other family needs: 4.6%
Other: 6%

*To stick to this guideline, total cost of RV, campsites, tow car, fuel, and repairs should equal sum of these two, or 42.5 percent.

If you have a net monthly income of $1,500, your monthly budget according to the formula above would break down as follows:

Food: $440
RV, fuel, campsite, supplies, repairs: $638**
Clothing: $71
Personal care: $44
Medical, dental, optical: $147
Other family needs: $69
Other: $90

**From this, also contribute to the reserve fund mentioned above.

If your net monthly after-tax income is $2,000 a month, your monthly budget might look more like this:

Food: $586
RV, fuel, campsite, supplies, repairs: $850
Clothing: $94
Personal care: $58
Medical, dental, optical: $196
Other family needs: $92
Other: $120

Keep in mind that these figures are based on retirees, and not on families that are educating children, caring for elderly parents, completing their own education, or taking a one-year sabbatical before returning to careers.

CHAPTER FIVE

Where's Home?

Most fulltimers find it easier to select one state as a home base where they can vote, pay taxes, license their RVs, and renew their driver's licenses. But creative planning can greatly reduce fulltiming costs; as long as you live nowhere in particular, you can "live" wherever you can get the best deal. The truly stateless fulltimer can use several addresses to maximize benefits and minimize costs.

To avoid paying state income tax, look into mail forwarding services based in states that have no such tax. When their address becomes your address, their tax haven becomes your tax haven. See Chapter 11, "Keeping in Touch," for information.

Health insurance rates are also determined by your home address. Here's an example of rates charged by a company that bases its fees on residency, using ten geographic categories. For a thirty-year-old male they range from a low of $54.21 to more than double that figure—$114.80—for the same policy in regions where medical costs are highest. By the time the same man is sixty years old, rates range from $114.37 to $305.42, a formidable difference!

The rates you pay to insure your RV and other vehicles are also determined by your home address, and it's very possible that the cheapest place for health care is not the cheapest for highway insurance. Also determined by your "home" address are state and local income taxes, inheritance taxes, and the cost of licensing the RV yearly.

States that have no sales tax—such as, at this writing, Alaska, Delaware, Montana, New Hampshire, and Oregon—are good places to begin a fulltiming life, because you can save hundreds of dollars by buying your RV in one of them. Contrast this with, say, New Jersey, where a $150,000 motorhome will cost an additional $10,500 because of the seven percent sales tax.

Even if you *buy* the RV in a no-tax state, though, you'll have to pay the tax if you *register* it in a state that does have sales tax. As long as you're on the go and can keep the rig licensed in a no-tax state, you're ahead of the game, but if you start putting down roots it's just a matter of time until you get nailed and have to pay up. Meanwhile, the RV continues to depreciate, so the day may come when you're better off to register it in a sales-tax state, pay the taxes, and reap other state benefits.

Nevada, New Jersey, and Rhode Island have the highest *state* sales tax rates, but the total bite in a given locale may be far higher because of additional city and county levies. New York's state sales tax, for example, is only four percent, but in most parts of the state you'll pay total sales taxes of eight percent or more.

At one time, we licensed our RV in one state and our boat in another, bought health insurance in a third, and paid income taxes in a fourth. While summering in one state, we opened a bank account there, but yanked it out quickly when we started getting state tax bills for the interest paid. We avoided opening bank or brokerage accounts in any state that had an inheritance tax, because of the danger of one of us having to pay taxes on our assets if the other died.

We never rented a safety deposit box anywhere either, without first learning whether if would be sealed if one of us died. We were truly homeless and used many different addresses to different advantages.

Using this kind of gerrymandering dishonestly, however, can land you in trouble with the government and could void your insurance coverage too. You can vote only at your legal residence, so once you have selected one, you're on thin ice when claiming others to suit your own purposes.

Taxes and fees change constantly, depending on the whim of politicians whose appetites, at this point, seem insatiable. So juggling your addresses requires careful study and constant vigilance. Taxes change, and so does your personal situation depending on the source of your income, your age, your net worth, and any emergency help you might need from state agencies.

Some states have lower taxes but charge higher fees for licenses and services such as vehicle inspections. And some states seem generous while you're alive, but will torque your spouse for inheritance taxes on half your jointly owned RV and savings if you die.

Some points to investigate:

◆ **Senior citizen benefits.** Once you're sixty-five, your state income tax might be reduced.

◆ **Source tax.** Some states are now reaching out beyond their borders to tax pensions earned in that state. This is one you may not be able to outrun.

◆ **Inheritance and estate taxes.** You may have to pay tax on inherited assets (including, in some cases, your half of your own motorhome if you and your spouse owned it jointly, as well as joint bank and brokerage accounts). Not all states charge inheritance taxes, but there's a federal tax for estates over $600,000. While that sounds like a lot, you may be surprised to find that your total worth is that much or more. Add it up and see a tax advisor about how to pass some of your wealth along to your heirs, tax free. An excellent guide is *The Zero Tax Portfolio Manual* by Vernon K. Jacobs, CPA. For information write Research Press Inc., 4500 W. 72nd Terrace, Prairie Village, Kansas 66208.

◆ **Personal property tax.** More insidious than a one-time sales tax, this must be paid anew each year on the worth of such things as household furnishings, collectibles, keepsakes, and other valuables including your wedding rings.

◆ **Intangible assets tax.** Certain assets are taxed yearly in some states. Florida, for example, has no income tax, but will tax you yearly on the value of stocks, mutual funds, accounts receivable, and certain other holdings according to what they were worth on December 31 of the previous year—regardless of their worth at the time the tax is due.

It isn't enough just to pick a state known for its low per capita taxes. You need to find the one that charges least according to your own needs, source of income, net worth, age, and changing circumstances.

CHAPTER SIX

Making the Break

As the man commented to a friend who was about to step off the tenth floor into an open elevator shaft, "Watch that first step. It's a big one."

The decision to leave behind a conventional house and belongings to become a homeless wanderer is not unlike taking that ten-story jump. In the process of leaping off the edge, there may be missteps, stumbles, and outright pratfalls.

Which possessions should you keep? Sell? Give away? As you begin your pullout, what do you tell your family, your neighbors, your closest friends—and when?

Three hackneyed expressions make excellent advice now:

◆ Don't burn your bridges.

◆ Don't go away mad.

◆ Make your words sweet, because you may have to eat them later.

For many people, the big decision to go fulltiming comes at a pivotal time of life such as retirement, graduation, marriage, divorce, or when the last child marries or goes away to college. We met one couple who went fulltiming because they'd lost everything they owned in a house fire, and were forced to make a new start immediately.

For us, things evolved very slowly and thoughtfully. There was no great, beckoning opportunity such as winning the lottery. Nor was there any significant milestone in our lives, either enabling or preventing our breakaway.

Gordon was decades away from retirement or pension, so money would be a problem. On the other hand, we hadn't suffered any precipitating cataclysms. In some ways, this made things easier for us, because the timetable was ours. In others it was harder because, like everyone else, we found it easy to procrastinate, and difficult to give up possessions, old habits, and a hard-won career.

Our first decision was that we wanted our parting with Gordon's job to be a happy one. We liked the company and are still friends with many of his former co-workers. We were fond of our neighbors too and wanted to sell our home to nice people for their sakes. Gordon gave three months' notice at work, allowing plenty of time for the company to choose just the right pilot to take his place.

Keep in mind that we were still in our young thirties. We were sure we'd have to get jobs again when our meager savings were gone, so we wanted the transition to be smooth and amicable.

Because our families lived elsewhere, we decided to break all our bonds with Danville, Illinois, where we were living at the time, and to sell out completely. However, you may prefer to leave more doors ajar, with the hope of returning to your home town someday. There are many advantages to leaving one cheek on the chair in case the music stops.

Some options (check with an accountant; everyone's circumstances vary):

◆ Sell the house at a profit and make a tax-free exchange for an RV.

◆ Sell the house at a profit and take the one-time capital gains exclusion that is available to home owners who are past age fifty-five and who have lived in the house for five years or more.

◆ Sell the house at a loss.

◆ Rent or lease the house. Its value will probably keep up with inflation better than most other investments you could make—but look carefully into the cost of landlord insurance, professional management while you're away, and income tax pluses and minuses. (In Florida, where every householder gets a $25,000 homestead exemption plus added exemptions for a handicap or widowhood, taxes on a modest-size home would double if you moved out and renters moved in.)

◆ Let the house stand empty, which means it will be there for you to use any time you like. However, you'll also have the expense of upkeep, insurances, taxes, and security. Be very sure the house is well protected and looks lived in while you're gone. Otherwise, the insurance company may claim "abandonment" and refuse to pay a claim if the house is robbed or vandalized.

If you do sell your house, you'll no longer have to worry about mortgage payments, skyrocketing local taxes, tenants who run off without paying, repairs, insurance, vandalism, or coming home to find that some sharp politician snuck through a variance that rezoned your neighborhood as a toxic waste site.

We met one couple who were having a wonderful winter in Mexico when they heard from a former neighbor that their tenants had moved out, leaving the house a shambles. They had to leave their RV, fly home, make major repairs to the house, and find new tenants. It took three awful, expensive, frustrating months.

In our case, we kept only a few family heirlooms and some antiques Gordon had restored to showcase condition. We had happy memories of starting our marriage with nothing and then saving, dollar by dollar, to buy the things we had accumulated. We knew that someday, when and if we settled down again in a house or apartment, it would be just as much fun the second time around.

When you sell out completely, you have the money in hand to spend on today's fun. You'll be free to settle down again according to your new ideas about location, decor, furnishings, and neighborhood. If you sell all the furniture, you don't have to worry about storage costs, fire, deterioration, changing fashions, and mildew.

The Sellout

We allowed six months for our home to sell, but a lot will depend on your neighborhood and on the economy in your area. We did learn that it pays to shop around for a realtor who will work for less than "standard" commissions. Interviewing several agencies, we bargained for lower commissions, a higher advertising budget, and other promotional gimmicks such as the promise of so many open houses. The house sold in mere weeks.

We were glad we hadn't signed with the first realtor we talked to, and that we didn't reveal our plans too soon. Play it cool and create your own timetable. If you mention to a close friend that you're thinking about selling out to go live in an RV, and she tells her friend, the realtor, you soon will be under siege. Remember, *you* are in control.

When the house went on the market, we began running newspaper ads for a few of our largest, least-used items. We didn't want to denude the house too soon because the realtor had told us that fully furnished homes sell more readily. By advertising only a few things at a time, we avoided being overwhelmed by phone calls, dealers, and the merely curious. We sold some extra furniture, the second car, the slide projector, and other specialty items through individual ads, shown by appointment only.

As soon as we had a contract on the house, we began gnawing through the inventory that filled ten rooms, a basement, the attic, and a 2½-car garage, in inverse order to our need for each item. Guest room furniture went first. Then hobby equipment, the freezer, the largest shop tools, the dining room set, and the living room furniture. Last to go were the washer and dryer, kitchen appliances, and our bedroom set.

Finally the time came when we had to open the floodgates. During the final weeks, we had massive weekend garage sales. If you're not a yard sale follower, attend a few to get an idea of how they work. The most common mistake for neophytes is to price things too low. Forget what you paid for an item back in the fifties or sixties. While some of it is now worthless junk, some things are worth much more than you paid.

Be forewarned that garage sale stalwarts can overwhelm you unless you stand firm. People started ringing our doorbell the night before each sale; others showed up for a 9 A.M. sale at dawn. Fortunately, we were able to price our things, arrange them in the garage, and keep the door locked until our advertised sale hours.

This is a nerve-wracking period in your life, so try to keep calm. Provide crowd control, if possible, by confining the sale to the garage, porch, or a roped-off section of yard. Lock the house while you're selling. Our sales brought huge crowds, and things could have gotten out of hand.

Start the day with plenty of change, preferably in a carpenter's apron so you'll have everything on your person. If you keep all the cash in a cigar box, it's too easy for someone to walk off with it while you're demonstrating how well the lawnmower works or are helping someone try on your roller skates.

Some other suggestions:

◆ Put a price on everything. It eliminates confusion, not just for the customer but for your spouse and anyone else who is helping you sell. Bits of masking tape work well and cost almost nothing.

◆ Have on hand a good supply of paper bags, newspaper for wrapping breakables, and boxes for packing large purchases.

◆ If you have a really large household, as we did, don't put out everything at once. It's easier to keep control if you spread the sale over several days. Also, you can adjust prices upward for items that sell better than expected and lower the prices on wallflowers.

◆ Beware of dealers who arrive early and offer a flat rate for everything. It may sound like a lot of money, but we made far more by extending the sale and lowering our prices on the last day. Yard sale regulars are great bargainers, but we held firm to our prices. When someone made a lowball offer, we invited them to come back on the final day. Most paid our asking prices rather than wait.

Other Sellout Choices

Garage sales are a gold mine, but you may be wiser to give some items to non-profit causes and take a tax deduction; check with your accountant. Antiques or good jewelry, given to a museum, could bring a handsome deduction. We donated our expensive books and records to a library. Gordon's high-ticket business suits went to a charity. The last of our unsold items we donated to a thrift shop, and we obtained a receipt for the IRS. Don't leave them for the trash collector.

Another choice is to hold an auction. It's painful to sell off bits and pieces of your life at garage sales. By turning over everything to an auctioneer, you can simply walk away and trust that the professional will work the crowd for the highest dollars. You're spared much of the work and all the sadness of selling. However, the auctioneer's commission is usually a hefty twenty-five percent.

As a last choice, you can call in a dealer who will haul everything away and pay you a flat fee. It's quick and neat, and you're spared the heavy labor of hauling, the annoyance of crowds and phone calls, and the hassle of haggling.

We found secondhand dealers to be the most rapacious, underhanded people we had to work with in the entire agonizing process of selling out. They sniffed over our goods like turkey vultures over road kill, hoping we didn't know the value of our hobnail glass or old baseball cards or antique toys. Certainly some dealers are honest and perhaps even generous, but if you must deal with one, call in a licensed appraiser—not the same one who is also trying to buy your goods—to give you a fair picture of what things are worth.

Storage: What's in Store

If you decide to keep some or all of your furnishings, you have several options: Rent your home fully or partially furnished. Or pile everything into the attic or spare room, lock that part of the house, and rent out the rest of the house. (When you buy a landlord's insurance policy, don't forget to insure your personal belongings separately. The tenant's policy will cover only their own possessions, not yours.)

You might ask friends and relatives to take anything they have room to store. It's free, and a trusted relative could even be enlisted to go through your things on your behalf. Say you're in New Mexico when you need an old medical record that's stored in the attic back in New Hampshire. Or you run short of cash and want Aunt Sue to sell the heirloom silver you've stored in her attic. If Aunt Sue has free access to your stuff, she can do more for you than just warehouse it.

This solution also has its drawbacks. First, you have the expense or labor of moving everything to Muffy and Bob's basement or to Aunt Sue's attic. Then, when Muffy and Bob are transferred to South America, someone has to find a new place and move your things there. The precious possessions that you thought were resting secure in that basement are now being shuffled around by heaven-knows-whom, to god-knows-where.

There is sure to be a wrangle if Aunt Sue's house burns down, or if Muffy's cat uses your antique rocker for a scratching post, or if your coin collection is stolen out of Aunt Min's spare room. And the day may come when Uncle Leftie swears that your stamp collection was not a loan, but that you gave it to him.

It may cost more to deal with professional storage companies, but it's often worth it. The good news is that, with so many people today living in small apartments and in homes with no attics or basements, there has been an explosion in the building of mini-warehouses. You see them everywhere. They look like long, windowless buildings, faced with row after row of doors and "garage" doors. You lock your own warehouse door, visit your goods whenever you please, and pay a modest storage charge by the month, season, or year.

Typical mini-warehouse sizes range from bins as small as four feet by eight feet by four feet to full-size rooms about ten by twenty-two by eight. The smallest of these minis, only four feet high, is suitable only for piled boxes, a motorcycle, or other small items. It rents for $20 or less a month in most places. At the upper end of the scale, you'll pay $100 a month or more for a large room, and more still if you use electricity to run a dehumidifier.

Most mini-warehouses are well fenced and may have twenty-four-hour security as well. Some have their own locks; on others, you supply the padlock of your choice. Some allow you access only during business hours; others are always accessible. When you're shopping for a mini-warehouse, compare not just price and size, but access, security features, and whether or not electricity is available. And don't forget that you'll need your own insurance.

If you deal with a moving and storage company, you have the protection and convenience of working with professionals. They pick up everything at your house, install it in their warehouse, and deliver it wherever, whenever you want. A good mover will put your household into individual plywood containers to prevent wear and tear and will put upholstered pieces on racks where they'll get good air circulation.

Look for a company that is bonded, that has a sprinkler system and circulation fans, and that stores furniture on platforms rather than on cold, damp cement floors.

Prices are high and are charged by the hundredweight (CWT), which usually works out to about forty dollars per room per month. Insurance provided by the storage company is also figured by the CWT and is usually well under your household's actual worth. Get additional coverage from your own insurer. The cost of moving into and out of storage is also high, charged at typical moving van prices.

The biggest problem with any storage facility, but especially an unventilated or unheated mini-warehouse, is that moisture, heat, and cold continue to batter your belongings. Make sure you don't put any liquids in with goods stored in unheated warehouses in the north. We once forgot that a box contained a bottle of medicine. It froze, shattered, and made a frightful mess.

Before storing any fabrics, wash and dry them thoroughly.

Atmospheric stains appear out of nowhere after several months of storage in even the driest attic. One of our friends retrieved her stored linens from a humid Florida warehouse and found they had turned to dust in a few months. We had better luck in storing freshly washed, dried fabrics that were sealed into plastic bags on a dry day.

Make sure, too, that all batteries are removed from stored items. We all use so many batteries today, in so many different items, it's easy to overlook one in a camera, wristwatch, calculator, toy, or flashlight. When batteries discharge and begin to leak, they ruin the item they are in, and often damage surrounding items too.

The Final Cut

At long last, you're ready to move into the RV. We thought we'd pared our possessions to the bone when we sold out but, once we started moving, we saw we'd have to become even more ruthless about what to keep and what to get rid of. Even if you can find room for your custom-made bowling ball and the marble bust of Beethoven, keep in mind that it costs you fuel dollars to haul and brake every ounce.

Clothing, books, hobby gear—everything should be looked at with fresh, unprejudiced eyes. It's better to sell your wardrobe down to the bare skin, and use the money to buy one or two versatile and practical new outfits, than to start out with closets filled with unmatched separates and shirts that need starching.

Still, you'll take too much. We all do. And that's when the battles begin over his space, her space, and our space. We'll get into that later.

Parting Is Such Sweet Sorrow

No matter how you choose to unload your household goods, there will be difficult, even tearing, decisions to make. You and your mate may disagree over what to keep, give away, or sell. And if it's to be sold, you may argue over pricing. Steel yourself for some rocky times.

Suddenly you will realize how many good times you had in this house, how comfortable you were in that old overcoat, and how much you both like the silly little lamp you bought during a trip to Atlantic City.

You'll agonize over how much you'll miss the morning sun coming in through the bay windows to kiss the African violets. You'll worry about managing without this or that. You'll cry together, and you'll cry alone.

In addition to your own bittersweet partings with things that you and your spouse love, expect some ugly pressures from other people too. Relatives will get huffy if they catch you selling things they gave you as gifts, or things they think of as family pieces that should be given (never sold, of course) to Little Barney or Cousin Sue.

Many friends and neighbors may expect you to give things to them and, in fact, you may be embarrassed to put a price tag on the hand-made quilt that Betsy has always admired, or the garden tool that Harvey always borrowed from you.

This is a time of great mental, physical, and financial vulnerability. Be alert against hurts of all kinds. This is the tough part, but it's soon over. Now, let the good times roll!

CHAPTER SEVEN

How to Choose a Home on Wheels

Camping on weekends and vacations is one thing; living aboard is quite another. Part-timers don't mind roughing it for a few days. If the bed is too hard or too short, they laugh it off. They can breakfast on cold beans if it means getting out on the lake earlier. And taking the path to the bath is simply a quaint camping necessity.

Forget maintenance, cleaning, and costs. The piper can be paid later. When the part-timer gets home, he can dump all the dirty clothes and bedding into the automatic washer and dryer, soak off the grime in a full-size bathtub, and turn over the rig to a trusted hometown mechanic for a checkup. He can pay the bills later as they straggle in and luxuriate in household living until it's time to go camping again.

Fulltimers, by contrast, have to find their own luxury, fulfillment, and comfort aboard, because the *RV* is home sweet home. The bubble bath or laundry or fall house cleaning can't wait until you get home, because you *are* home. The piper must be paid one tune at a time.

The RV has to hold everything you need, year in and year out. That includes the income tax records, Christmas decorations, off-season clothes, hobby and entertainment paraphernalia, tools and spares for the plumbing and wiring and drive train, as well as such homemaking supplies as the mending basket and the jelly jars.

Within these four walls you'll have to eat, drink, and be merry.

Here's where you'll recuperate from the flu, play cards with your friends on Saturday night, get dressed for the hoedown, pay the bills and do the bookkeeping, soak your corns, settle spats with your spouse, do the spring cleaning, and plan trips, take trips, and recover from trips.

The part-timer is probably concerned with how many folks the RV will sleep—the more, the merrier. Fulltimers, by contrast, need sleeping accommodations only for themselves; but the bed(s) must be exactly the right length, width, and firmness, and be accompanied by TV, reading lamps, and a place for bedside books.

The part-timer carries gear for a week or two, for whatever the purpose of the trip—bass fishing this time, photographing the bald eagle migration next time, snowmobiling the time after that. The fulltimer needs freshwater tackle and saltwater tackle, snow skis and water skis, old clothes and Sunday clothes—everything *including* the kitchen sink.

Vacationers take dining shortcuts, eating in restaurants and cooking with convenience foods. The fulltimer needs a real kitchen where economical, nutritious, life-giving meals can be created and served attractively on a comfortable dinette, seven days a week.

In recognition of these needs, indeed in *celebration* of these needs, let's take a look at the RV marketplace.

Types of Recreational Vehicles

Even longtime campers may confuse some of the terms used in the RV world, so let's define them.

First of all, this book is about homes that are mobile, not about mobile homes (or manufactured housing, as they are sometimes called). A mobile home is a large house on wheels, with no engine. It is towed by a hired truck and installed permanently in a trailer park, and it is about as agile as an anvil.

The subject of this book is the recreational vehicle (RV), a vehicle designed to go places and do things while also providing a place to eat and sleep. RVs fall into various categories, as described below:

Pickup campers are camper units that slide into pickup truck beds. Also called truck campers, they range from simple shells to elab-

RV categories. (RVIA)

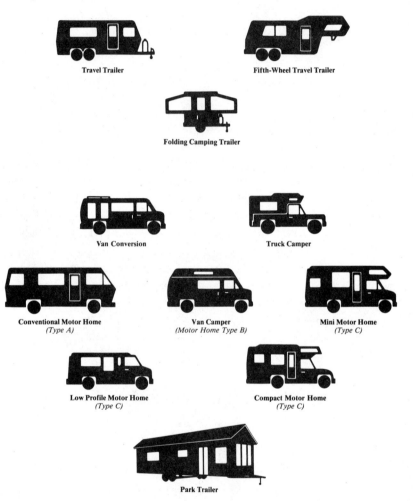

Travel Trailer

Fifth-Wheel Travel Trailer

Folding Camping Trailer

Van Conversion

Truck Camper

Conventional Motor Home
(Type A)

Van Camper
(Motor Home Type B)

Mini Motor Home
(Type C)

Low Profile Motor Home
(Type C)

Compact Motor Home
(Type C)

Park Trailer

orate units that include kitchen, bath, bunks, and dinette. Camper add-ons are available at prices from under $3,000 to about $7,500.

Motorhomes are complete units containing living quarters, engine, and chassis. They range from mini-motorhomes to large (Class A) motorhomes or motorcoaches. Class A motorhomes start in the $50,000 range; better models with expensive rear-engine diesel power sell for $150,000 to $250,000 or more.

Made in Canada, Triple E's Empress motorhome comes in five floorplans and in lengths from thirty-three to thirty-eight feet. (Triple E)

Travel trailers are complete living units towed by a car or truck. They come in many shapes, sizes, and prices, from little folding trailers that can be towed by very small cars to enormous wheeled estates thirty-five feet long or longer. Folding campers start at under $2,000 and average about $3,500; conventional RV trailers start at under $6,000 and average about $10,000.

Fifth-wheel trailers are a sub-category with an extension that fits over the bed of a pickup truck for easier maneuvering and towing. These sell for about the same prices as conventional trailers.

Park trailers also are travel trailers, but they are not designed for extensive towing. Most have peak roofs and expanding sections that can add a dining room or double the width of the living room. Larger park models may be single or double width, sporting such features as cathedral ceilings and bay windows, so the largest ones are more like mobile homes than RVs. Their average price is $15,000.

Van conversions may contain a microwave oven or tiny bath-

The fifth-wheeler gives you almost all the space of a same-length trailer but is easier to tow. (Shasta)

room, but generally are not suitable for fulltime living. They usually cost $25,000 or less.

Some Basic Choices

Your first decision should not be about the size, price, or shape of your rolling home, but whether you will drive it or tow it. For all their cute and fetching features in the showroom, RVs are *vehicles*. Safety, handling, weight, and fuel economy are paramount considerations. So is the cost of one vehicle versus two.

You can have one vehicle, such as a pickup camper or motorhome, an RV trailer plus a car or truck to tow it, or a motorhome that tows a small car.

The Case for Towing

Any RV that doesn't have an engine will naturally be cheaper than one that does. Because almost five trailers are built for every Class A motorhome, the choice of trailer brands, sizes, layouts, styles, and decors is better than in any other category.

When you get to the campground, you unhitch the trailer and you're home. Your car (or van or truck) is now free for local shopping and sightseeing. Depending on your travel style, fuel costs may be less than if you have to drive a big motorhome for every little errand.

There's an advantage to being able to trade or upgrade the trailer and the tow vehicle separately, with a choice of diesel or gasoline, as needed. And the tow vehicle can also provide extra storage, workshop space, or even, in some cases, an extra camper. If you tow a large trailer with a large truck that also has modest accommodations aboard, the trailer can be left in base camp while you make expeditions in the truck into the most remote areas.

The Case Against Towing

For anyone who is reluctant to wrestle a tow on the highway, and con it into and out of tiny campsites, there is no argument at all. Towing is out, period. And even if you and your traveling companion(s) are adroit and skilled drivers who love towing, there are other drawbacks.

If you cover a great many miles each year, fuel costs will probably be higher than in a single, aerodynamically efficient vehicle. So will costs for tires, because you have more skins on the road. And, because tolls are charged per axle, you'll pay more to drive toll roads. Check with your insurance carrier too and compare costs for coverage of a car and trailer versus a motorhome, versus a motorhome that tows a small car.

When you have a single, walk-through unit, you can pull over to the side of the road to take a nap or make lunch without going outdoors. With a trailer, you have to go out in the weather to enter your living quarters. Heat and air are separate, so it may be a nuisance (or impossible, if you don't have a generator) to start the air conditioner or furnace each time you stop for lunch. In a motorhome, by contrast, you can opt to leave the engine idling for short periods to run the heat or air.

It's illegal in most states to ride in a trailer under tow. That means your spouse has to be in the tow car with you underway even if he or she would rather be snoozing in the bedroom or doing needlepoint in the living room.

Narrowing the Choice

Only you can decide on the best rolling lifestyle to suit your comforts, frequency of travel, budget, and driving abilities. What we'd all like to have, of course, is a three-bedroom RV with garage, basement, attic, and vegetable garden. What we must settle for is a compromise: fuel economy and responsive handling versus space and weight; one vehicle versus two; the RV we covet versus the RV we can afford.

When we lived on the go fulltime, our home was a twenty-one-foot diesel mini-motorhome. We won't mention the brand because it is no longer made, but we still use it regularly and remain happy with our choice. It's small compared to what most fulltimers choose, but keep in mind that we're not retired. We travel quick and light, make a living on the go, and rarely stay in a campground for more than a few nights at a time. We like having everything with us, everywhere we go.

Our twenty-one-footer is large enough to have kitchen essentials, a comfortable dinette, double bed, and bathroom with shower. Yet it's short enough to park in city parking lots, in the yards of friends and relatives, and on the street outside a friend's home.

When we're doing television appearances in connection with our books, it's no problem to make the morning show. We sleep in the parking lot, have breakfast, dress, and walk in. We have slept in city parking lots after the theater, at trade shows, and at airports.

In a larger and more complex rig that wouldn't fit into a car-size parking space, our business life would be more complicated and costly. The retiree, on the other hand, will probably prefer more living space and less driving. In fact, there are retiree-only RV parks where you can stay by the season, the year, or the lifetime.

Here are some pros and cons of different types of RVs:

Pickup Camper

Pros: If you will be combining the fulltiming life with a business in which you'll use a pickup truck, this camper can be offloaded in the campground to form a wheelless, slightly odd-looking, but complete and cozy home while you take off in the truck. These campers are inexpensive to buy and, because you have separate truck and camper, you can change or upgrade either when the time comes.

A truck camper is ideal for those who need a pickup truck. The camper unit can be left, free-standing, at the campsite. (See photo of interior on next page.) (Fleetwood)

Interior design of a Fleetwood truck camper.

Cons: Because it was designed as a removable addition to an existing pickup truck, the truck camper gives you the poorest space utilization, weight distribution, handling, and riding ease of any camper you could choose. And you have to get out of the cab and go to the rear to enter the living quarters.

Motorhome

Pros: Large choice of sizes, styles, price ranges. Convenient to have everything with you, including your own kitchen and bath, at all times. Complete, self-contained independence. One of you doesn't like opera? Stay "home" in the parking lot, watching the fights on TV or babysitting the kids or the dog, while your spouse enjoys Mozart.

Lunch at the beach, museum, or mall? Go out to the RV and eat when and what you like, without having to pay restaurant prices. As a special bonus, you'll have your own bathroom out there in the parking lot too.

This Class A Winnebago Adventurer rear-diesel-engine model performs well even under the most adverse heat conditions. The Adventurer 34RQ offers superior mileage, lower per-mile costs, and long-term dependability while providing all the comforts of home with an abundance of interior and exterior storage. (Winnebago)

The Class A 1992 Winnebago Chieftain/28RT Itasca Sunflyer. (Winnebago)

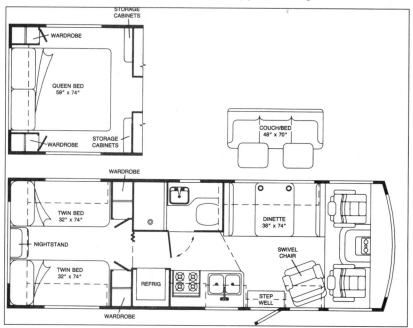

The entry-level Minnie Winnie mini-motorhome. (Winnebago)

The Class C 1992 Winnebago Minnie Winnie/24RC Itasca Sundancer. (Winnebago)

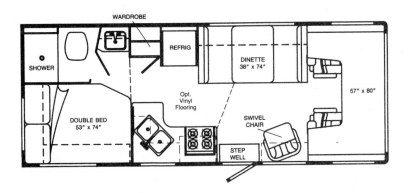

Stocking up at the supermarket? Everything goes directly into cupboards and the refrigerator before you leave the lot. Picking up clothes at the dry cleaner? Hang them right in the closet.

Cons: Unless you tow a small car (which in turn creates other inconveniences and expenses) you have to travel everywhere in the RV. When one of you goes to the dentist, everyone and everything goes to the dentist. If you forgot to shop for some essential when you went through the last town, you have to unhook the entire RV and drive back to buy it. And, if you want to go out to dinner and a show, it's a job to unhook and stow all the umbilicals, leave the campsite, and hook up again after an evening on the town.

When someone is working on the engine, your home life is invaded. When the motorhome is broken down, you have to set up housekeeping at the roadside, at the garage, or wherever the breakdown occurs. With a motorhome, all your eggs are in one basket, for better or worse.

Travel Trailer

Pros: A lot of "house" for the money. If it can be towed with a car or truck you already own and trust, you're off and running. Travel trailers come in so many types and qualities, you can shop for good, better, or best in any size from compact to queen. Get exactly the trailer for your needs, and just the right tow vehicle for the power, layout, seating, storage, and comfort you want. You can have the best of both worlds, leaving the trailer behind when you're touring.

Cons: In addition to the challenges of towing, as mentioned above, trailers are usually light in relation to their size, so windage can be a problem. The sheer size of a trailer-cum-car makes it difficult to "anchor out," which is what we call it when we overnight free in a

The Avion travel trailer. (Avion)

Avion's interior is elegant and stylish. (Avion)

friend's yard or driveway. And, the larger and more awkward the rig, the less able you are to reach smaller, more remote beach or mountain campgrounds.

You'll probably be more dependent on campground umbilicals, especially electricity, because 110-volt generators are not installed as commonly in trailers as they are in motorhomes. Most travel trailers now have simplified electrical management, in which the "house" battery is charged from the vehicle's alternator, but lighting and other 12-volt needs must be provided for.

Pop-up and Folding Camp Trailers

Pros: The lightest, most towable, and least expensive of all camping trailers, the fold-out is a good choice only for special situations and the most severely strapped budgets. However, they are available in many configurations, in canvas and hard-bodied models. Larger pop-ups have rudimentary kitchens and baths, and can be fitted with air conditioning.

Cons: In a typical layout, two double bunk "wings" unfold from the body of the camper. Unless you need both as bunks, they have little use except as a space to spread out gear while you're in camp. Living comforts are few, campground dependence almost total. Until you unfold the camper, you have no access to any of your own facilities. And setting up or breaking camp in bad weather is a burden.

Van Conversion

Pros: These are stylish, lean and mean on the highway, have a low profile that fits under canopies at gas stations, are agile on back roads and hills, and provide excellent riding comfort. A van can be fitted with an attached tent for an extra room. For the single fulltimer, with minimalist tastes and few belongings, the van provides unlimited possibilities.

Cons: Although many vans have toilets, you'll probably still be dependent on campgrounds for showers. Kitchens are adequate for warming up convenience foods but not for serious cooking. There isn't space, or water tankage, for much dishwashing or bathing. Some vans don't have standup headroom, and most have convertible beds that are awkward to make and uncomfortable to sleep in.

Down to Brass Tacks

Most RV manufacturers offer a large choice of layouts, and certain basic choices apply to both motorhomes and trailers. They include:

Built-in versus freestanding furniture. Until recent years, all furniture was built in by the RV manufacturer, but today you'll have a choice. Usually, freestanding pieces will be a conventional sofa bed, swivel chairs in the living room, and separate dining chairs instead of a built-in dinette.

Separate furniture may be more comfortable and stylish, but if you choose it you're sacrificing the spacious storage bins that can be put under built-in sofas and dinettes. You may also tire of having to stow the dining room chairs, so they don't break loose in a panic stop.

Bed size. There is no need to change your sleeping habits. All manufacturers offer a choice of double bed, queen, or bunk beds. Kings and full-size twin beds are harder to find.

Center hall versus side hall. In most layouts, you reach the bedroom through a center hall that also forms a dressing room/bath, or a side hall that goes past a separate bathroom. When you're shopping for a layout, think about traffic patterns, because in some you can't get from kitchen to bedroom if someone is showering or using the toilet.

Entry door placement. Although some trailers have both front and rear doors, most RVs have just one entry, and you might give some thought to it, especially if you expect to be entertaining in your RV or if you have children who are constantly in and out. In some motorhomes, the only entry is through the cockpit and everyone has to maneuver around the passenger seat to enter the "living room." One of our friends said she hated a center entry that was directly opposite the bathroom. Some doors open into the kitchen; others into the living room; others into a hall.

This is another area where the choice for part-timers may not apply for fulltiming. The vacationer hops in and hits the road, and wants easy access to the driver's seat. The fulltimer usually spends more time at "home" than at the wheel, so easy entry to the living quarters may count more than a convenient driver's door.

Windows versus cupboards. The bigger the window area in an RV, the less wall space is available for cupboards, closets, medicine cabinet, and mirrors. And windows add to your heat gain problems.

Construction Standards

In addition to all the lifestyle, comfort, and decor questions you must ask when selecting an RV, you will also want to know that you are purchasing a well-constructed home. The RV industry, represented by the Recreational Vehicle Industry Association (RVIA), has its own standards, which assure quality and consistency among member manufacturers.

The by-laws of RVIA require that its members certify that each RV they build complies with the American National Standard for Recreational Vehicles, the only nationally recognized consensus standard (part of which is delineated in Appendix 3). Look for an RVIA seal, affixed by the manufacturer near the RV's door; it certifies that the unit complies with that standard and with the National

Electrical Code.

RVIA inspectors make frequent, unannounced visits to monitor the manufacturing process and determine the level of compliance to the standard. A manufacturer who doesn't comply faces expulsion from RVIA.

A full ninety-five percent of all RVs sold in the United States are built by members of RVIA to RVIA standards. It pays to shop for a unit that bears this seal and to demand that repairs or replacements follow ANSI standards.

People Sizing

There's one last chore before making a final decision on an RV layout. Both you and your spouse should try sitting, standing, and lying anywhere in the RV where you'll be sitting, standing, or lying when you live aboard. You'll feel foolish in the showroom, but we urge you to sit on the toilet and close the door (there may not be enough clearance to do so), take off your shoes and stand in the shower (it may not be high enough), sit in the bathtub, and stand at the stove and kitchen sink (which may be higher or lower than you like).

If it will be a part of your everyday life to turn a dinette or a sofa into a bed, go through the procedure. It may be more awkward than you realize, and the resulting bed may have ridges and valleys in the worst places. Sit down at the table. Is there room for table settings for two? More?

(Fleetwood)

(Fleetwood)

(Fleetwood)

Bend over the bathroom sink as if brushing your teeth. It may hardly come up to your knees. Stretch out on the bed to see if it's long enough. Often beds look like standard sizes, but are not. And some overhead bunks don't provide enough headroom for sitting up in bed to read.

Remember that these living quarters, and all the plumbing and wiring behind the scenes, also have to reconcile with the needs of the vehicle. As a result, counter tops may be higher or lower than in a house. The microwave oven may be too high to reach with a hot, heavy casserole in your hands.

Everything may not be as it seems at first glance. Downsizing can be a virtue, but it can delude you if a sink is too small for washing dishes, or a shower stall too small to enclose your body, or a faucet so low you can't fill the tea kettle.

While it's tempting to choose the RV according to its living comforts, we must come back to the fact that it's also a vehicle. Can you check the oil, batteries, and radiator cap without dismantling the living room? Change a fan belt without taking the engine apart? Get at the generator to fuel and service it?

What's involved in filling the propane and water tanks, lighting the hot-water tank and refrigerator, emptying sewage and gray water, stowing cords and hoses, flushing out systems, changing the oil, getting at spare tire(s), leveling the rig, managing the electrical system, and doing all the other routine maintenance required by a home on wheels?

Can you find room (and access to pipes and wires) to add items that you consider essentials? They may include a water filter, generator, another air conditioner, additional lighting, a washer-dryer, an inverter to turn 12-volt juice into 110-volt power, more tankage, a dishwasher, or a trash compactor.

Only after these very important considerations are met can you start thinking about whether you want the sculptured carpet or the short shag, in beige or in robin's egg blue.

About Custom Units

Almost any RV, even in lower price ranges, is made to order, so you'll probably have plenty of factory-installed options, ranging from color schemes to major structural changes. Unless you have experience in RV living, however, we recommend starting with stock RV, new or used, to get a feel for the living patterns that will work best for you.

In a custom RV, almost anything is possible. That doesn't make it practical or wise. Exotic customizing adds to your costs and may reduce resale value. So don't opt for a built-in darkroom, sauna, or the flocked scarlet wallpaper until you're sure it's right for you for the long haul.

Finding Your RV

Look at as many RVs as possible—new and used, showroom and back lot. Even if you know you'll be buying a new unit, you can learn a lot by looking at used RVs, both at dealerships (where they're likely to be in top-notch condition) and through private owners (where you're more likely to see what a few years of wear and tear can do).

Even the largest showroom can't contain every model of every brand, so write and request brochures from any manufacturers listed in Appendix 2 that make the type of RV you're interested in.

Many manufacturers welcome your visit to the factory and will build to order if you're willing to pay the price. Top-of-the-line RVs, those in the $250,000-and-up class, are almost all built to order, rarely on speculation, so allow time for conferences, planning, and construction.

Giant RV shows are held around the country, and they are a dazzling, shortcut way to see hundreds of RVs all at once. They fill entire stadiums, fairgrounds, and enormous exhibition halls. For a list of major shows, write RVIA, Box 2999, Reston, Virginia 22090.

The more you've traveled by RV, the better equipped you are to choose the unit that's right for you. Still, many of us went happily into fulltiming straight from our tenting or vanning days, and lived happily ever after.

Equipping Your RV Home Your Way

Choosing the perfect RV is just the beginning of a long-term romance between you and the liveaboard life. Even if your RV is custom built to your own design, it won't truly be a home until it is finished, furnished, and fine-tuned.

It's here that you'll be making birthday cakes, Thanksgiving feasts, waffles on Sunday morning, and bean soup on Saturday night. In this RV you'll be entertaining friends, reading the Sunday funnies, sorting laundry, mending socks, and spending endless rainy days.

Fulltiming is a specialized lifestyle that requires specialized accoutrements. At first you may make do with paper plates and old army blankets, but you'll soon realize the importance of having the right sheets for making up odd-size bunks and the appropriate pots and pans for preparing Shamu-size meals in a guppy-size galley.

Remember, too, that the RV doesn't stay put like your house does. It accelerates, corners, maneuvers, and brakes to a stop. Every pound costs you fuel dollars; every ounce affects the way the RV will handle on the highway. You have to add equipment sparingly and place it carefully; for example, heavy items such as canned goods or a microwave oven should be well balanced fore and aft and kept as low as possible.

Decor

The fun part is to work within existing decor to keep the RV interior as color coordinated, uncluttered, and spacious looking as it was in the showroom. If you have swatches of the existing upholstery and carpeting, visit a paint store to pick up a handful of free color sample cards in your RV's shades. Then tuck them in your wallet so they'll be handy as you shop for bedding, bathroom furnishings, throw rugs, tableware, and accessories.

Smart use of color and light can create moods, make small spaces seem larger, brighten dark corners, and mask soil and smudges. When window coverings match the walls, and area rugs match the flooring, they blend into seamless expanses that seem larger. Contrasting colors, on the other hand, chop up an area and make it appear smaller.

Big prints overwhelm a tiny room. Hot colors (red, orange) make a small room seem stifling. Colder colors (blue, gray) add to the drabness of a rainy climate. Shiny fabrics, such as sateen and chintz, bring light to dark corners. Vinyl upholstery can be matte finish and buttery soft, or it can look cold, utilitarian, and cheap.

When you're choosing accents and accessories, think small. RV ceilings are low. Use long, thin, vertical mirrors or wall hangings to make them seem higher. Walls and furniture are downsized, so don't overwhelm them with large accent pieces.

Use practical items that both fill the space and put it to good use. For example, a picture on the wall is merely decorative, while a clock, barometer, vase, magazine shelf, or sconce is useful as well.

Throw pillows are popular accents. If you buy pillow shams instead, and stuff them with extra bed pillows or puffy ski jackets or your supply of knitting wool, you've created extra storage area at the same time.

Galleyware

Start with the bare-bones basics, then add to your galley gear as you develop your own RV cuisine routine. You may cook and eat much differently aboard than you did at home. Perhaps you'll use conve-

Expand counter space by using stove covers and sink fillers. Make your own sink fill-in using maple chopping block material or Corian. (Fleetwood)

nience foods more often, eat out more frequently, or cut down to only two meals a day, as many retirees do. You may cook out more too, because most campsites have a fire ring or a grill. (Cooking out is part of the breezy camping lifestyle, and it's a great way to meet campground neighbors.)

When choosing cookware, don't assume that you need an entire set or a matched set. It's better to choose the best pot and skillet, casserole and baking pan for each purpose. The same goes for silverware, dishes, utensils, and cutlery. In RV living, every inch counts.

Among those items that are especially handy in the RV are a pressure cooker, because it saves time and fuel; nonstick skillets, which minimize cleanup; an electric hotplate; a tri-level double boiler/ steamer, because it lets you cook several items atop one burner; and a couple of heavy pots with heavy, tight-fitting lids. (When you must shuffle several pots among too few burners, thin pans with loose lids

Appliance "garages" made for kitchen use are ideal for the RV galley, where all countertop aids must be stowed securely for the road. (Woodworkers' Store)

Microwave ovens are now standard equipment on almost all RVs. (Sharp Electronics)

let too much heat escape. Here is one place where heavier is better.)

For more about the RV galley, and dozens of mouthwatering, road-worthy recipes, see Janet's *Cooking Aboard Your RV*, which was published by Ragged Mountain Press in 1993 as a companion volume to this one. To order a copy call (800) 822-8158 and ask for book number 60336.

Bedding

Most RV manufacturers furnish the master bedroom with an innerspring mattress atop a solid wood platform. Unfortunately, innersprings are heavy and awkward to lift and handle. Opt instead for a good foam mattress, which will be more comfortable, lighter, and easier to move.

It's no longer necessary to buy real foam rubber, which is heavy and expensive, to get the comfort you need. Instead, look for a featherweight, manmade polyfoam mattress, which will be easy to lift whenever you need to get at under-bed storage, and easier to turn regularly to maintain firmness and freshness. Don't skimp on quality or thickness. Discuss the options with a foam specialist, who will explain the many types and qualities of foam available.

Now that the innerspring is out of the picture, you no longer have to settle for a sharp-cornered bed that wastes space and barks your shins. Do you sleep with your feet in the far corners of the mattress? Probably not. So have the bottom corners at the foot of the bed cut off, providing you more space for moving around the bedroom. Any custom mattress maker can whip out a foam mattress in the right size and shape for less than the price of a mass-produced innerspring.

If the bed in your rolling home is a standard twin, double, queen, or king, standard-size sheets and blankets are the best buys and come in the largest choice of colors. However, convertible and odd-size bunks, which are often used in RVs, present special problems. Standard bedding may be too narrow or too short. Worse still, some RV beds—especially convertibles—do not have a separate mattress that allows you to tuck sheets in. Unless you have a sleeping bag, you'll spend the night skating around on loose sheets.

When a convertible RV bed has to be made up each night and the bedding put away every morning, the job takes forever using conven-

To make the most of your RV bed, invest in a top-quality mattress pad. Wool fleece adjusts to the body, is cool in summer and warm in winter, and evens out upholstery ridges or buttons in a convertible bed. (Woolrest)

tional bedding. For these beds, there are a number of choices. Most big camping supply stores offer a selection of single and double sleeping bags for all climates. You don't have to worry about tuck-in or overlap, and some come with removable sheets for easy laundering.

The more sophisticated sleeping sacks come in all sizes from single to king and have a light side for summer and a heavy side for winter camping. All of them roll up in the morning in a few seconds, and unroll instantly at bedtime. Voilà! The bed is completely made up with sheets and blankets.

Our RV's bed is a standard-size double, but it's what is called gaucho style. That is, it's a settee by day and a bed by night. It must be made up completely each evening, and all the bedding put away in the morning. If you have such a bed and want to make bed making easier without using a sleeping sack, use fitted sheets. You probably will not be able to find fitted *top* sheets for sale, however, so here's how to make your own.

Buy a matching set of sheets, one flat, one fitted. Cut both in half across the width, and sew one fitted half to each flat half, using a

French or flatfell seam. You now have two fitted top sheets. Add matching fitted bottom sheets and whatever pillow cases or shams you need to complete the picture.

Inexpensive new "egg crate" mattress toppers do wonders in taming an RV bed that is too hard or lumpy. Because seams, cording, buttons, and crevices occur in many convertible beds, a thick and cushy mattress cover is a must.

Electronics

A television screen is no substitute for a crackling campfire and the camaraderie of fellow campers, but there are times when the tube is a welcome companion. A VCR is also a must, especially if you spend a lot of time in areas where TV reception is scanty. You'll probably want a good stereo, with tape and CD players, too.

Among specialty electronics to add to camping pleasure are a good CB (Citizen's Band) radio system, closed circuit television (it's especially useful on a large motorcoach to increase visibility to the rear), and a computer set-up.

Many campgrounds now offer telephone and cable TV hookups, so be prepared to utilize them. (If the campground charges extra for cable TV service, find out exactly what is offered; sometimes the cable is hooked only to the campground's own antenna and brings in only local channels. If your own antenna is good enough, you may not need their hookup.) You may also want to add a rotating antenna with a control that can be operated from inside the RV, or even a dish antenna. Folding models are available for RV rooftops.

If you're doing extensive renovations aboard an RV, start planning your electronics early, because wiring, antennas, cables, shielding, remote controls, user comfort, speakers, secure mounts, and ventilation all have to be planned before new paneling goes in. This is also a good time to add a sophisticated multi-function security system.

For a Quieter Ride

In furnishing the RV, try to find ways to make the rig quieter on the road and at rest. Opt for the thickest carpeting and padding, with a minimum of vinyl flooring. Wood and tile flooring may look good, but won't swallow sound as carpeting can.

Fabric upholstery is a better choice than plastic, at least as far as noise absorption is concerned. A fabric shower curtain absorbs sound; plastic reflects it. Plastic, wood, or metal blinds clatter; fabric curtains are silent. Padded, fabric-covered cornices dampen sound; wood cornices echo it. Fabric lamp shades soften sound; metal and plastics magnify it. A butcher block galley counter drinks in sound; tiles shout noises back at you.

Wherever possible, choose the softer or thicker or less brittle alternative. Add a chenille toilet seat cover, a thick bath mat, quilted bedspreads. Heavy, lined window coverings absorb sound and also insulate better against heat and fading. Melamine dishes are quieter than metal or china. Ovenproof plastic bakeware rattles less than metal.

To soften the clatter of pots and pans underway, slip a coffee filter between each piece. The filters will also protect nonstick linings, which could be scratched if they vibrate against other pans and lids. Never nest nonsticks so that the bottom of one pan grates against the lining of another.

Rubber sink mats can be used in many places to quiet and to cushion. Use one in each side of the double sink, one in the shower pan, and another on the floor of the refrigerator. Inexpensive carpet samples can be used to line cupboards. Simply lift them out for vacuuming or shampooing.

Arrange pantry items so glass doesn't clink against glass. When foods (juices, salad oil, vinegar, instant coffee, soda) come in plastic as well as glass, choose plastic. Cut the ribbed cuffs off worn-out socks and slip one over each glass bottle in the cupboard to keep it from clinking and breaking. The cuffs can be washed and reused over and over.

One of the noisiest parts of the RV is the stove. Always use the grate hold-downs provided by the manufacturer and, if you store pans in the oven, pad them with pot holders. Any time you dampen vibration and noise, you're also saving wear.

Use thick, cushioned drawer lining to keep kitchen utensils quieter. Foam liner, intended for use in tool boxes, is sold in hardware stores. Knives should ride in their own holder, for their safety and yours. If you carry any big, breakable item such as a bean pot or clay cooker, wrap it in bubble wrap. It's sold by the yard at professional and do-it-yourself moving companies, and it can be reused time and again.

Replace the bed's wood headboard with fabric. Cover a wall with sheet cork. It will absorb sound and also turn the space into a bulletin board. Sheet cork or a thick, textured wall covering can also be used to re-face the refrigerator door (most RV models have a removable panel to fill with the material of your choice).

Do you have accordion doors that clatter underway? Replace them with sound-absorbent materials (like those used to make "breakout" rooms in hotels and restaurants.) They'll be quieter on the road and provide more privacy in camp. Is the bathroom door too thin to provide privacy? Upholster it on one or both sides with padded upholstery vinyl.

Lighting

It's likely that you'll want to add a few interior lights to the RV, supplementing the basic system with lights that suit your individual needs—a night light near the baby's bunk, reading lights over each pillow, mood lighting over the sofa, or a bright bulb over the table where you'll play cards into the wee hours.

Visit a large RV store, or consult an RV supply catalog, to see what is available in light fixtures and in both 12- and 110-volt bulbs. If you need new wiring to add lighting, you may have to call in an expert. However, much can be done with existing wiring.

You might, for instance, change to a new-style fixture, substitute a warmer bulb for one that is too bright, put a double fixture in place of a single one, replace a short fixture with a longer one, or replace a light fixture with a wall plug or with track lighting—all with your present wiring. Just make sure you're not exceeding the capacity of each circuit.

Trash Storage

Suddenly one waste basket isn't enough. Most municipalities ask us to separate garbage from trash, and to separate trash into numerous categories—five different types of plastic, colored glass, clear

Many attractive 12-volt wall lamps are available through RV and marine suppliers. (RV Supply, Inc.)

glass, newspapers, other kinds of paper, tin cans, aluminum, hazardous waste, engine oil. And the RV-dweller has the added complication of adjusting to rules that vary from place to place.

Unfortunately, RV manufacturers have lagged behind in the trend toward recycling and often provide barely enough room for a single trash container, let alone multiple recycling bins. So, to avoid the unpleasant task of sorting everything after it's been thrown together, most of us compromise by making two or three compartments, and separating the most important categories.

You can take three steps. First, minimize your use of disposables. Second, seek out every unused inch in your RV where a trash storage bin might be placed. The most common place to find otherwise wasted space is in a galley corner, behind drawers. This space can be accessed from above. Cut a hole in the galley counter, and nestle a plastic waste basket into it. Then use the piece cut out of the counter as a lid. (Sometimes a similar dead space can also be found in the bathroom.)

Third, shop hardware and home stores, supermarkets, and RV supply stores for plastic trash storage containers in just the right size and configuration for your needs. They can be tall and thin, lidded or open, short and squat, round or rectangular. Some are divided into two or more compartments; some are on drawer-type frames that can be mounted under the counter and pulled out.

Trash compactors are available for RVs, but they are seldom standard equipment. If you camp in areas where strict separation is required, a compactor may be of little use anyway. Garbage disposals are even more uncommon in RV use; garbage would greatly complicate your gray-water woes.

Basement and Attic

Much of same sports equipment you stored at home in your basement, attic, or yard shed can go on the road with you and add to your fun. If you can find room for it inside, that's better for security and aerodynamics, but the RV offers plenty of spots where you can tack on extra equipment.

Tow a boat, carry an inflatable boat on the roof rack or in the "basement" storage areas underneath, or hang a folding boat on the side of the RV. Mount special racks in any suitable spot for skis, water skis, a canoe, golf clubs, tennis rackets, or fishing poles. Sturdy bike racks are available ready made, to mount on your RV or tow car. If you have toddlers, consider carrying a small inflatable swimming pool too. Add one or two roof pods, if necessary, to carry small items.

Modern RV awnings are a wonder, allowing you to unfold a spacious front porch with the flick of a wrist. Carry a couple of folding chairs in the basement or rooftop, to set up a patio wherever you go. The more you enjoy outdoor living, the more patio furniture you'll want to add—folding tray tables, a screen room, a gas grill, more chairs, strings of lights.

About Keepsakes

They are the music of our lives. Some, such as the bronzed baby shoes and the bowling trophy, are simple melodies. Others are entire

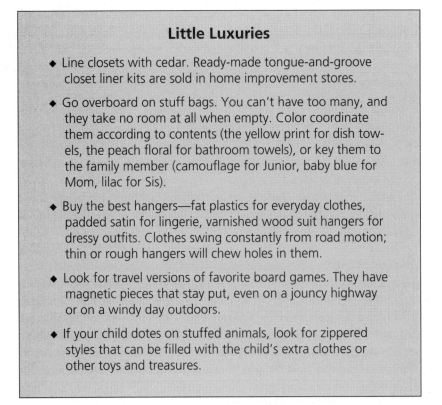

Little Luxuries

◆ Line closets with cedar. Ready-made tongue-and-groove closet liner kits are sold in home improvement stores.

◆ Go overboard on stuff bags. You can't have too many, and they take no room at all when empty. Color coordinate them according to contents (the yellow print for dish towels, the peach floral for bathroom towels), or key them to the family member (camouflage for Junior, baby blue for Mom, lilac for Sis).

◆ Buy the best hangers—fat plastics for everyday clothes, padded satin for lingerie, varnished wood suit hangers for dressy outfits. Clothes swing constantly from road motion; thin or rough hangers will chew holes in them.

◆ Look for travel versions of favorite board games. They have magnetic pieces that stay put, even on a jouncy highway or on a windy day outdoors.

◆ If your child dotes on stuffed animals, look for zippered styles that can be filled with the child's extra clothes or other toys and treasures.

symphonies—the big album of wedding photographs, a lifelong collection of salt and pepper shakers, your jazz records.

To fit all the tools of life into an RV, possessions have to be pared to the bare bones, and useless memorabilia must be left behind. Yet during our first year of fulltiming we found ourselves wishing that we had some remnants of our past life to share with each other, with new friends made along the way, or simply with our secret selves.

It's one thing to talk about what you did, where you've been. It's another to have something tangible—a photograph, a seashell, a recording—to recreate sounds or smells or sights out of the past.

When you break up housekeeping, one solution is to get rid of everything. Another is to keep it all, and warehouse it. (But you'll probably never see it again, let alone sort and utilize it.) A third and, we feel, more sensible solution is to make keepsakes manageable and enjoyable in the fulltiming life. Here's how.

Miniaturize It

Do you have to take the full-size version of it? A professional recording house, or even a good hobbyist, can transfer your record collection to tape and improve the sound quality in the bargain. Your old home movies, or all those hundreds of fuzzy old slides, can be put on videotape and edited at the same time.

The photographer who did your wedding album may still have the negatives. Have him make an album of wallet-size shots to replace the eight-by-tens.

Go through your scrapbooks, taking out items that you'll enjoy showing to others on the road (the blue ribbon you won for your carrot cake; the clipping of you and the Little League team you coached to state championships). Now make one compact, new scrapbook. When you strike up conversations with new friends in camp, such souvenirs sum up your past and your interests in a quick, interesting, visible way. When you're sorting all those boxes of old report cards, term papers, and homemade greeting cards, make scrapbooks for each of the children and grandchildren too.

Do you have more house plants than Cypress Gardens? Replace them with small and very pleasing miniature house plant collectibles such as a bonsai or a cactus dish garden. Do you collect glass or ceramic or stuffed animals? Start a new collection of tiny ones—they have a charm all their own. Do you dote on your power tools? Look at the Dremel line of miniature tools. Many do full-size work.

Extract from It

Could you find one, favorite Lladro piece or one Boehm bird or one golf trophy that will represent to you the rest of the collection you left in storage? It can be the center of attention somewhere in your RV. If you visit your warehouse once in a while, you could exchange one sample for another.

Items that aren't too heavy can be held in place with a stickum such as florist clay. Or, you may want to make a custom cupboard or holder. Never forget the bumps and grinds of highway living, and protect your keepsakes accordingly.

Frame It

Measure the most likely section of unbroken wall space in your RV and buy a clear, frameless poster frame that will fit it. Then fill the frame with a collage of snapshots and portraits—large and small, old sepias and bright new color prints, formal and whimsical. Butt or overlap them, like a crazy quilt. We have one in a big, thirty-two-inch by twenty-six-inch frame that seems to create a happy, seamless jumble of memories, generations, friends and family, punctuated by ticket stubs, prize ribbons, and other memorabilia. We never tire of looking at it.

Other things fit into frames too. Frame a piece of Grandmother's tatting, or the pressed flowers from your wedding bouquet, or your child's baptism dress. Special, thicker frames can hold medals, prizes, a collection of rare seashells, car badges, Dad's pocket watch, an antique fan—anything that isn't more than about an inch thick.

Make It Useful

Cut out the best part of an old, worn quilt, Spanish shawl, or afghan and turn it into throw pillows you can use in your RV. Build in a special spot for the antique clock and continue using it as your primary, livingroom timepiece.

Start using your collection of spoons, antique candle sticks, porcelain cups and saucers, salt cellars, or whatever. Carry as many as you comfortably have room for, and bring out new ones each day. The day you have been saving them for is *here*.

Use It Up

Read those books you've been saving up, then donate them to a library. If you have a basket into which you've been throwing souvenir matchbooks, use them to light campfires. Not very serious about that bundle of stamps or postcards? If they have no value as collectibles, stick the stamps on the cards and mail them to friends as you travel.

Do you have a button collection? Sew them on a plain T-shirt to create a work of art and wear it. Collections of pins, flies, charms, or badges can also be sewn on a hat or vest. Do you have a collection of fabric scraps? If you don't have time to make a quilt, make a couch throw or a skirt—something you can really use.

Most of all, cherish the past but don't mourn it. You're making new memories every day. The sooner you wear out that old souvenir T-shirt or baseball cap, the sooner you can wear the new ones you'll buy along the way.

CHAPTER NINE

Rest Insured

It can cost a king's ransom to replace your most basic necessities if you lose your household. If you ever have to start over, you'll need the hefty grubstake that good insurance can provide. And even if you never face a *total* wipe-out, the proper insurance can help you avoid financial catastrophe.

Fulltimer Coverage

Imagine yourself in any of the following situations:

◆ Your cat scratches the child in the campsite next door, and the family demands that you pay the medical bills.

◆ You go on a business trip, and your suitcase is stolen at the airport.

◆ You're entertaining campground neighbors on your site's patio when your folding chair collapses under your guest.

◆ Your safety deposit box is rifled in a major bank heist.

◆ Your sister and brother-in-law are storing your expensive Oriental rugs in their attic while you're on the road, and their house burns down.

◆ There's a fire in your RV, and your stamp collection, the family silver, and some expensive cameras are burned beyond recognition.

Your homeowner insurance covers all this, right? Well, not necessarily. If you're no longer a homeowner, you can have the best RV insurance policy in the world and still not have all the coverage you used to take for granted.

As a fulltimer, you need to insure the RV, its contents, and its liabilities. You also need a Comprehensive Personal Liability (CPL) policy to cover such things as the cat scratch or the collapsed chair, and floaters to cover those valuables that are carried aboard and those being stored elsewhere.

We can't say it too often: When you're a fulltimer, you have special problems and needs—needs that non-fulltimers often do not understand. One of our liveaboard friends lost a very expensive set of heirloom silver in an RV fire. Can you imagine trying to convince an insurance investigator that you had sterling silver flatware in a *motorhome*?

Even the special "personal effects endorsement" offered with some RV policies is designed more for the part-timer, who may carry cameras, skis, fishing gear, or other personal belongings, than for the fulltimer, who travels with an entire household. It doesn't cover more than a small fraction of the value of expensive jewelry, paintings, silver, heirlooms, and keepsakes. You'll need special policies for each.

Before you move aboard, consult an insurance agent to review the coverage you have and find out what you'll need for the unique life you'll be taking up. Then make sure the new policy is in effect before the old ones are cancelled to avoid even a moment's lapse in coverage.

If you're going to rent out your house while you're gone and plan to store some of your personal belongings there, cover them in your landlord policy. If you're simply going to leave your home intact and unoccupied, your existing coverage can continue as if you were a part-timer—but read the fine print in your policy: If the insurer can make a case for abandonment (e.g., uncollected newspapers at your house, or a neglected lawn) it could void some or all of your coverage.

If you tow a car or boat behind your motorhome, or if you tow a travel trailer with a car or truck, they will be insured separately. As a result, you'll need additional coverage for items you carry in the tow vehicle, such as the shop tools or outboard motor.

Additional coverage may also be available through other sources. For example, a warehouse may offer (or even require you to buy) insurance for items you store there.

It's possible that your present underwriter can't offer the coverage insured

you need, simply because many insurance firms are unfamiliar with the fulltiming lifestyle and have no provisions in their policies for it.

According to Brock L. Benn, a vice-president at Alexander & Alexander and a specialist in motorhome insurance, you'll probably pay higher premiums as a fulltimer, because typical RVs are used only about fifty days per year. So even though you may spend weeks or months in one spot without moving, and aren't facing any more road hazards than the part-timer, you present a higher risk in terms of fire and other losses.

Here is Benn's insurance advice for the fulltimer:

♦ Inventory your possessions, using videotape or a notebook, and store the record somewhere other than in your RV.

♦ If you need more coverage than the standard RV policy provides, get additional personal effects insurance. It costs about $15 per $1,000 in coverage.

♦ Valuables such as jewelry, guns, cameras, and collectibles should be covered by special floater policies. Again, you'll need a motorhome insurance specialist because many companies won't write floaters unless they also write your homeowner policy.

♦ Towing a car behind a motorhome, and using it for local errands, may reduce your premiums. The reasoning is simple: When you're on the road in an $8,000 car instead of in an $80,000 motorhome, less is at risk.

♦ Don't lie about your state of residence or your fulltimer status. It could void your coverage.

♦ Higher deductibles reduce premiums on collision and comprehensive, but this is a "comfort level" decision. Most companies offer deductibles of $100, $250, $500, $1,000, or higher. Ask for quotes and determine whether the savings will be meaningful.

Comparison shopping for bargain rates will be difficult, Benn admits, because sources for fulltimer coverage are limited. If you're having trouble finding a policy for fulltiming, call Alexander & Alexander at (800) 521-2942.

Getting Paid

Once all the right insurance is in place, you must take the steps that will make it possible to collect on claims. You need a careful record of the inventory in your RV so you'll know exactly what is lost in a fire or what is missing after a burglary or a collision. And, Brock Benn warns, some underwriters will also want to see a bill of sale or a professional appraisal to document the worth of valuables covered under floater policies.

One way to take a household inventory is simply to start with pencil and paper and list everything aboard, plus what you paid for it, and when. An easier way would be to record the inventory on audiotape. Or use a camcorder or still camera to make a visual record. Remember that you're making a record, not a prize portrait. Go for completeness and clarity. We prefer slides for this purpose, because they store in very little space, yet can be projected on a very large screen to magnify small details if necessary.

Make note of serial numbers, model numbers, and identifying features. Pan across the set of silverware, focus tight on marks or numbers, get a shot of Mom in her expensive leather coat. Line up all the appliances, and items in every closet, drawer, and storage bin.

Don't underestimate the value of everyday items. A few pots can easily cost $100; a set of good cutlery can cost a fortune. Even a set of stainless steel flatware can cost hundreds of dollars, and a pair of men's canvas shoes fifty dollars or more. So list *everything* that is part of your household—in, under, or atop the RV.

In the living room for example, list the carpeting, curtains, drapes, wall cloths, books, records, plants and planters, musical instruments, and entertainment electronics.

In your porch or patio area you may have a grill, awning or folding umbrella, hoses, electrical cord and pigtails, and folding chairs. In the kitchen you have not just costly tableware, cookware, and appliances, but food, cleaning supplies, curtains, and lighting fixtures.

In the bedroom, don't forget books and tapes, the TV and VCR, expensive cosmetics and toilet articles, clothing, and several hundred dollars in bed linens (the mattress alone probably cost $200 to $300). You may think you don't have any expensive jewelry, but costume pieces add up too.

Your office may contain a computer, FAX, cellular phone, and other very expensive electronics, not to mention software and irreplaceable files.

Our bathroom is the size of a phone booth, but we counted up an impressive inventory in towels, the shower curtain, toiletries, electric razor, over-the-counter drugs, and prescription medications.

Don't forget to list items stored in the roof rack, bike racks, or "basement" storage areas—tools, spare parts, pet supplies, the folding shopping cart, luggage, out-of-season clothing, and holiday supplies you use only once a year.

Items that can be stolen easily, such as cameras and electronics, can be scribed in some hidden spot with your driver's license or Social Security number. While this I.D. may not help the authorities retrieve a lost item for you, it will prove that the item is yours if you do have a chance to claim it.

Consider getting a professional appraiser for the valuables you carry aboard. Once the inventory is done, keep a copy with you and send others elsewhere for safekeeping. Update it regularly as you add new equipment or as jewelry increases in value. Review your insurance coverage regularly too. Many homeowner policies increase coverage automatically with inflation; your personal effects policy probably doesn't have this feature.

Storage of Valuables

If you want to leave some of your belongings in a safety deposit box, think carefully about what to store and where to store it. It makes sense to have two or more signatories to the box—perhaps you, your spouse, and a close family member who could get into the box if you need something from it while you're on the go. If, however, the box is in a state where all financial instruments are sealed when one signatory dies, you could lose access to your own safety deposit box for weeks if your spouse or any other co-rentor dies. Ask.

Let's say, though, that you want to store things that are too large for such a box, such as silver holloware, works of art, or a large coin collection. Commercial vaults, not to be confused with mini-warehouses, are found throughout the country.

Such vaults have maximum security, including fenced parking lots, closed-circuit surveillance, and guards. The cost is high, perhaps $2,000 a year or so for a vault about three feet by four feet by two feet, plus optional insurance. For a list, write the National Association of Private Security Vaults, 3562 N. Ocean Blvd., Fort Lauderdale, Florida 33308, or call (305) 565-7466.

When choosing a vault, look into its security features, annual costs, and ease of access. Ask whether the facility is open all the time or just during business hours, and whether you're allowed unlimited visits or just a certain number per year.

Dave Fisher, an outdoor writer who specializes in hunting, lost everything in a fire. He wrote us, "We had a summer I would not wish on anyone. The loss of everything is not the worst part; it's losing it all at once . . . no keys for the car, no license, not even a toothbrush."

No security system is secure against all theft. No insurance can cover the total cost, heartbreak, and time lost when you suffer a complete loss of your rolling home and its contents. Still, you can ease the pain by setting up the right protections and insurances to make recovery as quick and complete as possible.

CHAPTER TEN

Managing Money on the Go

Imagine yourself a stranger everywhere you go, unable to walk into a bank where you're known, or pay by check at the supermarket or autoparts store, or ask a friend to cash an out-of-town check for you. That's life on the go.

The banking/credit/money transfer scene has undergone dizzying changes in the last few years. Such changes mean higher costs for banking services, easier access to your money at some times and outlandish hassles at others, and enormous penalties for mishaps such as a small overdraft.

Banking

First, forget all your old banking habits and shop ruthlessly for the best prices on the services you now need. When you're on the road you probably will do all your banking by mail or electronic transfer anyway, so there's no reason to stick with your old accounts or your neighborhood bank. In fact, the answer for you may not be a bank or savings and loan (S & L) at all; you may choose to open an account at a brokerage or credit union, or to deal primarily in cash.

Look also at other options that make sense in your new circumstances, such as a senior citizen's account if you're fifty-five or older, or a low-activity account designed especially for people who write only a few checks each month.

When comparing such packages, weigh all the perks—such as free life insurance or a free credit card—against per-check charges, the cost of any extra services, penalties, interest rates, fees for allowing your balance to fall below a certain minimum, or charges for writing more than the allotted number of checks per month.

Beware, too, of inactivity fees. Believe it or not, banks commonly charge for the privilege of holding onto your money. Fulltimers who stay out of touch for months at a time, thinking their money is quietly earning interest, sometimes receive nasty surprises.

After you've narrowed the choice of accounts, take another keen look at the list of benefits. Some of them, such as a slick monthly magazine, an insurance policy that pays only if you're killed in a plane crash, or discounts on hotels, are of little or no value to the RV fulltimer.

Banking today is a giant shell game, constantly shifting, so it's no longer wise to park your money or your loyalties permanently. Keep abreast of costs and reshuffle the deck as necessary. (Beware, though, of penalties for closing an account too soon. Not to be confused with penalties for early withdrawal, these are fees banks charge to offset the inconvenience they say you cause if you close an account within, say, six months or a year after opening it. Such fees can be charged for *any* accounts, not just CDs.)

Now that you're fulltiming, you'll probably want to look for such account features as:

◆ Best checking account based on the way you'll use checks on the go. Charges vary wildly, so choosing the wrong package can be costly.

◆ Best deal on electronic transfers. If you'll spend time in Canada, Mexico, or other countries, compare international transfer costs too.

◆ Best "extras" for your needs, such as a fee-free credit card, free traveler's checks, or low-cost overdraft protection.

◆ Safety. It goes without saying that bank safety is a special concern these days. Even if all your money is in federally insured accounts, a bank failure might cause a delay in access to your funds, or loss of interest, so it's best not to have all your nest eggs in the same banking basket.

Cashing Out

We had some rude shocks when we first went fulltiming. Instruments we thought were as good as cash turned out not to be. A Florida bank refused to honor the cashier's check we'd brought from our home bank; a discount store refused to take our traveler's checks for a basketload of supplies; a savings and loan balked at redeeming our savings bonds.

Here are some ways to get cash on the road. Most of them should be put in place before you leave, because it's much more difficult to get new accounts or credit cards after you no longer have an address or telephone number.

Credit cards. With most major credit cards you can get cash at a bank or automated teller machine (ATM), and sometimes at other outlets as well. Some cards, such as Discover, also offer emergency hotline help for cash emergencies such as a highway breakdown. For a cash advance, you pay a transaction fee, which could be a percentage or a flat rate, plus applicable interest. Most cards charge interest on cash advances from the day of withdrawal, even if you pay the bill each month and are not subject to other interest charges. More later about credit cards.

Debit cards. If your Visa or MasterCard is not a credit card but a debit card against your savings or brokerage account you pay no interest, because you're withdrawing your own money. However, there may be an annual fee and a charge for each transaction.

ATM cards. Issued free by your bank, an ATM card can be used to get cash automatically at any member bank, street kiosk, airport, supermarket, or mall. For the fulltimer, the best ATM card is the one belonging to the largest network, with the most outlets most convenient to your travel route. Some networks are local, some regional. Others, such as the Plus System, which has 60,000 ATMs in fifty states and sixteen countries, are universal.

When comparison shopping, ask about transaction fees, which may vary according to whether you're using your own bank, a member bank, or a commercial outlet. Take precautions when using an ATM, especially at isolated machines, and keep your personal identification number (P.I.N.) in your head, not in writing.

Traveler's checks. A traveler's check is more theft-proof than cash, but it won't be accepted by everyone, every time. Traveler's checks are issued free with some savings accounts. Otherwise you'll pay about one percent. Even free checks cost you money, however, because money invested in traveler's checks is tied up and earns no interest.

When shopping for traveler's checks, ask exactly what you must do if they are lost or stolen. If you have to travel miles to report a theft, or wait days for your money, you could be stranded. Replacement rules and times vary, and the process seldom is as quick and easy as you think.

Read the fine print about your responsibility. If the company can prove you were negligent in handling traveler's checks, they may refuse to pay. In one scandal a few years ago, people were denied refunds for stolen traveler's checks because they had signed them, at the issuing bank, with erasable ballpoint pens. Thieves simply erased the signature and penned in a new one, then added a matching countersignature.

Savings bonds. Series EE savings bonds, available for as little as twenty-five dollars (fifty dollars maturity value) are as safe as traveler's checks, but they earn interest. At this writing savings bond interest is 6.5 percent if the bonds are held to maturity—a better rate than is currently offered by money market funds or T-bills. Moreover, the interest is tax deferred until you redeem the bonds. You might stock up on them during your last few years at work, then spend them on the go when you're in a smaller tax bracket.

Their downside is that they must be held for at least six months before you can redeem them, and they can be cashed only at savings institutions. That means you're out of luck on nights, weekends, and holidays, when thrifts are closed. Nor can you use them in other countries. Savings bonds can't be cashed outside the United States, even in branches of U.S. banks.

Bonds are no longer issued immediately. You must get an application from your bank or S & L and send it to the Federal Reserve. Service takes two to three weeks.

After one southern S & L balked at cashing bonds for us, we wrote the U.S. Treasury and were told that institutions that sell such bonds are *required* to redeem them, as long as you have adequate identification and do not ask for "unreasonable" amounts. Now we cash only a few hundred dollars at a time, offer a passport and a driver's license as I.D., and stand up for our rights. If you meet all the rules and are refused, report the institution to Savings Bonds Division, U.S. Treasury, 1111 20th St. N.W., Washington, D.C. 20226.

Money by wire. Money sent via Western Union arrives across the country in as little as fifteen minutes, so it's instant cash in an emergency. It can also be used to send cash to Mexico or Canada (although international transfer takes longer).

Wire transfer is fast, but it's cumbersome and expensive. You can ask someone to go to a Western Union desk in person, with cash, or you can charge a transfer against a credit card. Costs range from about $15 dollars to send $100, to $37 to send $500. To claim your cash, you'll need identification, such as a driver's license.

Wire transfers between banks usually cost a flat rate, so they are a better deal than Western Union if you're sending large amounts; less competitive for small amounts. Things can get sticky if you're not a depositor at one or both banks, but it's worth a try. You can also arrange a cash transfer via the American Express Optima card.

Other methods. Here are ways to get cash in a real pinch.

◆ Have someone send you a cashier's check via Express Mail or an overnight express service. You may have trouble cashing a cashier's check in a city where you have no account, but most banks are willing to accommodate if you have a good appearance, good I.D., and are willing to pay for a long-distance call to verify the check.

◆ Have someone send you cash via registered mail. It takes longer than regular mail because it must be signed for by each person who handles it, but if cash must be mailed, this is the safest method.

◆ Have someone send you a postal money order via a fast method such as Express Mail or Federal Express. Money orders are inexpensive (75 cents for a $500 value) and safe. On the downside, post offices aren't open nights and holidays, and a small post office may not have enough cash on hand to cash a large money order.

Hang On to Your Cash

You'll have to get cash less often if you use checks and credit cards wherever possible. Our rule is to try personal checks first. They're *always* accepted for bills paid by mail and when the plate is passed at church, *usually* accepted for campground fees, prescriptions, and medical and dental charges, and *occasionally* (but don't rely on it) accepted for stamps and other postal supplies, flea-market buys, restaurant meals, groceries, auto parts, fuel, and purchases in variety stores. For your own convenience and credibility, some banks suggest that you have your driver's license number printed on your checks.

When checks fail, we try a credit card *if* we can charge the item at no extra cost. Always ask, especially at fuel stations and small businesses; some merchants charge a premium price for credit card purchases. Many gas stations have three price structures: cash, their own credit card, and other credit cards. Small businesses might want an additional four percent or so to put it on the plastic.

We're assuming that you prefer not to carry large amounts of money aboard. However, if you do feel more comfortable with a stash of cash, invest in a fireproof safe that can be mounted in a hidden spot, in the most theft-proof, crash-proof manner you can devise (such as welding it to the frame).

Ironclad I.D.

If you find that your driver's license isn't enough identification, get a passport. We've always carried ours, and it has been a big help in establishing our identity in situations where a driver's license alone was getting us nowhere.

Good I.D. is crucial to the rootless wanderer, but it's important to safeguard personal information. Now that some states have passed laws prohibiting the practice, most merchants no longer ask for a credit card as additional I.D. for cashing a check. Be suspicious of anyone who asks for a credit card as I.D., because it's of no use to an honest merchant. Unless you have used it to make a purchase, he cannot make a claim against your card even if you gave him a bum check.

Never reveal a telephone credit card number and never write down your personal identification number in the same place as the account number.

A new scam is being worked by thieves who tap your bank account if they can get the number. A signature isn't needed. Don't give your account number to anyone who calls you; don't use deposit slips to write grocery lists or as substitute business cards when you want to give your name and address to campground friends.

About Credit Cards

Even if you've never been a credit card user in the past, plastic can play an important role in keeping your cash cloverleaf flowing. But be aware that not all credit cards, not even all Visas or all MasterCards, are alike.

Interest rates differ among issuing banks, and also according to limits set by state law. Some bank cards charge interest at a set rate; others at a variable rate tied to the Federal Reserve prime rate, which changes frequently.

You can write to RAM, Box 1700, Frederick, Maryland 21702, for the current issue of *CardTrak*, a monthly newsletter listing rates at 500 institutions worldwide. A single copy costs five dollars. In a typical list at this writing, we see annual fees ranging from zero to thirty-nine dollars, and interest rates ranging from 9.5 percent to 21 percent or more. Most lending institutions have toll-free numbers, so you have nothing to lose by shopping around. Call for several credit applications, then read the fine print and apply only for the cards that will cost least according to the way you will use them.

Below are some features to consider when selecting a credit card for fulltiming.

Cost of Using the Card

♦ **Annual fees.** Fee-free cards are available; others cost thirty-five dollars or more per year. Often, cards with the lowest annual fees charge the highest monthly interest. If you get a card that carries no annual fee, and pay it off each month, you pay nothing for the convenience of having a credit card, unless you incur transaction fees or penalties.

♦ **Penalties.** In addition to interest, charges are made for late payments and for charging more than your limit. At People's Credit, the plan offered by *Consumer's Digest*, each of these transgressions costs fifteen dollars.

♦ **Interest charges.** If you pay the bill in full each month, you won't care that interest rates are in the twenty percent bracket. If you get your mail regularly, and pay bills by their due date, this convenient credit costs you nothing. Once you get sucked into the interest vortex, however, it isn't always easy to claw your way back out. When you carry a balance, interest rates begin at once with each purchase and are calculated on the average daily balance.

If your mail sometimes is delayed and you want to avoid getting caught with interest or late payment charges, work with a credit card company that allows you to pay the bill even if you don't receive it. To do this, keep track of all your credit purchases and send a check to pay the amount owed each month *before* the due date. Some companies aren't equipped to deal with your payment without all the data contained in the stub that comes with the bill, so ask first.

If you're dealing with a Visa or MasterCard debit card from your bank or broker, you're simply withdrawing your own money from your own account and are not subject to interest charges. Another plus is that you can have a very high spending ceiling, limited only by the size of your account. The disadvantage to these cards is that you get no "float": As soon as the merchant reports the purchase, your account is charged. With other cards, you get a grace period, usually twenty-five to thirty days. Too, brokerages usually charge a fee of twenty-five to thirty-five dollars per year for cards that are available from banks for nothing.

Kickbacks

With the popularity of the new "affinity" cards (Visa or MasterCards connected with another business or organization) have come all manner of paybacks connected with credit card use. Every time you use an affinity card there is a payoff to your favorite college, cause, or charity, or to you in the form of frequent-flyer miles or some other benefit. The Discover card, for example, pays you back a percentage of your purchases each year, in cash. All major credit card companies also offer prestige or "gold" cards, which cost more per year but also offer higher kickbacks, benefits, or privileges.

Extras

With most major credit cards, you can get a cash advance almost anywhere in the world. Compare bottom-line costs, including interest and transaction fees.

If you use the credit card in your business, you might benefit by getting a card designed especially for that purpose. They offer such things as monthly breakdown by type of expense, or a yearly breakout of costs by category. This is a tremendous help with bookkeeping and taxes.

Another benefit offered automatically by some cards, and at additional cost by others, is warranty protection that insures you against loss or breakage of any purchase charged to that credit card. However, it's not as simple as providing a receipt and complaining that the item doesn't work. You'll have to fill out forms and perhaps provide serial numbers, a copy of the manufacturer's warranty, or a copy of the police report if the item was stolen. In some cases you can have the item repaired and submit a bill; in others, you must send the item to a service center specified in the contract or to the credit card company itself.

You may also have to submit a copy of your RV or homeowner's policy, to prove you don't have duplicate coverage. Because items stolen from an automobile may not be covered by such warranties, payment for thefts from your rolling home could be tough to collect.

Most cards also offer optional insurance against credit card theft or fraud, and another insurance that pays your balance if you die or become disabled. Discover, for one, offers insurance (which varies according to state law) that makes your payments if you're unemployed under certain circumstances. Insurance that takes over payments is, of course, of little value to those who pay their balance in full every month.

Read the fine print in your card contract to acquaint yourself with your rights and obligations when your card is stolen, or when you are charged for merchandise that you never received or that arrived in unsatisfactory condition. Sometimes you're protected only if the purchase was bought or ordered within, say, fifty miles from "home"— which in your case may be a forwarding address in a state you never visit.

Brokerages

Just as it may no longer make sense to stick with a hometown banker, it is wise to rethink your brokerage, too. We were paying top commission rates to a "full-service" broker who was available to us only during Eastern-time business hours and who could only offer us a limited selection of funds. We switched to a twenty-four-hour broker, and now we are able to trade via telephone at any hour. We also have a wider choice of funds, and we pay lower commissions.

If we choose, we can do the entire trade by touch-tone telephone, although, to be honest, we're reluctant to rely on push-button trading when we're on the go and a real person can't get back to us to verify a trade or ask a question.

The discount route may not be for everyone, because it means doing more of your own research and relying less on Good Ole Phil calling to tell you about a new issue or suggesting that you bail out of Tanking Enterprises.

When shopping for a new broker, keep in mind that commissions vary greatly, and so do services. Small traders generally pay higher fees than high rollers; the deepest discounters usually do not offer twenty-four-hour service. And while some mutual funds offer round-the-clock service and no commission (load), they deal only in their own family of funds and cannot sell you individual stocks. They may not offer any check writing privileges, and probably cannot offer a credit/debit card as a brokerage can.

Some twenty-four-hour brokerages to look into are Fidelity (800) 544-7272, and Charles Schwab (800) 435-4000.

Additional Financial Finaglings

Other wealth. Two of the best bank accounts for fulltimers are a pantry filled with food and a stock of spare parts.

Power of attorney. Everyone today needs a will, living will, and other legal documents, but the fulltimer has added reason for giving power of attorney to one or two trusted confederates. When you're far from home, this person can act on your behalf in hundreds of useful ways. Discuss it with an attorney.

Joint bank account. An inexpensive way to empower a trusted friend or relative to act on your behalf is to open a joint bank account with him or her. In what we call the Friendly Account with Janet's mother, we keep a small balance that Mom can use to pay bills that come due when we can't be reached. She can draw on this account for family birthday gifts or funeral flowers, and deposit checks that arrive when we are out of touch.

Joint accounts can, of course, present problems in cases of the inevitable deaths and taxes, so keep balances small and manageable. Be wary of sharing a safety deposit box or bank account with a relative in a state where accounts are frozen and boxes sealed when one party dies. You could lose access to your valuables for weeks.

Other joint ownerships. Because so many of today's families are made up of people who are not married or related, lawyers keep busy untangling the many wrangles that result. Imagine these scenarios:

◆ You're fulltiming in an RV that is half yours, half your father's. He dies, and your rolling home now belongs half to you and half to your father's estate, which is to be divided among yourself, your two sisters, and your father's disabled brother. If you can't afford to buy out the others' shares, you're homeless.

◆ You and your friend go fulltiming in the RV he owns. When he has a stroke and is hospitalized, his children take over the RV and even deny you the right to visit him in the hospital. You're stranded, homeless, and alone.

◆ You and a friend are fulltiming in your RV. Your friend is at the wheel when the RV collides with a car, injuring its occupants. You're stuck with the lawsuits.

It's popular today to dismiss marriage as "just a piece of paper," but society also looks upon it as a legal contract. As a spouse, relative, or legal heir, you have certain rights that the law does not extend to your lover, best fishing buddy, or anyone else—no matter how pure and passionate the personal contract between you—*unless you get it in writing*. Where rights and possessions are at stake between or among partners who have no legal relationship, see a lawyer now to avoid the possibility of bitter, costly, and perhaps futile battles later.

Information Services

If keeping up with the day-by-day dealings of Wall Street is essential to your financial management, look into DOWPHONE, which costs $15 for sign-up and up to $1.50 per minute to use. Call as often as you like, and pay only for time used to get the information you need. By calling one toll-free number you can get real-time quotes on stocks, options, commodities, and indexes, as well as weather reports, sports, and financial news. For details, call (800) 345-6397. If you have a computer, modem, and telephone hookup, you can also access such information through databases such as Prodigy and CompuServe.

CHAPTER ELEVEN

Keeping in Touch

Mail on the Trail

Whether it's a letter from Aunt Hattie, a pension check, or a charge account bill, we all want our mail to reach us securely and quickly. On the other hand, we're also pursued by tons of junk mail that we *don't* want. It's tricky to keep the postal spigot running full force while filtering out as much unwanted mail as possible.

The more important the content and speed of your correspondence, the more you'll depend on the FAX machine you carry on board or on Federal Express, UPS Red or Blue Label, Express Mail, and other special services. And that in turn can mean higher fulltiming costs.

As a fulltimer, you will need to establish one permanent mailing address, and a means for getting mail from it to you. If you'll be fulltiming for a long time, handling your mail will eventually become drudgery to anyone upon whom you rely to forward it, and when friends and family go on vacation, get sick, or have busy periods, your mail problems may take second billing.

Not so if you use a paid professional forwarding service; nor do they snoop into your personal affairs. If you're getting perfumed letters from Spain, or dunning letters from a collection agency, or advertisements about baldness cures, you may prefer that the mail doesn't go to Uncle Barney on its way to you.

We, however, are lucky enough to have Janet's mother available to forward our mail. We can ask her to throw away the seed catalog but forward the L.L. Bean catalog and the alumni bulletin; to sieve out checks and deposit them for us, and to contact us immediately if she senses an emergency. When we are in other countries where forwarding costs are very high, she throws away excess tonnage, trims borders off letters, and chooses which things to send airmail and which by surface mail.

When we are out of touch for long periods, Mom can intercept bills and pay them. When we're in one spot for a long time, we fill out postal forms that allow her post office to forward first-class mail automatically, without delivering it to her. When we hit the road again, the forwarding is stopped and mail accumulates at Mom's until we settle in a new spot.

The chief advantage of having a trusted family member handle your mail is that you can get completely customized service, always with your best interest in mind. Despite all their other advantages, none of the other mail forwarding options listed below can think for you like Mom or Sis or Good Ole Charlie. However, since such people are rare, many fulltimers use services like the ones described below.

Forwarding Services

Many options are available, from very-low-cost mail forwarding services that are included in some camping club memberships to high-tech services that also offer voice mail and other advantages. Compare not just price, but also speed and accessibility. Some services have toll-free telephone numbers and twenty-four-hour service. With others, you can call only during business hours, on your quarter.

Family Motor Coach Association, 8291 Clough Pike, Cincinnati, Ohio 45244. FMCA membership, which offers mail forwarding, emergency message service, and other benefits, is $35 per year.

Fast Forward, Box 917729, Longwood, Florida 32791; (800) 321-9950 or (407) 774-3222. Using their address allows you to claim Florida residence. (Florida has no state income tax, but does have an intangible assets tax—$20,000 per person exemption.)

Home Base, Box 65656, Lubbock, Texas 79464-5724; (806) 794-9644. Provides the fulltimer with Texas residence (no state or local income taxes), mail forwarding and message services ($7.50 or $15 per month, depending on whether your usage is light or heavy, plus postage and some calls), and other services including FAX, voice mail, emergency medical information, campground reservations, discount buying service, competitive insurance rates, a driver's license requiring no test, emergency locator service, and bill paying. With your authorization, Home Base will charge everything to your Visa or MasterCard. Calls are taken mechanically twenty-four hours a day; the switchboard is open during business hours only. Their numbers are toll-free in the United States (including Texas) and Canada.

M & D Associates, 5801 Carolyn Dr., Ft. Worth, Texas 76180; (800) 525-2691 or (817) 485-8074. Yearly dues are $100, or take a six-month trial membership for $60. (These rates do not include postage or shipping materials.) Once you're established as an M & D client, dues are adjusted to reflect mail volume. If your forwarding postage amounts to less than $14 dollars, dues are only $28; $70 in postage means $70 in dues; for each additional $8 dollars, add a $6 dues increase, to a maximum of $150 a year.

M & D offers twenty-four-hour phone service, including a message service that costs $12 a month or, if it is paid in advance and used with the mail service, $75 per year. Mail instructions and messages can be given over the toll-free number in the United States and Canada.

Also available from M & D is a bill-paying service for $10 a month plus $1 per bill paid. A deposit equal to 1½ times your normal bills is required. Payments are made twice a month, to insure meeting deadlines. Once M & D becomes your personal and business address, you're welcome to claim Texas as your tax home as well. That means no state income tax, and no county personal property tax.

Mail, Messages, and More . . ., Box 2190, Henderson, Nevada 89009-7009. Offers mail forwarding, holding, and remailing via UPS, Federal Express, or Express Mail according to your wishes. Also offered is toll-free voice mail with password security, accessible from any push-button phone; free lost pet service; free emergency locator service; and faxing of important papers as necessary.

Annual fees are based on mail volume, ranging from a minimum of $30 if your volume is less than $19 in postage yearly, to $60 for mail requiring $61 postage, up to $150 per year. (All fees are plus actual postage.) Voice mail is free for mail forwarding members, but a per-call fee is charged depending on telephone charges. You'll be asked for a deposit of $80 up front for personal service or $130 for business service, plus your annual membership.

Mail, Messages, and More grants you total control of what mail you want forwarded and how often, and you also can authorize them to accept certified or registered mail on your behalf. Fulltimers whose address is Henderson are eligible for a competitive insurance rate, and if you register your vehicle here, no smog check is required. For providing the special rural address necessary for these benefits, an additional $30 per year is charged.

Mail Trail Inc., Box 418, Waverly, Florida 33877; (800) 321-7443. Answers live seven days a week, 9 A.M.–7 P.M. No state income tax; Florida does have an intangible assets tax.

Postal Express, 3000 Market St. #351, Salem, Oregon 97301; (503) 363-2677.

Travelers Remail Association, 6110 Pleasant Ridge Rd., Arlington, Texas 76016; (800) 666-6710. This gives you a Texas address.

Travelers Mail Express, Box 10121, Eugene, Oregon 97440.

Managing Mail

Once you have an address, the next step is to eliminate as much mail flow as possible. Arrange for automatic bank deposits of your checks, automatic investment, and automatic bill paying where feasible. Notify those correspondents you no longer care to hear from. One effective way to get off some mailing lists is to mark an envelope Refused, Return to Sender, and give it back, unopened, to the mail carrier.

Get your name off junk-mail lists by writing Mail Preference Service, Direct Marketing Association, 11 W. 42nd St., New York, New York 10163-3661 and Equifax Option, Box 740123, Atlanta, Georgia 30374-0123. Be sure to give your complete name and address. You may have to write more than once if you are listed under more than one name. Later, you'll probably have to write again. Mailing lists multiply like rabbits.

When you order something by mail, note on the order blank:

"Temporary address. Do not add to <u>any</u> mail list." If you underline the word any, it emphasizes that you don't want it on their list or on lists they sell to others.

Subscribe only to magazines you can't buy on the newsstand. Ask your broker how you can reduce mail poundage such as stock proxies and annual reports, perhaps by giving proxy power to someone else. Inquire about electronic checking account statements in which you receive just a one-page statement, not cancelled checks.

Once you select an address, carve it in stone. Trust us on this one. Once any address gets written down, mail goes there forever. It's impossible to keep all your friends and relatives, let alone businesses and banks, abreast of your ever-changing addresses. Although it's a constant fight to convince Aunt Maude that your mail *must* go to Albany, even though she knows full well you're in Albuquerque, insist and persist. You can't notify all the Aunt Maudes in your life every time you move on and, if you notify some and not others, there will be hard feelings.

To keep your temporary addresses from being carved on someone *else's* stone, enlist your mail forwarder in keeping these addresses secret. Otherwise, both of you will fight a losing battle with Aunt Maude and her legions.

When she is handling our mail and someone demands a right-now address, Mom can say something tactful such as, "Oh, just send it here. The post office handles all that automatically," or, "They're on the go again. Send your letter here so I can send it via Federal Express with their next mail packet." Commercial mail forwarding services can be more blunt. They will refuse to give your address to anyone without your authorization.

The only other mail option we can recommend, if you alternate between only two addresses per year as many fulltimers do, is to have stationery printed with both addresses, like this:

John and Mary Brown

Shady Pines, Space #32	P.O. Box 142
Bar Harbor, ME 09887	Key West, FL 33333
May 1–September 30	October 1–April 30

Keeping Your Home Address

Another choice, if you're going to be fulltiming for a year or less, is to keep your home address—even if someone else lives there. The U.S. Postal Service forwards all first-class mail free, directly from the post office, within the United States for one year. Non-first-class mail is forwarded free for up to sixty days. See your postmaster for details. (If yours is a small post office, send a cheery post card or even a box of candy or some silly souvenir once in a while, just to remind the hometown crew that they are appreciated.)

Forwarding from the United States to Mexico and Canada also is free, but you'll probably have to pay to receive the mail on the other end. Postal strikes in Canada have made things very inconvenient for us in the past, and mail to Mexico can be very chancy, although some Mexican states are somewhat more reliable than others. Once you leave the U.S., mail forwarding becomes more complicated and expensive, and if you venture beyond Canada or Mexico, even more costly.

If you are using your home address as described above, the U.S.P.S. will continue to forward newspapers and magazines at your expense after the sixty-day limit. You leave a check to cover costs, then send additional money as needed. The upside to all this is that the mail comes into the post office, gets a new label, and goes right back out the same day. With forwarding services, the delay could be several days; if it goes to a friend or relative, it could sit there for weeks.

The down side is that, after a year, the post office will not continue to forward mail sent to your old address. If you're not home by then, you'll have to supply a new address.

There's also a chance that mail sent to your old home will go astray, and there are sure to be some snafus with mail labeled "Do Not Forward. Return to Sender." Usually this is very important mail, such as a new credit card or a bill, and it may orbit the globe for weeks before you receive it. If you're using this type of mail forwarding (instead of having someone remail everything in a separate packet), you might try writing to your credit card company, alerting them to the fact that this may happen. Then request that they do not change your permanent address unless they are notified by you.

Much depends on your having a good relationship with your present mail carrier, who will be responsible for forwarding any mail sent to your present address after you leave. We treat ours like a member of the family; he is solid gold.

One more point about dealing with the postal service. Your instructions must be in writing, and signed. Laws requiring this are for your protection, so allow plenty of time for changing your forwarding address each time you move on.

Receiving Forwarded Mail

Half the battle is to get the mail headed your way, but more headaches await on the receiving end. Wherever possible, we prefer to have our mail go to a friend, relative, business associate, or other personal address, or to General Delivery, rather than to a campground we have never visited before.

Although, thank heavens, most campgrounds are highly sensitive to the value of mail, we've been in some where all guest mail is thrown into a box for anyone to root through. If your travel plans change and you go elsewhere, it may sit there forever. If you do want a campground to safeguard your mail, it helps to write ahead to announce that you're on the way and to ask that your mail be held there until you arrive or send further instructions.

If you're using General Delivery, do some research in advance so you can have mail sent to a small town or to a branch post office most convenient to your campsite. If it goes to a large city, it ends up downtown at the main post office where traffic is heavy and parking is impossible.

General Delivery mail can be held for a limited time, usually ten to fifteen days, before the post office is required to send it back where it came from. So if you are delayed, notify the postmaster *in writing*. (Here's another advantage to working only with small post offices. People are friendlier, and they receive so little General Delivery mail that they are likely to remember your name and give more personal service. In the few cases when we were delayed beyond the ten days, we've phoned ahead and assured the postmaster that written instructions were on the way. Each one bent the rules for us.)

In some small town post offices we've been welcomed like old friends because our mail had been piling up and they were curious about us. As an added precaution, we usually send a postcard ahead to the postmaster, indicating cheerfully that we are on the way and asking that a lookout be kept for our mail.

Even after you and the mail both arrive, it's not over until the mail is safely in your hands. Take identification to the postal window; it may be required. Suspicious clerks don't want to give mail to the wrong people, and that's good. Also, it can help the clerk find your mail. If your name is a difficult one like Groene, pronounced GRAYnee, it isn't enough to ask for it verbally, because it's filed under GRO and they hear GRAY, or Haney or Raney.

We once checked into a resort to find that all our mail had just been sent back to our permanent address, because a family named Greene had just checked out. Starving for mail, we felt as if a feast had been snatched from under our forks. After that, we started writing ahead to *any* address where we could be receiving mail.

Presenting your name in big, block letters is even more important in areas where another language is spoken. In Mexico, the clerk may look for the Bennetts under V, and the Yardleys under LL. In French Canada, when the O'Rourks request their mail, the clerk may look under Au or Eau. Write it down.

No matter how well you have covered all the bases, leave a forwarding address with each campground and post office before you move on. If you don't know where you're going next, leave your permanent address. If you don't, and if mail arrives after you've left, it will be returned to its sender.

One way to make sure you get all the mail that has been forwarded to any one address is to have your mail forwarder number the packets. Checking in by telephone, you can compare notes on how many packets were sent, and you'll know when it has all arrived.

Always keep in mind that Federal Express, UPS, and other services cannot go to General Delivery or to a post office box address. Because most mail-order merchandise is not sent through the mail, don't order anything unless you can supply a street address.

Some other tips:

◆ If your mail forwarder knows where you are at the time any certified or registered mail arrives, he should give your address to the mail carrier. Once signed for, it is considered delivered, and it will have to be re-registered or certified to get the same protection when it is forwarded to you.

◆ Make sure your mail forwarder uses enough postage. If it arrives Postage Due, and the campground or other receiver refuses to take delivery, it could end up heaven-knows-where.

◆ Although it's very tempting to arrange that mail be waiting for you at General Delivery when you arrive, it's sometimes better to get there first and then decide on the best place to have the mail sent.

◆ Rates keep changing, so we won't quote them here, but good values for small packets include Priority Mail, Express Mail, and Second Day Air via the package delivery services. If you use one of the large mail forwarding services that deals daily with these services, you won't get hit with the additional pickup charge.

◆ If you're in a desperate hurry for a delivery, decide on the best course of action for each situation, because Special Delivery is no longer the only choice. Express Mail is, according to our local postmaster, faster.

◆ If the campground office is closed when the mail carrier brings your Special Delivery, it goes back to the post office, and a note will be left for you at the campground office. And if that little note goes astray, it may be days before you collect your mail. Certified and registered mail also goes back to the post office if there is no one to sign for it.

◆ Federal Express and United Parcel do not consider Saturday a working day, so weekend service costs a hefty premium. However, Saturday deliveries of Express Mail are standard. Two services are available: post office to post office, and post office to addressee. If you arrange by phone for someone to Express Mail something to you, specify whether you want it to go to the post office or to some personal address. Another advantage to Express Mail is that it can go to a post office box; Federal Express and UPS cannot.

◆ Renting a post office box has many advantages to the fulltimer who stays in one general area. Mail waits safely in the box until it's convenient for you to collect it. Box access hours are usually much longer than post office window hours, perhaps even twenty-four hours a day, so you can pick up the mail nights or on weekends if you like. Private postal box services are also springing up around the country.

The Mail-Order Maze

Merchandise-by-mail has caused fulltimers more grief and relief than anything but the tire pump. Whether or not you've been a mail-order user before, you may have special need for it as a fulltimer.

If you have a credit card for no other reason, it can be lifeline to mail and telephone orders in such situations as:

◆ Emergency delivery of a hard-to-find spare part when you're miles from the nearest dealer.

◆ Quick and efficient gift giving without your having to buy, wrap, and mail a package.

◆ Getting exactly the right size, color, or quality in clothing, linens, and other supplies. By always dealing with the same catalog house, you are assured of consistency. For example, we know what size L.L. Bean hiking boots fit us, and what shade of yellow towels from Sears will match our bathroom. Mail-order saves time and fuel.

◆ Tremendous choice. Even in a large store, you probably won't have the choice of items that you can find in one catalog. Despite the size and weight, we carry Sears catalogs. We order from them constantly for ourselves and for gifts, and we use them as price guides when we're shopping for a big purchase such as an appliance.

◆ Mail order gives you access to the specialty and oddball merchandise that is often needed in fulltiming. Through catalog shopping you can find anything from a 12-volt VCR to an automatic pet feeder. Through specialty catalogs, you can also get all your needs for any hobby, no matter how exotic, from ham radio to raising hamsters.

Mail ordering also has its negatives, and they are worse for fulltimers. Here are some ways to cope.

◆ Most mail-order firms do not deliver to post office boxes or General Delivery; you must provide a street address. Sometimes you can specify that an item be sent by mail or not at all, but don't count on it. Most mail-order outfits simply aren't set up to use the mails.

◆ Returns, follow-ups, credits, and warranty work get much more complicated when you're on the move. Sometimes it's better to deal with local merchants or national chains.

◆ Shipping costs are increasing. Many catalog houses charge ten percent or more for freight and handling. We once sent a check for a long list of items, most of which were out of stock. Although the company sent us a full refund for the merchandise that was not available, we ended up paying $4.50 in shipping and handling for the one $4 item we received. Now when we order several items from a company that charges a high minimum shipping cost, we write on the order, "Do not back order, or fill order partially. If you cannot fill the entire order, please cancel it and return my check. "

◆ Sales tax may be charged. Compare the bottom line.

◆ Packages are not forwarded free, so that means a big increase in your shipping costs if an order doesn't arrive before you move on. You might state on each order something like, "If order cannot be shipped to arrive before (date), cancel order and refund my money by return mail." When ordering by phone, ask whether the item is in stock for immediate shipment.

Additional tips on mastering the mail-order maze:

◆ When you receive duplicate or unwanted catalogs, put them in the campground's literature exchange bin. Someone else might need them.

◆ Keep meticulous records of telephone and mail orders, including warranties, verbal promises made over the phone (get the name of the person), confirmation numbers, dates of all orders and correspondence, and every scrap of paper that comes with the merchandise. Usually, exchanges can't be made without key reference numbers.

The Next Best Thing to Being There?

Although fulltimers come in all sizes, shapes, ages, and incomes, all have similar contentments and complaints. Chief among their pleasures is the freedom to move on as they please. One of their most common gripes, on the other hand, is telephones. Here are some tips on telephoning on the go.

Using Your Phone Card

At this writing, telephone credit card use remains a problem. Although laws are making it tougher for telephone companies to block your access to AT&T, Sprint, MCI, or whatever other company you choose to use, we are still encountering difficulties.

Your primary defense is to know the access numbers for your long distance company. If you simply dial "0" plus the phone number, following the instructions on the pay phone, the call will go through promptly, but you'll be billed by whatever carrier handled the call, sometimes at prices far higher than those charged by your chosen carrier.

If you're getting a lot of bills from telephone companies you never heard of, call your primary carrier and ask how to access their service from wherever you are. And when you find you can't reach that service, complain to the campground or other merchant whose pay phone you're using, as well as to the FCC, 1919 M St. NW, Washington, DC 20554.

When you check into a campground that has telephone hookups, always ask for a full rundown of how charges are computed for the calls you make from your own campsite.

Call Home America, a service designed for families whose children are away at school or who otherwise want their loved ones to be able to call home at their expense, might work for you. (Ideally, someone in your family will already have it and will allow you to call home on it.)

Say you call one of your children, or the neighbor who is keeping an eye on your home, several times a week. You can get an 800 number for that phone for only (at this writing) $3.75 per month plus 19 to 24 cents per minute. You can give the number to anyone else whom you want to be able to call that number toll free (at your expense). People can't call the toll-free number to reach you if your number changes constantly. It must be assigned to a permanent phone. For information on this service call (800) 594-3000.

Cellular Phones

A *mobile* phone is a dedicated unit that is mounted in the RV, so don't confuse the mobile with two other types of cellular phone. A *transportable* cellular phone has a battery pack and antenna, so it can be used outside the RV; a *portable* phone is a tiny unit with a built-in antenna and a miniature power pack and can be used almost anywhere.

Although one type can usually be converted to another, you'll get the most energy and space efficiency by opting for the model you plan to stick with. For most of us, a mobile phone is best because an automotive antenna is better than a telescoping portable one, and it's tied into the RV's battery system, with less worry about replacements and rechargings. And mobiles, with prices starting under $300, are cheaper than transportables (starting at about $350) and portables ($500 or more).

Phone prices are going down, and cellular coverage is going up. Today, you're seldom far from a cell. On the downside, service charges are high (about one dollar per minute), although prices may go down as digital technology comes on line. By 1995, analog phones

Numbered for Life

AT&T's new 700-number service may appeal to you if you want to avoid the hassles that come with changing phone numbers every time you move. It's different from Call Forwarding, MCI's Follow Me, and other services, in that it provides you with one telephone number you can keep forever, no matter where (within the contiguous United States) you move. Each time you move on, you call in your new telephone number, and anyone who dials your 700 number will be routed through to you. If the caller is not on an AT&T line, he must dial a five-digit access code first.

At this writing the price is seven dollars a month for the service plus fifteen to twenty-five cents per minute for every call made to you. You pay for all calls, welcome or not, and for calls that come to you through a campground switchboard, even if you're not there.

This is not a number you'll want to give to everyone, but it is an option that may suit your fulltiming lifestyle.

will give way to digitals, which means better communications and more glitch-free data transfer.

If you're new to cellular phoning, you may be surprised to find that such features as Call Trace, Caller ID, Automatic Callback, Automatic Recall, Call Waiting, and Call Forwarding are now available from some carriers. These services are frosting on the cake, however. Choosing a carrier involves far more than buying bells and whistles.

First, look at the coverage area. There's no point in paying for phone service you cannot access; nor can anyone just pick up a phone and find you. Usually the caller has to know what area you're in and then use a touch-tone phone and a series of dialing exercises to ring your chimes.

One fulltimer couple, for example, used phones primarily to call their only daughter, who lives in an area that does not have a cell. They decided that a cellular phone would not be a wise investment.

Second, read price lists carefully and compare costs. Most carriers charge you for both incoming and outgoing calls, busy signals, and unanswered calls. Many cellular companies also require you to use their choice of long distance carrier; if you want to use another, you have to dial in extra access numbers. And it's one thing to subscribe locally; "roaming" costs can make your bills skyrocket.

Technology is changing so rapidly, it pays to keep inquiring, shopping, and learning.

Other Ways to Communicate

Don't assume that you have to run out and invest in a cellular phone; you have many other choices. Some campgrounds have landline telephone hookups, so you can make calls from the comfort of your "living room." If you have a computer and modem, you can communicate worldwide over telephone lines via databases. Or, you may prefer to send and receive faxed messages.

Many fulltimers prefer less expensive, more relaxed options. You might, for example, have an answering machine hooked up somewhere and call in for messages when you get around to it.

Some camping clubs and mail forwarding services (including all those mentioned in this chapter) offer message-taking or voice messaging. Telephone companies, too, offer complete voice mail services.

One nationwide paging service is Sky-Tel (800) 759-8355. Because such paging services reach areas within only a twenty- or thirty-mile radius of major cities, they are of interest only to those fulltimers who are in business or who prefer to camp near metropolitan areas.

Emergency Air Travel

Bill and Marilyn W. were in California when they received word via their message service that Bill's father had had a heart attack in Ohio and was not expected to live. The Hendersons, fulltiming in Mexico for the winter, learned during a routine call home to Michigan that Sue's sister had been hospitalized after an accident at work. Sue's young nieces would be put into a foster home unless Sue could get home immediately to care for them.

We were fulltiming in Fort Lauderdale when word came that

Mother had pneumonia in Albany. Unless Janet could get there at once to give her home nursing care, she'd have to be hospitalized.

There are times when an emergency is too immediate for you to get there by RV. So one or more family members have to leave the RV at a distant spot and fly home. Airline fares have been a turbulent, confusing shell game in recent years, but a recent wrinkle, "bereavement" or "compassion" fares, gives travelers a break on last-minute ticket purchases. However, these fares, like everyday fares, are a puzzle because rules vary from airline to airline.

If you have to fly home in a family emergency, your best contact will be a good travel agent—preferably one who works on salary and not on commission (although ethical travel agents will try to find the best fare under any circumstances). Also, you want a travel agent who is willing to call each individual airline for the latest information rather than working only with his network or database, which may lag hours or even days behind.

Most travel agencies are open only during business hours. If tragedy strikes at night or on weekends, your next choice may be to arm yourself with a handful of change and call individual airlines, or to go directly to the airport and go from counter to counter looking for the best deal on the earliest flight possible.

Here are some things you should know about bereavement fares.

The emergency. Not all airlines offer compassion fares. Among those that do, different yardsticks are applied. Death of a family member is considered an emergency by all airlines, but in the case of Mom's pneumonia, or Sue's trip home to take care of her sister's children, the decision could be up to the telephone reservation agent or the agent behind the counter at the airport. In borderline cases, ask to talk to a supervisor; underlings may not have authority to grant special exemptions.

Documentation. Airlines have been the victims of fraudulent sob stories, so they may require you to present a letter from a doctor, a copy of a death certificate, or written confirmation from a funeral home. Others may ask only for the name of the doctor, funeral home, or hospital. Provide as much information as possible.

Consanguinity. Usually, "family" means a spouse or close blood relatives. Compassion fares may not apply if the death in the "family" was a cousin, uncle, or in-law. If possible, shop around. Some airlines have an ironclad policy defining what relationships are "close" and which do not qualify. Some judge on a case-by-case basis.

Restrictions. Make sure you understand whether the bereavement ticket is fully flexible/refundable, fully non-flexible/non-refundable, or carries some possibilities for alteration. For instance, you want to get there as soon as possible, but you don't want to commit to a return date because you don't know how long it will take to settle the estate, nurse Mom back to health, or see Dad through a crisis.

Some airlines will waive advance purchase requirements in an emergency, but will impose the same restrictions as apply to Supersaver tickets (e.g., stay over a Saturday night, or fly only Sunday through Thursday). Although it's hard to think or care about the return trip now, try to allow for some flexibility on that end.

Senior citizens. Many airlines offer books of four tickets that are good for domestic flights from anywhere to anywhere at very low prices. Such tickets carry their own restrictions involving advance reservations or blackout dates, but are an excellent buy. You can sometimes, especially in an emergency, fly standby without advance reservations. If you're over fifty-five, ask whether you can get a discount. Different age limits apply depending on the airline, but sixty-two is the most common threshold.

The full-price senior citizen deal may be better than bereavement fare. And most airlines allow each senior to take a companion of any age at the senior citizen rate.

Money angles. We have recommended throughout this book that fulltimers carry at least one credit card for emergencies. Virtually all airlines accept major credit cards, traveler's checks, and cash; rarely can you use a personal check. Some airlines require you to pay the full tariff up front and then will refund the bereavement discount later after you've sent in the required documentation. Some airlines do not refund this discount in cash, but only in the form of a voucher that can be used on a future ticket.

Bereavement fares are usually not the cheapest way to fly. Fully restricted, non-refundable tickets, purchased well in advance, are usually cheaper, but who can predict an emergency in advance? When one strikes, there is a good chance that you can get a break of thirty to thirty-five percent over regular coach fares.

If your message service brings bad news, tell the airlines your story fully and honestly. Shop around if possible. Play by the rules, and be patient with those who are trying to help. They are doing you a favor, usually spending extra time and earning less commission. When you need to get somewhere in the fastest way possible, compassion fares can help take some of the financial sting out of a personal loss.

12

The Fulltimer's Pets

To put this in pet language, Whoa! Before including a dog, cat, or other pet in your fulltiming family, consider the joys and penalties. The dangers and disruptions are so many that our friends, whom we'll call Jeff and Joan, chose an extreme solution and had their beloved old cat put to sleep rather than subject him to the rigorous, roadway life.

Pets, for all their winning ways, mean more expense, more problems finding and keeping campsites, more potential for wrangles with camping neighbors, and lots more time spent on pet care than ever before. Pets get carsick, scared, thrown around in panic stops, hurt in accidents, and killed along the roadside. They get bored, bitten by bugs, thirsty and hungry, and restless when they can't run free. We've heard countless horror stories about innocent pets involved in highway accidents and about owners who delayed their trips for days because the cat disappeared, or whose budgets were strained by unexpected veterinary bills when the dog needed an operation. Pet ownership isn't to be taken lightly, especially when you live on the go.

Many campgrounds won't admit pets at all. When they do, rules are strict. Even then, you may have problems if the dog barks when you're not aboard, or if the cat squirts on the neighbor's tires.

Do you really want a pet on board? If the answer is a thoughtful, pets

loving, and selfless yes, here are some ways to make fulltiming fairer to both yourselves and your pet(s).

Preventive Medicine

Well before leaving, see your hometown vet and make sure your pet's shots, tags, and all necessary certificates and documents are up to date. Carry these papers as carefully as cash. They'll be vital if your pet bites someone, if you cross national borders, or if the animal becomes ill and needs treatment by a vet who hasn't seen him before. Most kennels require these papers and sometimes require extra shots before boarding a pet.

Explain your travel plans to the vet and ask if the areas you'll be visiting present any special, local hazards for your pet. Heartworm preventive is needed almost everywhere, and you may need to alter the pill schedule. Histoplasmosis is endemic in scattered parts of the United States and Canada. Lyme disease and Rocky Mountain spotted fever are regional, tick-born ailments to which pets are susceptible. Your vet knows what dangers await where.

If new immunizations are needed, have them done well enough in advance that the pet can recover if he has an adverse reaction, and can develop an immunity fully.

Carry ample supplies of vitamins and medications. If your pet gets carsick, he probably will get over it as he adjusts to life on the road, but meanwhile a tranquilizer or a motion sickness pill might help.

Consider, too, having your dog or cat spayed or neutered before you go. The vet can explain the many advantages to the animal's health and welfare.

Guarding Against Loss

Buy or make a pet I.D. tag on which you can change your address each time you move to a new campsite. You could use a capsule-type I.D. or a luggage tag that opens so you can change the message often. In it, place a note with your campground address, the dates of your stay, and a third-party contact if you have one. A regular I.D. containing your "home" address is of little value, because it could take days to get word to you, even if your pet is found a block away from your campsite.

Subscribers to the mail forwarding services of Mail, Messages, and More, Box 2190, Henderson, Nevada 89009, automatically get free pet locator service. For $8.95, you get a tag to put on your pet. If the pet strays, anyone who finds it can call a toll-free number. When you check in at the same number, a message about your pet will be on your Voice Mail.

If you're a dog owner, you might want to join the National Dog Registry, P.O. Box 116, Woodstock, New York 12498; (800) NDR-DOGS. A one-time fee of thirty-five dollars covers all your pets, each of which is tattooed with your Social Security number (tattoo costs vary according to locality). A medallion that explains how to call the registry via a toll-free number can be attached to a collar. If your pet is lost, you call the registry and report where you are and how to reach you. Anyone finding the pet will see the medallion, look for the tattoo, and call the registry, which then gets you and the pet back together. The registry claims a ninety-eight percent recovery rate.

Safety and Comfort

Look in pet and camping supply stores and catalogs for equipment that will make the trip safer and more pleasant for you and the pet. If your RV floors are cold, get a 12-volt heated pet bed. You'll find such things as portable kennels that fold up when not in use, folding fencing, and special leashes and swivels that allow the pet to be staked out in the most comfortable corner of your campsite. Also available are poop scoopers, leakproof or automatic feeders and watering bowls (although your pet may be reassured by old, familiar bowls, at least at first), and non-skid place mats that protect the RV floor as the pet feeds or drinks.

It's also a good idea to keep a pet life vest on board if you like waterfront camping or if you will be doing any boating. Dogs and cats can swim, but they can't get back aboard a boat, climb the side of a pool, or hoist themselves out of a bulkheaded waterway. If a pet goes overboard, say experts at Ralston-Purina, a life vest will allow you to lift it by the harness; lifting it by the collar could injure it. And don't, says Ralston-Purina, take a pet whitewater rafting. In an upset, it may not be able to swim to safety.

If you're really serious about pets, get a towable kennel trailer. Designed for hunters, these trailers provide a cozy home for the dog(s) underway and at rest, as well as storage room for equipment and shotguns.

On the Road

People are protected by seatbelts, but in a hard stop or accident a loose pet becomes a projectile. The pet could be hurt; so could you if you're the first thing it hurls into. Find a safe place for it to ride, install a divider in your vehicle, or keep the pet in a travel cage that is safely anchored.

Pets need plenty of fresh air, but don't let a dog hang its head out a window; flying debris could damage its eyes. Also, never leave a pet in a closed vehicle, even on a cloudy day. It's thoughtless, risky to the pet, and illegal in some municipalities. After only a brief time in an overheated car or camper, an animal dies. You'll not only lose a cherished pet, you might be prosecuted, fined, and perhaps even jailed for animal abuse.

When driving, stop often and give the pet a brisk walk and a drink of water. Always leash the animal *before* opening the car or RV door, because even well-trained animals sometimes run when frightened or confused. The chances of recovering a pet that bolts away from a rest stop along a busy interstate are not good. Don't risk losing yours.

If your pet is a caged bird, gerbil, or hamster, it too needs special care in the fulltiming life. Movable objects such as swings and toys should be taken out of the cage. Road motion could make them swing hard enough to injure the pet.

Don't let a bird ride on your shoulder or fly free in the RV. It could escape or, worse still, be smashed against the windshield in a collision. Carry the cage in a safe spot that has gentle air flow and is out of direct sun.

Underway, don't leave water in the cage. Spills make for a damp cage where harmful organisms can grow. Instead, provide juicy fruits and vegetables. Then make sure to offer plenty of fresh water as soon as you park.

Having pets aboard can enrich the fulltiming life, but they can complicate it, too. (Terry)

Pet Life on the Go

With a good guidebook, you can find campgrounds that admit dogs and cats. Even so, it's best to call ahead to confirm that your pet will be allowed, and under what circumstances. Sometimes "pets allowed" means that your dog can be housed in the campground kennel, free or at extra cost, but will not be allowed to stay in your RV.

Most state and national parks (but not all; check ahead) allow campers to bring pets if they are kept on a six-foot leash. You and the pet will be evicted if the pet disturbs other campers or any of the park's plants or wildlife, and the definition of "disturb" can vary. If the dog so much as startles a squirrel, or the cat jumps at a bird, the ranger might call it a crime against the native wildlife and send you all packing. Private campgrounds are more lenient, especially if previous campers and their pets were on their best behavior. If former guests allowed their dogs to bark annoyingly or make messes, or have washed them in the public bathrooms, you're sure to find a No Pets sign at the campground entrance.

Campground living means close quarters, and tempers can fray. We once parked next to an RV in which a big dog began barking the moment his owners left for the day's fishing and didn't stop until they returned. When they were home, the dog didn't make a sound. Annoyed as we were, we didn't blame the poor dog. Left alone, and surrounded by strange sounds, he was probably baffled and frustrated. Because of these thoughtless pet owners, that campground soon adopted a No Pets policy.

If you're fulltiming with pets, be meticulous about their manners. It isn't enough to bury the dog's droppings. Be careful too about where the dog and cat piddle. If a pet wets on the neighbor's wheels, it's offensive to the other camper and highly corrosive to the metal.

Leave the pet alone as little as possible, and not at all if it barks while you're gone. Never bathe a dog in the campground showers, pool, or beach. Take it to a professional groomer.

Cats can suffer liver damage from DEET, an ingredient in some insect sprays, so be cautious when using tick repellents. Check all pets often for ticks and, if the pet seems sick, get to a vet. It could have a tick-born disease that can affect *you* next. Early treatment is important because relapses can occur after the pet appears to recover. Ticks also can cause pet paralysis.

All pets are potential targets for thieves, so fulltimers should be aware of the dangers. Rare cats and dogs or valuable birds are easy targets; some thieves specialize in feisty dogs, entering them in illegal dogfights. There is also said to be a criminal traffic in stolen pets, which are sold to labs for experimentation. On the road, just as at home, safeguard the family pet.

Housekeeping Problems

Four-footed friends track in sand and mud, so vacuum frequently and use a carpet deodorizer. Change kitty litter more often than ever before. Be meticulous about airing and frequent floor cleaning and carpet shampooing, because in the small area of your RV home, odors can build up more quickly than you realize. Your guests will notice, even if you don't.

Start fighting fleas even before you move into the RV. Spray everything well with a flea treatment that kills fleas in live, larvae, and egg form. (Some powders and sprays kill only living fleas.) Follow directions carefully—incorrect use wastes money, reduces effectiveness, and can endanger your family or the pet.

You may need to respray weekly, monthly, or only after two or three months. Some products have residual power for months; using them more often than needed won't help.

If you're moving out of the RV for any period, make sure your flea control program is up to date. Fleas spend most of their lives in the carpet, furniture, or floorboards and jump onto the animal only long enough for a hearty meal. If you and the pet move out for a few weeks, you need a product that will go on killing new fleas as they hatch.

CHAPTER THIRTEEN

Driving the Big Ones

"I'd love to have the biggest motorhome I can afford, but driving one scares me." It's a common feeling.

If all your driving experience has been in cars, we have good news for you. High off the road in a big motorhome, you can see farther ahead and behind, so you're better able to slow down for trouble ahead, change lanes, and otherwise keep control. People see *you* better too. It's less likely that someone will pull out of a side street in front of you.

Of course, larger units are more difficult to maneuver in a tight, defensive driving situation. They take longer to stop, longer to get up to speed. And, if you have to pull off the road to let an emergency vehicle past, it might take some time to find a spot large enough.

Clearance

Learn the height of your motorhome in exact feet and inches, and make a label to stick on the dashboard so you or other drivers will never be in doubt. Underpasses, bridges, and fuel station canopies are usually marked, so you won't have to guess, but in some other places, such as fast-food drive-up windows, you can't be sure. One old trick is to mount a whip antenna on the front bumper, to the exact height of the tallest point in your rig. If it hits, you can back away before scrap-

Equip your car with the big mirrors needed for towing. They'll increase the width of your car to trailer width or more and allow you to get the feel of the wide load. (G. Groene)

ing off the air conditioner.

If you're about to start towing a big trailer for the first time, get a feel for your new width by mounting towing mirrors on your car (if this is permitted in your state.) Once you realize that something this wide will fit on the road without knocking all the mailboxes off their posts, you know the vehicle behind you will fit too, no matter whether it's 30 or 300 feet long.

You now know that you can tow anything of a given width down the interstate forever. Problems arise only if you want to turn a corner or back up. It's time for Lesson Two.

Steering

The steering geometry of every rig is different, depending on length, overhang, and positioning of the wheels. And, because you can't see what the outside rear corner is doing in a turn, you have to learn to guess where it will be. A good way to get the feel of steering is to borrow a small trailer, such as a utility trailer, and practice in a

Practice driving in uncrowded places until you know exactly where all the corners of your RV will end up when you make a turn.

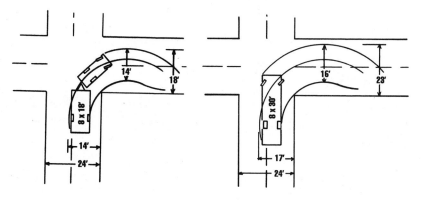

wide-open place such as the far corner of a parking lot. Get used to making the trailer do what you want it to.

If you continually get confused backing up a trailer, here's a tip from truckers: Hold your hand on the wheel at six o'clock; the trailer will head the direction you move your hand.

Later, set up pylons or plastic trash cans and practice backing, parking, and maneuvering with your RV trailer. Set up a typical highway corner, and keep practicing until you know just how wide you must swing to clear the corner with the rear wheels.

The other problem with vehicles that have long overhangs is the departure angle; that is, the angle between the road and an imaginary line from the rear wheel up toward the rear bumper, clearing the lowest point in sight. In other words, you want to be able to judge whether a ramp angles up too sharply. Otherwise, you'll scrape some-

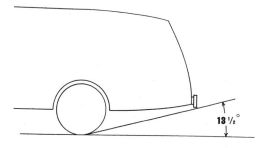

Departure angle.

thing that's covered with dollar signs—usually a gas tank or plumbing fitting. Some vehicles have protection built in; on others a heavy steel roller can be added. Otherwise, you must defend yourself with a knowledge of your departure angle, and drive so that you never exceed it.

Courtesy

Extra courtesy gains fulltime RV drivers a safety edge for ourselves, and helps keep other drivers from seeing us as "those blank-blank old road hogs." If your rig is big and cumbersome, always notice when you're holding up the parade. If a line forms behind us, we pull off the road and watch the world go by. Courtesy is always appreciated, and there is a selfish motive: In a panic stop, you'll have fewer vehicles to pile into you.

In the Campground

Many times we've seen an RV driver make a braying ass of himself by loudly chewing out a copilot for "letting" him back into an overhead branch, a sand trap, or a chuck hole. Tell it to the marines. As driver-captain of this land yacht, you're in charge. Anything that goes wrong is *your* fault.

A Boeing 747 can be parked on a pinpoint at the airport without a word, so there is no reason why fulltimer teams can't develop clear hand signals that communicate in complete silence. When you're shouting to be heard over the noise of the RV engine, you only call attention to yourself as you miss the hitch for the forty-fifth time.

As we said, you the driver are responsible for whatever happens, so don't just blunder anywhere your partner points. Before attacking the campsite, both of you should get out of the RV and look things over carefully. Note the location of the hookups in relation to your outlets. Discuss any special problems, such as low-hanging branches, a sharp tree stump that could damage a tire, or a struggling seedling you want to avoid.

The sidekick's job is to stay within sight of the driver, either directly or in the mirror or rear-view television. Hand signals can indicate right or left, point to the sewer outlet, or show that you have "this far" to go. Tell the copilot exactly where you want to stop, so the signal will be given when you reach the right spot.

Hand signals speak loud and clear, allowing you to park on a dime without calling attention to yourself. (G. Groene)

art continued on following page

During the parking, the sidekick can also monitor such things as whether the backup and brake lights are working. As the tires turn

slowly, look for cuts or breaks. Note any fluid leaks or bearing squeals.

Campers are nice folks who want to help, especially if you're alone. But don't let someone's offer of assistance turn your attempt to park into a shouting match in which you find yourself letting him tell you where you can put your own RV. Get out of the RV and take all the time you need to walk around the campsite, decide where you want to go, and tell the neighbor what kind of signals to use.

Driving a big RV is a new and different skill, and more than a pushbutton pushover. Still, it's a skill that can be learned, and enjoyed with confidence and safety. Go ahead. Drive yourself happy.

The Rental Car Puzzle

We have already discussed the pluses and minuses of having a big tow car and a travel trailer, versus a motorhome towing a car, versus a single-vehicle operation. The big drawback to having only one set of wheels is that it's expensive and cumbersome to take a big RV to the supermarket, and it's inconvenient when everyone must go every-where, even to the dentist, at once.

Alternatives to using a big RV to do small errands include renting

RV Driving Tips

A long-haul truck driver of our acquaintance suggests trying these big-rig tricks, and any new ones you can dream up to add to your visibility, predictability, and safety. For example:

◆ In hilly country where there are passing lanes, plan ahead to get into the slow lane *before* someone comes up on your right side.

◆ "Get a run at" hills—making sure you have a good head of steam before starting up the hill.

◆ On multi-lane highways, pick the lane that is moving at the speed most comfortable for you so you don't impede others.

◆ Magnify all your best driving manners—turn signals, stop signals, headlight dimming, and a flick of the headlights to show a trucker that he has passed you safely.

◆ When passing another vehicle, don't pull back into the lane until you're a good distance ahead; you should see *both* headlights in your right (flat, not convex) mirror.

◆ Mount a convex spot mirror on both sides of your vehicle.

◆ In mountainous country, use engine compression to hold down speed on downgrades to prevent brake failure.

◆ Leave a minimum three-second "cushion" between you and the vehicle in front.

or carrying bicycles or motorbikes, walking, or taking public transportation. Just for fun, because the idea is so radical to Americans who are accustomed to having a car, compare the cost of owning and towing a car to renting a car, say once a week, to do all the nuisance errands—shopping, the post office, and so on. Add up what it will cost you to own, insure, and maintain a car, then call around to see what is available on rentals. Costs vary around the country, but even in very high price areas, you can usually get a weekend special.

Here are some tips on car rental.

Cars are usually available in six classes, ranging from Economy (e.g. Geo and Nova) to Luxury (e.g. Cadillac Sedan de Ville). In between are the Compacts (e.g. Pontiac 1200), Mid-size (e.g. Olds Calais), Full-size 2-door (e.g. Buick Regal), and Full-size 4-door (e.g. Buick Century). Usually we get an Economy for fizzing around on errands; we rent larger cars if we need them for business or major hauling.

Pricing is a giant shell game, made more complicated by all the discounts, frequent-flyer bonuses, weekend specials, coupons, and other gimmicks that differ from company to company. Although we qualify for various discounts through half a dozen organizations we belong to, we can usually do as well or better without them because so many restrictions apply. Don't lose sight of the bottom line.

If you're price shopping, the best bet is to go to an airport during off-peak hours and counter-hop to comparison shop. Free telephones at airports connect you with other firms, often cheaper ones, that don't have counter space at the airport. We've almost always been able to get to an airport and shop for a good rental easily, without reservations. You may strike out, though, during a big convention or bowl game that ties a city in knots.

Some other points about car rental:

◆ Special models are available through National for the hearing impaired, for handicapped drivers who need hand controls, and for skiers who want tire chains and a ski rack.

◆ Understand exactly what your existing RV insurance covers. You may not need the optional (and very high priced) coverage offered by the rental company. Add-on insurance is one of the biggest expenses in car rental, so be alert for alternatives. Some rental companies now include it; sometimes it's included automatically if you charge the rental on certain credit cards.

◆ Always ask about special promotions. You may save a bundle by taking the car on a weekend, midweek, off-season, or for a specified block of time.

◆ Fill the gas tank just before you return the car. If the rental firm fills it for you the per-gallon price is much higher.

◆ Some companies "redline" residents of certain areas and charge them more than others for the same rentals—one more penalty we pay for living in a litigious society—and it has to do with the right of an injured person to sue the rental company as well as the driver. If you live in the Bronx, for example, you may pay a fifty-six-dollar surcharge to rent a car in Connecticut. The practice varies greatly among car rental companies, and among destinations. If you find yourself getting redlined, try another rental company.

◆ If you are reserving by phone, get a confirmation number.

◆ Check into used-car rentals (Ugly Duckling, Rent a Dent)—but again, look at the bottom line, including insurance.

◆ When renting from discount-priced local companies, ask what support they offer if you break down out of town. The national chains have nationwide support; with the independents you may be on your own.

◆ Before taking off, walk all around the car checking for damage or missing pieces, and report them now, in writing. That's your only defense if you're accused later of causing the damage.

◆ If you want a one-way rental, check into "drop" charges. They vary widely among companies.

◆ If you are concerned, as many people are today, about million-dollar lawsuits, look into the one-million-dollar liability insurance available on Hertz rental cars in cooperation with Alexander & Alexander, and Firemen's Fund.

Should You Lease a Car?

When Bob and Mary L. went fulltiming, they knew they wanted to tow a car behind their big motorhome, but they didn't want to dump a big down payment, followed by high monthly payments, into the car they had in mind. They'd just sold their home and furniture and were liquid, footloose, and fancy free.

They had a cash buyer for their old car, one that wasn't suited for the fulltiming life they planned, and they didn't like the idea of putting all that money back into another car. It was beginning to feel good to have it as part of their nestegg.

So they leased a car.

Once a rarity, leased cars are now driven by almost a million people, and leasing seems to be catching on. On the plus side, there is no down payment. If you were going to ante up, say a $2,500 down payment on a new car, you could invest the money instead at about nine percent on today's market. Instead of tying up money in a car, you have it in the bank or bonds or T-bills, drawing interest available for emergencies. Meanwhile you pay only a manageable, monthly lease fee. If you use the car as a business deduction, the advantages of leasing are even clearer (ask your CPA).

However, there is a dark side to leasing, one that spells Buyer Beware. One pitfall is hidden charges. Some lease contracts start out at a temptingly low monthly rate but balloon after a certain date. Read the fine print in your contract.

Bob and Mary's story could end happily or on a sour note, depending on several factors including luck. Most leases don't include repairs. If the car is a lemon, the L.'s will have to pay all the maintainenance bills on top of their monthly lease payments.

If their plans or goals change, and they want to turn in the car before the completion of their contract, there is a big penalty. And if they turn it in in bad condition, they'll be charged for repairs.

The lease is close-ended, which was a smart move on Bob's part. He knew that some leases leave you, at the end of your obligation, with the car worth "fair market value" *as determined by the leasing company*. After four years, when Bob's lease ends, the residual value of his car will be X percent of the sticker price, and the L.'s contract says that they can buy it for that if they choose. (Percentages and lease times could vary, but Bob had stated a figure rather than a vague "fair market" value.)

The other precaution Bob and Mary took was to talk to their insurance company. In many cases, insurance for a leased car covers just the cost of the car, not the monthly payments. If it's totalled or stolen, you have to collect what you can, but continue paying off the lease—even if you collect far less than what you still owe on the car.

In reading the original contract, Mary spotted a provision for some fancy add-on fees for paperwork and nonsense and got them deleted from the final draft. And Bob noticed that there was a mileage limit he felt was too low. So he had it hiked in the final contract.

The L.'s have been smart on another score. They know that, no matter how rough the sledding in the future in doing repairs or meeting their rental payments, it's their baby. Although some used-car agencies run ads offering to take a leased car off your back, sub-leasing is contrary to the contract *and* is a felony in four states.

When you're buying a car, you look at much more than the sticker price. Likewise in leasing, look beyond the monthly payments. The deal could be a dream, or a nightmare.

(14)

Mini-Hobbies for Your Mini-Home

Most of us need absorbing, rewarding pastimes to enliven our "off-duty" hours. Hobbies are even more vital to fulltimers, who may have to pass rainy days and long evenings in areas where they have no friends, no TV reception, and no local entertainments. No one wants to be cooped up in a box that measures eight by twenty-five or thirty feet, with nothing to do and no room to do it in.

Here are ways to miniaturize your present hobbies and suggestions for new hobbies that might suit your skills and interests.

Radio

Although the CB craze is not what it once was, these radios still play an important role among people who make the highways their home: truckers, emergency services personnel, traveling salespeople, and RV fulltimers. Through CB you can make friends, ask directions, find out where to get the best buys on fuel on the road ahead, and learn how to get around traffic tie-ups and detours.

A CB is essential when you're traveling in company with another RV or in a caravan. For the greatest convenience, you'll need a CB in the cockpit and another in your living quarters.

Other radios that make for interesting hobbies are VHF, which requires a special license and will give you a window on the boating and fishing world; scanners, which allow you to eavesdrop on emergency channels; and radios that receive aircraft frequencies so you can listen to activity at the control tower.

Ham radio is to CB what caviar is to sardines. The equipment isn't inexpensive, and you must invest hours of study to get even the most basic license. You'll also need room aboard for a radio shack, plus a good source of power and an efficient antenna.

In return for this investment you will have a fascinating hobby for the entire family. It's not uncommon for husband, wife, and older children all to get ham licenses. Through ham, you can converse with people all over the world, talk to your friends and relatives via phone patches, help out during disasters when other communications are down, and join "nets" that keep you in touch with people who share your interests in almost any field. And if you plug into the local ham club when you're in a new community, you will have an instant circle of buddies.

For information on becoming a ham, contact the ARRL (American Radio Relay League), 225 Main St., Newington, Connecticut 06111; (203) 666-1541.

Sewing and Crafts

Many of us would be lost without a sewing machine, not just for the love of making clothes but because sewing and mending save money (and can be used to *make* money, if you're good). In an RV, there are three important rules for successful sewing:

•Keep the machine in a secure place where it won't break loose in curves and panic stops. It's heavy.

•Allow extra space for patterns, findings, and work in progress, but try to finish one project before starting the next. Carrying tons of bargain fabric on the road costs fuel dollars.

•Get yourself a roomy cutting table. I found an inexpensive folding cardboard table-topper in a fabric store. It stows under the mattress and provides a smooth, clean surface atop the dinette table or the campsite picnic table.

More compact sewing hobbies include quilt piecing, lap quilting, knitting, macrame, needlepoint, embroidery, crewel, and huck weaving. If space is tight, rediscover these traditional favorites.

Hang Out at the Library

As busy as most fulltimers are, there are days when you're at loose ends. You're a stranger in town, without friends, and it's the off season, so the campground is deserted. You're tired of malls, and movies cost too much.

The library is one place that brings both of us unending entertainment and learning, even though we have very different abilities and interests—and it's free.

We find libraries in towns of every size. Now we schedule at least one day a month for a library stop and usually end up coming back for more. We can easily spend all day, taking a lunch break in the parking lot in our RV.

It's true that, as a stranger passing through town, you probably cannot get a library card or borrow books. But if you think libraries are nothing more than literary takeouts, it's time to get reacquainted.

We have found libraries offering everything from language lessons to lectures, from free movie classics to classes in local history or wild flowers. Most libraries have story sessions for children. Some have displays or small museums, extensive collections of recordings, listening booths, VCRs, and tapes. Larger libraries have typewriters or computers for the use of patrons. There's almost always a coin-operated copy machine, coin phones, a pleasant reading room with comfortable chairs, and other reading areas where you can sit at tables or desks and make notes. Most reference rooms also have special sections for regional and local books covering everything from history to folklore, city directories to the most recent Yellow Pages.

Librarians—who are worth their weight in platinum—have helped us find everything from out-of-town phone numbers to lists of little-known sites we wanted to visit to an address we needed to order a spare part for an old outboard.

Book Swaps

Some campgrounds have their own "libraries"—book swap boxes or shelves. If you find yourself at one that doesn't, urge the manager to start one. All it takes is a clean cardboard box, a couple of books as "seed money," and a sign inviting campers to "Take One, Leave One; Honor System." In most cases, the box will soon brim with excellent reading, because many people will leave more than they take.

(By the way, here are three reading essentials for the RV life: Charles Kuralt's *On the Road with Charles Kuralt* and *A Life on the Road*, and John Steinbeck's *Travels with Charley*.)

Discover the Ag Center

While the library is the heart of a community's cultural life, the office of the County Agricultural Extension is the core of its natural life. When you're on the go and need to know how to deal with specific local fruits, vegetables, fish, or game, or hazards such as poisonous plants, it is here you'll find expert help.

Workshop

The secret to success in any workshop hobby is having the right equipment, the raw materials, and a place to use them. We met one van-dwelling hobbyist who towed a travel trailer that housed a complete workshop with a workbench and plenty of drawers and pigeon-holes.

Just as the RV galley is a specialized work area that should be furnished with the right stuff rather than kitchen castoffs, the workshop should be equipped so that every inch and every ounce do yeoman duty. It may pay to bite the bullet and buy new tools that are appropriate for the RV life.

Dremel makes a complete line of serious small benchtop tools and accessories. You can carry a Dremel drill press, router attachment, scroll saw/disc sander, vise with swivel head, table saw, and enough accessories to build an ark, all in the trunk of a car. For information, write the Dremel Division, Emerson Electric Company, 4915 21st St., Racine, Wisconsin 53406.

Other trusted names include Skil, known for its circular saws and now a line of full-size benchtop tools, Stanley, Black & Decker, and Craftsman, with its international Sears network of spares and support.

One of the most effective mini-workshops we've ever seen was a suitcase-size kit designed by a man whose hobby was clock repair. Opened, it formed a lighted work shelf. Closed, it corralled a creditable collection of tiny replacement parts.

We met a fisherman, a retired U.S.A.F. colonel, who had a compact workshop he used to make lures and other custom fishing gear for

You can equip your workshop with down-size tools and have hours of pleasure as well as the means to create accessories for the RV, make repairs, and perhaps even turn out saleable items. (Sears Craftsman)

himself and for sale. On sunny days, he set it up on the picnic table at his campsite. He continued to work as he jawboned with anyone who stopped by, and inevitably made several sales in the bargain.

Miniature projects that fit well (and often sell well) in the fulltiming life include dollhouse furniture, toys, jewelry, model planes or boats, and wooden name plates made with a router.

Gardening

Among ex-fulltimers, one of the most common reasons for settling down again is, "We missed our garden." However, gardening can be a portable hobby. We met one family who had two dozen pots of herbs, which they set in dishpans and carried in their shower underway. After they parked, they moved the plants to a sunny spot. They always had plenty of fresh parsley, basil, cress, and the like.

Small gardening projects include bonsai, which requires artistry and skill, or sprouting edible seeds such as mung beans, alfalfa, and wheat, which even a child can do. Trade plants and cuttings with like-minded fulltimers. You can even make pin money at it, by starting house plants and selling them at flea markets.

One of our most enjoyable summers was spent in a North Carolina campground where campers were invited to work in the communal garden. By the time we moved on in the fall, we'd eaten our fill of fresh produce.

If you own your own campsite, you can landscape it. Or, if the campground needs groundskeeping, you may be able to trade your gardening talents for some free rent.

Treasure Hunting

This one is addictive. You live on a hopeful high, believing that the Big Find is just around the corner. Every treasure hunter on the beach has a story about finding a handful of coins or a valuable ring, and treasure hunters occasionally find ancient Spanish coins on Florida beaches after heavy storms.

We met one couple who found a BB-size gold bead near an old Indian mound, and a seventeenth-century brass candlestick at low tide outside an old fort. On the site of a long-abandoned village in Vermont, we found part of an old cookstove, a large silver spoon (in two pieces) and a 1910 revolver that had rusted into a solid mass.

As a practical tool, a small metal detector helps find small screws or other tiny metal parts if you lose them in the grass while working on the RV. The more you spend, the more sophisticated a metal detector you can buy. The cheapest models "see" any metal, so a lot of time is wasted in digging up aluminum cans and other junk, but even these are useful and fun.

One warning: It's illegal to use, or to have in your possession, a metal detector in a national park or national historic site. When in such areas, remove the batteries and otherwise render a metal detector inoperable. In any case, it's just good citizenship never to detect or dig in a site archaeologists may want to excavate someday.

RV travelers love square dancing. Wherever you travel, you can almost always find a square dancing or clogging group. (Fleetwood)

Square Dancing and Clogging

Group dancing continues to be a national craze, especially among campers. Once you learn the steps and lingo, you'll fit in wherever you go. It's an international language spoken in campgrounds everywhere. Chances are there's a square dance at least once a week at almost any large destination campground you visit, and you'll happen into countless hoedowns in camp and in town as you travel.

Volunteer Work

If you've been active all your life in church and charity work, fulltiming presents special problems, because you're a stranger everywhere you go. That will change quickly once you check in with the local Volunteer Bureau, a church of your own denomination, Habitat for Humanity, Meals on Wheels, or other services. Even if you can spare only a few hours a week and will be in town for only a month, there is work for you.

If you have a special skill, such as teaching literacy via the Laubach method or transcribing for the blind, or have always worked with a national group such as the Red Cross, contact national headquarters before you leave and ask how you can keep active in your field as you travel.

If you have a talent that would entertain elderly shut-ins, volunteer yourself to nursing homes as you travel. You might give a lecture-slide show on your travels, call a square dance, tell tall tales, or play an instrument.

For those of us who are never in one spot long enough for any kind of volunteerism, one-on-one projects can give you a sense of useful purpose. We keep a list of homebound friends of friends and relatives of relatives, and we send a constant barrage of mail as we travel. We rarely get mail in return from these folks, usually because they are too ill to write, but the payback is in imagining their happiness when they get an upbeat message on a picture postcard from a faraway place.

CHAPTER FIFTEEN

Home, Sweet Campground

The more we travel, the more we are dazzled and amazed by the variety of campsites in this great land of ours. You can still find a cozy nook, without hookups or facilities of any kind, in a Corps of Engineers area for free. And you can pay forty dollars a night or more to loll in Lucullan luxury in a resort that has a health club, sauna, golf course, stocked fishing lake, fulltime social director, and fireworks on Saturday night.

We've tried them all, and we love them all—even the grubby campsite next to the railroad track, if it's close to our business or sightseeing goal for the day. If you're like us, you'll choose different campsites for different reasons: wilderness sites for solitude, resorts for the social whirl; the campground closest to the theme park, the overnight stop handiest to the highway; the site with the best view of shuttle launches or the one closest to the beach.

Finding a Campsite

For advance planning we rely on our Kampgrounds of America (KOA) Directory and the indispensable guides published by Allstate (formerly Rand McNally), Woodall, Wheeler, and TL Publications. If we are on the road and searching only for an overnight stop, we rely on highway signs. Some of our happiest camping experiences have been serendipitous, simply jumping off the road to look over a campground because we saw a sign.

In shoulder season, it is seldom a problem to find a site. During high season, however, it's wise to call ahead for reservations. In cold climates in winter, when many campgrounds are closed, advance planning and reservations are also advisable.

We also stop at almost every highway welcome station we come to—not the tourist traps that want to sell something in exchange for advice, but those run by local, regional, county, state, or provincial agencies. Here, we stock up on free maps, campground directories, and brochures describing state or regional attractions. Often operated by dedicated volunteers, welcome stations have provided some of the best advice, from the most cheerful and knowledgeable people, in our travels.

Lists of state campgrounds are available free from each state's tourism office. If you don't have the address, it's a safe bet you'll reach the right place by writing: Division of Tourism, State Capital (you do know your state capitals, don't you?), state, zip code; or Division of Tourism, provincial capital, province, Canada.

For information about camping in national parks and lands write:

Bureau of Land Management, Recreation Sites Information, Public Affairs Office, 1800 C. St., N.W., Washington, DC 20240

National Park Service, 18th at C St., N.W., Washington, DC 20240

National Forest Service, USDA Office of Information, Box 2417, Washington, DC 20013

National Refuges, U.S. Fish and Wildlife Service Public Affairs, Washington, DC 20240

U.S. Army Corps Projects, U.S. Army Corps of Engineers, 20 Massachusetts Ave. N.W., Washington, DC 20314; Att: Public Affairs

Cutting the Cost of Fulltime Camping

When you're a part-timer, nightly camping fees seem like a bargain compared to staying in hotels. But to the fulltimer, $18 a night adds up to $540 a month—a sum that in some parts of the country will still get you a smart, spacious, two-bedroom, two-bath apartment big enough to hold your RV four times over.

If you average $15 per night for camping, that is $5,475 per year. Here are some ways to chop the cost of nightly camping.

Join a membership campground chain. As a member of a nationwide chain, you'll pay only a dollar or two per night to stay in any member campground. Investigate the deal carefully, because an initial investment of $4,000 to $8,000 is required.

State camping permits. It may pay you to establish legal residence in a state that gives its residents a break on camping fees—especially if you want to spend a large part of the year there. In Florida, for example, a resident can purchase a year's permit for state campgrounds for under $200. Your only cost is a few dollars per night for electricity. There's a two-week limit per stay. Total cost for 365 days: about $1,000. See if your state has a similar deal. Most states also have some special discount for senior citizens and the handicapped.

Golden Eagle Passport. Anyone over the age of sixty-two can receive, free, a passport that is good for a fifty percent discount on camping fees in any federal campground. In the Ocala National Forest, for example, campsites with electricity are $9. Passport holders would pay $4.50 per night, or a total of $1,642.50 per year. You can stay only fourteen days in any one site, and your site won't include a sewer hookup. Golden Access Passports are available to the handicapped of any age. They too get a fifty percent discount.

Own your own campsite. We've seen mobile home lots for as little as $6,000, and condo campgrounds with pool and other facilities for $10,000 and up. You'll pay your own utilities and taxes plus, in a condo park, a monthly maintenance fee. Resale value will be a question mark, depending on what happens to real estate prices in the future. Another choice is to buy country acreage that is zoned for mobile homes, put in your own well and septic tank, and come and go as you like.

Monthly or seasonal rates. These vary greatly around the country depending on high and low season, electricity costs, and taxes, but we found most campground owners eager to sell monthly or seasonal deals—unlike government parks that limit your stay to two weeks or so. Too, some campground landlords want to look you over for a spell before quoting their most enticing long-term rates. Because the big discount might also involve a lease or a non-refundable advance payment, a trial period is in your best interest as well as the landlord's.

Freebies. Because our motorhome is only twenty-one feet long, we fit in metered parking spots, so we often park on the street or in lots at trade shows. We have also spent a lot of time in friends' driveways or backyards. Working as we go, stopping here to do a lecture and there to do a writing assignment, we ask if we can plug in—or at least park—for the night at our business destination. Most business parking lots have twenty-four-hour security, and although they are noisy sometimes, it's more than worth it because we're already "there" when we wake up in the morning. We avoid supermarket lots and overnight rest areas, for security reasons. (We keep on the go all the time, so we've never been hassled by police or angry neighbors. Since we're just there for one or two nights, nobody gets nervous about our becoming permanent squatters.)

Private deals. Let's say you intend to spend every summer for the rest of your life at Camp Lazydaze on Lake Fishalot. You approach the owner about a twenty-year lease, lifetime deal, or some other mutual commitment. With the help of a lawyer, you and a campground owner can work out an agreement that is fair and binding.

Tradeoffs. Regional camping newspapers carry ads asking for RV campers who will tend a campground in exchange for a free site. If you work the right deal, you'll do a fair amount of work, have a fair amount of free time, and will spend nothing for camping. We have also traded a month's camping for specific tasks, such as photographing a brochure. Barter any of your marketable skills—carpentry, gardening, electrical repairs, painting.

Camp stamps. This one is a little complicated, but camp stamps (somewhat like food stamps) get you a fifteen percent discount at National Forest (not National Park) campgrounds. Just make sure to have yours in hand before arriving at the registration window. They aren't sold at the forest itself, but at retail outlets, Ranger District

Headquarters, and local Forest Service offices. Stamps can also be used in conjunction with Golden Eagle and Golden Access passports.

Camping Clubs

The benefits are more than social, so look into camping club membership even if you're not a joiner. With membership you may get discounts, mail forwarding, emergency road service or medical evacuation, a monthly magazine, group insurance rates, message service, and much more. Dues are modest, usually twenty-five to fifty dollars per year.

Brand-name camping clubs. Contact the manufacturer of your RV, and ask how to join an owners' group. Most major brands, from Avion and Alpenite to Shasta and Winnebago, have such clubs. A list of names and contacts is available from RVIA, P.O. Box 2999, Reston, Virginia 22090.

Canadian Family Camping Federation. Write to Box 397, Rexdale Ontario, Canada M9W 1R3 for information.

Escapee Club. This organization of fulltimers has about 16,000 members and its own co-op campgrounds. Contact them c/o Kay Peterson, Rt. 5, Box 310, Livingston, Texas 77351; (409) 327-8873.

The Family Motor Coach Association. Membership is about 75,000 motorhome owners in 261 chapters. Chapters are divided not just according to geographic area but also according to special interests—fulltimers, singlehanders, musicians, Elks, the disabled, hams, treasure hunters, members of Coast to Coast Resorts or Thousand Trails Resorts, golfers, and a long list of brand-name camper chapters including three for GMC owners—one for owners in general, one for GMC preservationists, and one for owners of GMC bus campers. To join a chapter (and you probably will want to join more than one) you must first join the national FMCA. For information write 8291 Clough Pike, Cincinnatti, Ohio 45244 or call (800) 543-3622 or (513) 474-3622.

Good Sam Club. More than 800,000 campers belong to this international club, which has 2,200 chapters throughout the United States, Canada, and Europe. There are also special-interest chapters for square dancers, ham radio operators, singles, the deaf, U.S. Marines, and computer owners. For information about joining Good Sam, write TL Publications, 29901 Agoura Rd., Agoura, California 91301 or call (800) 234-3450.

Handicapped Travel Club Inc. For a membership application, send a #9 or #10 self-addressed stamped envelope to 667 J. Ave., Coronoda, California 91118.

International Family Recreation Association, P.O. Box 6279, Pensacola, Florida 32503 and **National RV Owners Club,** P.O. Drawer 17148, Pensacola, Florida 32522. The first group has 8,300 members and is for all travelers with an interest in camping; the second has 6,000 members and is for RV owners only. Trips of seven to ten days are arranged, with visits to a series of theme parks, festivals, and other points of interest.

International Travel & Trailer Club. Write 15320 Crenshaw Blvd., Gardena, California 90249 for information.

Loners of America. Publishes a newsletter covering matters of interest to lone RV travelers. Write them at Rt. 2, Box 85E, Ellsinore, Missouri 63937.

Loners on Wheels. Singles travel together for fun and mutual help. For information, write 808 Lester St., Popular Bluff, Missouri 63901.

National Campers & Hikers Association. This group is for family campers; its yearly camp-vention brings thousands of campers together. Special chapters include those for motorcycles, tents only, retired military, and the handicapped. Write c/o Fran Opela, 4808 Transit Rd., Depew, New York 14043.

National RV Owners Club. Write to Box 17148, Pensacola, Florida 32522.

North American Family Campers Association. Publishers of Campfire Chatter; c/o Harold F. Coakley, 3 Long Hill Rd., Concord, Vermont 05824.

RV Elderhostel. Special Elderhostel study groups for RV owners. Some courses occur at universities where parking and hookups are provided for RVs; in others, instructors accompany caravans that study along a route such as the Oregon Trail or the Gold Rush route through Alaska. Contact them at 80 Boylston St., Suite 400, Boston, Massachusetts 02116; (617) 426-7788.

SMART (Special Military Active Retired Travel). Members are 2,500 military retirees in twenty chapters and two social groups. Contact P.O. Box 730, Fallbrook, California 92028; (619) 723-2463.

Camping Resorts

Camping resorts are usually open year round, offering indoor and outdoor activities including swimming, fishing, health club, tennis, golf, and more. Most offer memberships; most also accommodate non-members. Some are local. Others are national chains, including:

ACI Parks, 12301 N.E. 10th Pl., Bellevue, Washington 98009

Coast to Coast Resorts, 64 Inverness Dr. E., Englewood, Colorado 80112

Outdoor Resorts of America Inc., 2400 Crestmoor Rd., Nashville, Tennessee 37215

Thousand Trails, 15375 S.E. 10th Place, Bellevue, Washington 98007

U.S. Vacation Resorts Inc., 7075 Ontario Rd., San Luis Obispo, California 93401

RV Rallies and Caravans

If you'd prefer to go with a group because you're new to RV travel, are traveling solo, or would prefer to be with other RVs when you venture into terra incognita, write for information from:

Adventure World R.V. Tours, The Seachest, Broad Park, Preston, Plymouth PL97QF, England

Creative World Rallies and Caravans, 606 N. Carrollton Ave., New Orleans, Louisianna 70119

European Caravan Federation, P.O. Box 1, Langport, Somerset, England TA109HP

Sicverl, 3-5 rue des Cordelieres, 75013 Paris, France

Trails-a-Way Compass RV Tours, 120 S. Lafayette St., Greenville, Michigan 48838

Verband Deutscher Wohnwagen-Hersteller e.V., 6230 Frankfurt 80, In der Schildwacht 41, Germany

Campground Chains

Best Holiday Trav-L-Park Association, 1310 Jarvis Ave., Elk Grove Village, Illinois 60007

Kampgrounds of America (KOA), Box 30558, Billings, Montana 59114 (Write for information, or pick up a free directory at any member campground.)

Yogi Bear's Jellystone Park Camp-Resorts, also Safari Resorts, 6201 Kellogg Ave., Cincinnati, Ohio 45230; (800) 558-2954

16

Put the RV in ConseRVation

Being homeless, rootless, and routeless is not without its culture shocks. One of the blows to the ego is that some people look down on RV campers as gas hogs, nature tramplers, and the all-time chief polluters of the outdoor world. You can expect some dirty looks on the highway and a few nasty cracks from tent campers and backpackers.

We know what it is to be on both sides of the finger pointing. During the ten years we lived on the go fulltime, the RV was our summer home. In winter, we lived aboard a sailboat, using only the free energy supplied by the wind. One year, our fuel consumption for the entire season was the twelve gallons we had used to recharge the batteries once a week.

We sailors called powerboats "stinkpots" and looked at them much as canvas campers looked at us and our RV in summer. It was silly, but it did help us laugh at ourselves when we were looked down upon by campers who thought they were more "pure" because they were backpacking, biking, or canoeing.

Fulltimers can only hope to make others understand and see the good in us, but we *can* recognize the good in ourselves and go on truckin' without apology, knowing that our lifestyle is conservation at its best.

Look at it this way. Back in what we now call "real life," we lived in a huge, drafty, older home that had a furnace the size of Rhode Island

and a bathtub that held as much hot water as the YMCA pool. Our internal combustion inventory included two cars plus a fume-belching arsenal of yard care equipment. We lived in the Midwest, where temperature extremes forced us to run either the furnace or the air conditioning almost every day. Winter days were so short, the lights went on at 3 P.M. and sometimes burned throughout the dark day.

We exchanged all that space and energy dependence for tiny living quarters that follow the seasons. The RV furnace is seldom lit; the lights rarely are used during the day. When we *do* run the heat or air conditioning, it's for an entire home that has less cubic footage than *one bedroom* in the average house.

The consumer needs of most RVs are minuscule compared to even the smallest homes. A typical RV water heater holds six gallons or less. The largest RV refrigerators (and few of us have the largest) are only about ten cubic feet—the size of the smallest kitchen refrigerators. Most of our entertainment electronics work on 12-volt power, which we supply ourselves by charging our batteries underway.

We RVers are abstemious with water, not just because we have to fill our own water tanks but because we have to *empty* our waste water tanks too. Homeowners may let a faucet drip for a few days until it's convenient to fix it. Not so in the RV, where every drop wasted is a drop closer to an empty tank!

RV owners can't let the faucet run until the water is cold because we know that our tanks have only twenty to fifty gallons in reserve. And if we let it run until it's hot before stepping into the shower, it never takes more than a pint or two because the pipe run is so short.

Our toilets flush for a week on the amount of water used in a water-saver household toilet in a day. Few of us have automatic dishwashers, icemakers, disposals, compactors, washers, or dryers. Where we do have electric servants, from power tools to the vacuum cleaner to kitchen appliances, they are chosen for light weight, small size, and energy efficiency in ways that most house dwellers never think about. We know the cost of energy because we pay for it day in and day out at the gas pump, at the campground, in charging the battery, and in running a generator.

Fulltimers develop a sharp eye for value, long wear, compactness, and versatility in everything we buy, from clothes to tools. When we say we are self-contained, that means we can take care of ourselves when necessary without hookups. When you're making your own electricity, running your own waterworks, and operating your own sewer system, it gives you a conservationist perspective the hard way.

It's because they are self-contained that many RV fulltimers are thoughtful enough to stay out of state and national parks, and off the highways, during busy holiday weekends when vacationers need the roads and tenters must have the toilet and shower facilities that campgrounds provide.

It's true that RV travel requires plenty of fuel, but who says a fulltimer has to be on the road every day or even every week? Most fulltimers have to budget for fuel more carefully than anyone else, because they are fully or partially retired on a limited income.

We know people who think nothing of commuting sixty miles per day to work, driving fifty miles to see a movie, and covering a couple of hundred miles sightseeing over a weekend. And most families these days drive their children anywhere that is more than half a block away. Fulltimers, by contrast, use more gallons per mile, but make every mile count for something.

The fulltimer thinks twice before unhooking and stowing all the umbilicals and wrestling the rig out of a campsite. Errands are lumped together; trips are planned carefully to make every mile count. Once at a destination, a fulltimer can settle down for a while, make friends, and savor the local scene for a week, a month, or a season—unlike the rushed vacationer who pulls up stakes every day.

Simply put, some people use more fuel than others, and living in an RV doesn't necessarily make one a fuel glutton. This isn't the place to go into a discussion of big RV versus small, or gasoline versus diesel. Our point is that, no matter how efficient the RV, the fulltimer uses it with the utmost conservation in mind because it wasn't bought to be a station wagon or a sports car. It is, above all else, a *home*.

What You Can Do

Now that you're committed to fulltiming as a way of life, and have made the wide world your home, you have more reason than anyone else to do your part in saving the earth. Here are some conservation points that apply specifically to the fulltimer way of life.

Prevent Sun Damage and Heat Gain

Get insulated window coverings that keep out the cold or hot sun. Any good custom drapery maker can design attractive curtains with double or triple linings. If possible, buy an RV with double-glazed windows. When replacing skylights, opt for double-glazed types. Have solar film professionally installed (do-it-yourself installations are usually doomed to failure) on at least some windows.

Check regularly for air leaks and caulk them. In an RV they're rare compared to the many gaps found in a house, but some voids may be found around the furnace, refrigerator, or other through-the-wall installations.

Get awnings for the side, for individual windows, and to shade the side of the RV over the refrigerator coils. Make, or have made, a cover for the windshield. You might even order two, one in a dark fabric to absorb heat on cold days and another in white to use in hot climates. Park in the shade in hot climates, in the sun when it's cold.

Get a high-quality, heavy-duty spare tire cover, not just a thin cover with a cute logo on it. Sun fade is as destructive to tires as road wear. When you're parked, use sun shades on all the tires.

Use polishes with ultraviolet inhibitors. Don't wash the RV in the sun. It's not good for the paint, and you'll waste more water through evaporation. (Observe campground rules; washing RVs may be prohibited, or it may be permitted only in certain areas or during specified times.)

Going Solar

Although solar energy hasn't yet become practical for most households, it makes special sense in the RV life because you can use it to charge batteries, and batteries run RV lights, television, radio, and much more. Add solar panels to the roof as you can afford them. A full-length and well-illustrated book, *RVer's Guide to Solar and Inverter Power*, is available from RV Solar Electric. For more information about solar panels and other solar accessories, contact RV Solar Electric, 14415 N. 73rd Street, Scottsdale, Arizona 85260; (800) 999-8520.

Also consider getting one of the portable solar water heaters sold by camping or boating suppliers. One brand, called Sun Shower, is a

Put the RV in ConseRVation

The more solar panels you can add to your RV, the more independent you'll be. (Kyocera America Inc. and RV Solar Electric)

complete unit including water bag and shower spray. If you devise a permanent hanger for it in your shower stall, you can hang it outdoors to heat the water in the sun, then bring it inside to use in the comfort and privacy of your own bathroom.

Another solar accessory that has proved practical for RV use is an overhead hatch with a solar-powered exhaust fan. It fits into standard size hatch openings and is easy to install.

Outside the RV

Fulltimers have storage problems that other RV campers don't have. It's bad enough that the living quarters are stuffed and overloaded, but in addition, each time you step on the gas pedal fuel must be used to get all that inertia rolling.

The problem compounds, though, when possessions start spilling over from inside the RV to the roof, sides, or front bumper, because now you're adding both dead weight *and* aerodynamic drag. (Carrying things on the front bumper may also interfere with air flow to the radiator.) Try to keep the exterior as sleek and uncluttered as the designer intended.

If you must add exterior storage, keep it as aerodynamically clean as possible. You can tell just by looking at them that some roof pods, side mirrors, awning containers, and air conditioners will cut through the air better than others. Depending on the configuration of your rig, an aftermarket fairing (you've seen them on eighteen-wheelers) may be available to channel air flow more advantageously.

Consumables and Recycling

Most of us have been recycling for years, but new habits have to be learned on the road because each campground and community has its own rules. In one town you may be asked to separate only a few categories such as aluminum, newspaper, and clear glass; in another you might have to separate just trash and garbage; and the next may have elaborate sorting rules involving different types of plastics, clear and colored glass, and aluminum foil separate from aluminum cans.

In those campgrounds where everything goes into the same bin, you can still maintain your own voluntary recycling program for at least some items. Crushed aluminum and steel cans take up little space or weight and can travel with you until you find a recycling center.

Water, too, is a resource that most of us learn to use and re-use. Letting a faucet run until the water is hot? Catch the surplus in a pitcher and use it to water plants or rinse sprouts. Draining a big pot of spaghetti? Save the water for washing dishes. Rinsing dishes? Save the clean, slightly soapy water and do a batch of hand laundry or wash the dog.

In the coin laundry, use cold water wherever possible. Clean the dryer filter before every use. Use concentrated detergents and measure out only as much as the manufacturer recommends.

During droughts in some areas, campgrounds ask that gray water

Waste storage is almost always inadequate in RVs. Devise ways to separate and store trash for recycling. (Rutt Custom Kitchens)

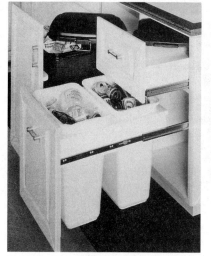
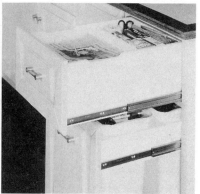

be emptied onto nearby trees. Otherwise, dispose of this water only in designated places. Don't use formaldehyde in black water tanks; buy only the new, biodegradable toilet chemicals. Although water conservation is considered a virtue, when the ratio of solids to liquids is too great it can create a problem in your own black water tank and even greater problems in campgrounds that have septic tanks. Unless water is in short supply, flush generously.

Used engine oil and all other automotive chemicals, dead batteries, and worn out tires and tubes must be disposed of according to state or local law. If you've picked up a heavy load of road salt, be careful where you wash the RV. Salty runoff can damage plants.

The Campfire

Although most fulltimer RVs have a gas stove with oven and perhaps a microwave, most of us still enjoy campfires as part of the camping experience. Observe local fire laws, and be aware that they can change from day to day according to weather conditions.

Learn to start wood fires with tinder and kindling rather than chemicals. Minimize the use of charcoal. You might carry a gas grill that hooks up to your main propane tank. Or gather wood for cooking. Or bring the electric broiler outdoors. If you do cook with charcoal, use an electric starter and/or bellows rather than chemical starters and dispose of the ash according to campground rules. Remember that charcoal looks cold even when it's scorching hot; keep children away from it and make sure the coals are cold before leaving them.

When you have a wood fire, don't add anything except clean burnables and well-seasoned wood. Packaging that contains metal or plastic pollutes the air and leaves junk in the fire pit.

Additional Environmental Tips

♦ Don't feed wildlife or try to tame it. If you have a pet, remember that you and the pet are the outsiders in parks and other wildlife refuges.

♦ Invest in rechargeable batteries and a charger. Disposable batteries are expensive and contribute toxins to landfills.

♦ Don't pick any plants except where allowed, and then don't take more than your share.

♦ Take care not to damage trees and bushes at campsites. Don't hammer nails into trees to hang clotheslines or hammocks. Don't tie anything to them, either, because even the smallest abrasions can create voids where bugs or disease can get a foothold.

♦ Carry a screw-type stake and put the dog's chain through that, rather than around a tree or shrub. Shop for the kind of chain that is enclosed in a plastic sleeve.

♦ Don't add to erosion problems by driving on fragile beaches, shoulders, deserts, or fields.

♦ Don't pick sea oats or other natural dune protectors.

♦ Consider adding a screen room to provide both shade and bug protection without chemical sprays.

♦ Instead of towing a car or a boat, and hanging bicycles or motorbikes on the RV, consider renting what you need, when and where you need it. Club Nautico is a nationwide organization in which members get a big discount on boat rentals everywhere they go. Contact them at 5450 N.W. 33rd Ave. #106, Fort Lauderdale, Florida 33309; (800) BOAT-RENT. Most tourist areas have bikes or mopeds for rent; they may be available right at the campground.

◆ Rediscover public transportation. Ask at the campground what is available. In many areas, free shuttles are run between campgrounds and major attractions or shopping areas. At others, city bus stops are only a short walk away. You save fuel, tolls, and parking fees, and make friends during the ride.

◆ Save fuel by starting each city visit with a guided tour. When we want to see a tourist area thoroughly, we first take a guided tour such as the Conch Train in Key West, one of Boston's tourist trolleys, or a Grey Line tour. Instead of touring with one eye on traffic and another on the map, we can relax and see the sights while an experienced narrator regales us with local yarns. When we do take off on our own after that, we have a better idea of how the streets lie and how traffic flows.

◆ When you're losing Freon, find and fix the leak immediately. Gone are the days when it was cheaper to buy Freon in cans and top off the air conditioner every few weeks.

◆ Disposing of unneeded antibiotics? Don't flush them if the campground has a septic system—they could kill helpful bacteria.

◆ If you break a mercury thermometer, carefully collect the bits by using a toothpick to push them into a glass bottle. Then cap it and turn it in at a hazardous waste facility. Don't vacuum it, or the vacuum cleaner will be permanently contaminated.

◆ Line closets with cedar and/or use one of the new, natural citrus fresheners. Moth balls contain naphthalene, which you don't want venting into your living quarters. If you do use mothballs, seal clothes in tightly lidded containers.

◆ Don't use formaldehyde mildewcides either. Depend instead on frequent airing and washing of stored fabrics.

◆ Don't buy clothes that need dry cleaning.

◆ Buy food, shampoo, and cleaning products in bulk where possible, and repackage in reusable containers. Foods, however, should be stored only in food-quality plastics—not soap dispensers or garbage bags.

◆ Don't use a disposable if it's available in reusable form. The list includes disposable razors, emery boards rather than a nail file, disposable pens (refillables are making a comeback), and paper products for the kitchen.

◆ Don't accept merchants' paper or plastic bags. Take your own canvas carry bags when doing any shopping. You'll not only cut down on disposables, you'll find endless uses for these bags in the RV life—and their hefty web handles make them far easier to carry than paper or plastic sacks.

◆ Good arguments can be made both for and against disposable diapers. If you use cloth diapers, or any other contaminated items that need special laundry treatment, ask at a medical supplier for the hospital-type plastic laundry bags that dissolve in hot water. Once put into these bags, laundry does not have to be handled again. It goes into a washer, bag and all. Use very hot water (both to dissolve the bag and to sanitize the wash) and effective disinfectants that will decontaminate the wash and the washer.

◆ Report illegal dumpers, poachers, and polluters. Most states have a toll-free wildlife hotline where you can blow the whistle on illegal hunting, trapping, fishing, or wildlife abuse of any kind.

◆ Join adopt-a-beach, adopt-a-highway, and other cleanup programs.

◆ Volunteer for a season as an unpaid worker in a state or national park. You'll be rewarded with a free campsite as well as with new friends and a feeling of real accomplishment.

◆ Don't get so caught up in recycling that you lose sight of the fact that you shouldn't have bought the item in the first place. Mix your own drinks using powders or concentrates, and you'll have no aluminum cans to store, transport, and recycle. Buy fresh fruits and vegetables and have no cans to squash, no cardboard packaging to burn, no plastics to recycle.

◆ Buy good wood-and-fabric folding chairs. Repaint them as needed and sew up new canvas seats and backs as the old ones wear out. They'll outlast plastic and aluminum chairs by decades.

◆ Keep all the RV's filters clean. An air conditioner with a clogged filter has to work harder. A vacuum cleaner with a full bag has to work longer. A stove exhaust with a greasy filter uses just as much energy to move half as much air.

◆ Don't hold up the parade. RVs are not as responsive and speedy as cars, and much of the resentment against them comes from drivers who are in a hurry. Try not to drive during rush hours or holiday weekends. If a line of traffic piles up behind you, pull off and let them pass. They'll appreciate it, and you're less likely to get involved in a rear-ender or a pileup.

◆ Rediscover the old ways. Our grandparents knew how to reverse a collar to double the wear, let hems up and down as fashions changed, re-sole shoes and boots, turn dress scraps into baby clothes and baby clothes scraps into quilt pieces. There was no waste, few disposables, and no land-fill crisis in those days.

A few years ago, we found ourselves in a very poor village on a tiny atoll in Indonesia. The only litter on the beach was nature's leavings—broken seashells, coconut husks, and a few twigs. It wasn't that the people were neat. It's just that they had almost nothing made of glass, aluminum, or plastic. The few consumables they did have were used and reused until they were nothing but dust and rust.

It's bad enough that we are smothering in our own trash. The worst of it is that much of it would be considered treasure in other countries, where people would use and reuse it. Traveling in the Bahamas, we noticed that some Haitian boats left with a cargo of nothing more than empty glass and plastic bleach bottles picked from local dumps.

Those of us who choose to roam can learn from these people that less is best, not just for a simple, happy life but for Mother Earth too.

Portable Professions

If you're independently wealthy, or retired with enough income to bankroll your fulltiming life, you can skip this chapter. Most of the rest of us face one of the following scenarios. You are either:

◆ Fully in the work force, currently ineligible for pension or Social Security. You are looking for a way to stay on the road while making enough money to live on, build for the future, and eventually retire.

◆ Fully in the work force in a profession that requires such frequent moves that it's more economical to live in a portable home.

◆ Retired or disabled, but with only a bare-bones income. You need supplemental income for now and something to put away for the future.

◆ Young but temporarily retired, on sabbatical from a job you will return to after fulfilling your dream of fulltiming. You want an occasional job that will allow you to keep up with your fast-changing field.

◆ Sick of your present career and eager to start a new one that involves full-time travel.

Once almost unheard of, midlife career changes are now common-place. Some changes are gentle ones, such as leaving a corporate career as an engineer and forming your own engineering consulting firm. Others are very difficult, involving years of additional education or other new training. A helpful guide is *Second Careers: New Ways to Work After Fifty*, by Caroline Bird (Little, Brown).

If you want serious career opportunities, they are available to full-timers. There also are not-so-serious work opportunities out there for those whose only aim is to keep truckin'.

Here are some avenues to consider.

Workamping

Theirs is the happiest of stories: Greg and Debbie Robus realized their own dream and then began devoting their lives to helping others do the same. Both have college degrees, Greg in parks administration and Debbie in elementary education. Working as a park ranger for the Corps of Engineers, Greg began to see a need for linking up fulltimers who needed extra income with parks and other employers who needed dependable, but not necessarily year-round, workers.

Debbie, a kindergarten teacher, had experimented with newsletter publication in the field of needlework, her hobby. So the couple sold everything they owned, bought a computer, moved to a farm in Arkansas, and founded *Workamper News*.

The bimonthly *Workamper News* offers free classified ads of 100 words or less to employers who can offer jobs to RVers. A typical ad might read: "Wanted: Neat, semi-retired couple to work in small, family campground May–September. Free campsite with hookups, and small salary."

Ads offer fulltime, seasonal, part-time, or temporary jobs that are ideal for those fulltimers who want to stay free, but who need the occasional boost to the bank account. Some ads are invitations for bids to work for a government park, usually at twenty-five to sixty dollars a day. Others offer jobs in marinas, guest ranches, farms, orchards, mobile home parks, RV parks, cabins, and motels. One ad is from a company that needs experienced RV drivers to work for movie companies.

No matter what your talents or background, *Workamper News* may list just the job you need. A couple who were living in a thirteen-foot trailer landed jobs at Silver Dollar City, a theme park in Missouri, and lived a fairy tale life in calico and buckskin. They were soon able to afford a more spacious RV and lived happily ever after.

Professional musicians sing the song of the open road, often playing to RV parks or church groups. A licensed nurse and her husband, a Mr. Fix-It who carries all his own tools, find work as they travel the country where and when they please, using *Workamper News* as a resource.

Workamper News also prints ads for volunteer positions that offer no payment but do provide a free campsite with utilities. While most of the jobs assume that the reader is an RV fulltimer who will bring his own housing with him, some employers offer a cabin or apartment.

In addition to the free ads, the Robuses publish paid ads from both job seekers and employers, and they also offer a referral service. Workampers, as these members of the fulltimer family call themselves, fill out a resume and job preference form. For five dollars (plus two dollars for each update), it is kept on file, matched up with employers in each field and geographic area, and mailed out by the Robuses to prospective employers.

Greg and Debbie are kept busy reading their fan mail from happy campers who are able to stay solvent thanks to workamping, and from delighted employers who find workampers reliable, industrious, and highly qualified (usually because they are retirees from industry or the military).

Workamper News subscriptions are $18 for one year and $33 for two, plus additional postage for Canada, Mexico, or overseas mailing. A sample, three-issue subscription is $12.75. For information, write *Workamper News*, 201 Hiram Road, HCR 34 Box 125, Heber Springs, Arizona 72543.

Word Processing

The work-at-home movement is hot and getting hotter. Although not all such jobs can go on the road with you, it's possible that you might be able to connect, via computer and modem, with some word processing jobs. If you have background in legal, medical, or other specialty word processing, or a wide network of industry contacts, it will be easier to keep the jobs coming.

We also heard of an accomplished word processor whose onboard computer center serves as a mobile school in which she trains others as word processors. She runs ads offering to make her RV/office available to businesses in need of word processing training.

It is possible to make a living on the go in your RV if you find a product that catches the public eye, then market it tirelessly. (Sears)

Arts and Crafts

Create items at your leisure and sell them at flea markets as you travel. Or if you'd rather not deal directly with the public, visit boutiques as you travel and ask if they'd like to sell your wares. Ski shops, for instance, may take sweaters on consignment, and larger shops may contract with you to knit for them. Homemakers with knitting machines are paid about twelve dollars per hour in the Northeast to fill large orders placed with them by catalog houses.

Consignment, of course, has its pitfalls, especially if you leave your products behind and are miles away when a merchant goes out of business, declares bankruptcy, or otherwise goes south with your goods or money. Diversify, and deal only with established and reputable outfits. Among them, if the quality of your work justifies it, are museum gift shops and non-profit craft stores operated to benefit artisans.

Xavier Roberts, whose Cabbage Patch dolls took the world by storm, began as a simple hobbyist working with an old German craft called "needle sculpture." He found a theme that worked and parlayed it into an empire.

Your success might be in anything from country crafts to custom Christmas ornaments. But in the crafts field as in so many others, having the talent to make the crafts is just the beginning. You must also be a savvy, persistent salesperson and a self-starter who can keep turning out the work on a regular schedule. Keep in mind that public taste can be fickle, so it's best to find products that both sell well and suit your talents, interests, equipment, and work space.

Writing

To anyone in the creative arts, fulltiming can be the best of all muses. It certainly was for the famous romance writer Janet Dailey, who set out in a travel trailer to write a series of novels set in every state in the Union. Fulltiming can also, however, be a tremendous hurdle for the hungry writer.

Writing and photography supported our ten years of fulltiming and have continued to provide us income and adventure now that we are part-timers again. But before you rush out to follow our lead, let us clear up some popular misconceptions about freelancing.

Many people imagine they'll have such an exciting life as fulltimers that *National Geographic* will beat a path to their door, or that they'll write the Great American Novel while gazing out over the passing panorama. Countless times, people have told us, "Oh, the stories I could write if I had time," or "I could write a book about my adventures." It might come as a surprise to those folks to discover that fulltiming itself will not magically turn them into writers.

Writing for a living is not something you do when you "have time." It's a demanding, agonizing discipline that you work at just as others work at dentistry, truck driving, or selling cars. Writing the material is only half the battle. You also have to merchandise it.

Unlike handicrafts, which can be sold at flea markets and art shows, articles, books, plays, and poems have to be sold to publishers. This can be done in two ways: You can market the material yourself by mail, which is cumbersome and expensive, or you can send it to an agent, who will market it for you.

Unless you're already a highly successful author, no agent will take you on a commission basis, so forget that option unless you're prepared to pay handsomely for reading fees, critiques, and other services that rarely lead to literary success. You'll probably have to paddle your own canoe, at least in the beginning.

If you're already a selling writer, fulltiming will open some doors and shut a few windows. If you're not already writing, don't take off in your RV expecting to become an instant writer. Even if you begin writing at once, which is unlikely because you'll have so many other things to do, and even if you start selling those writings immediately, which is even more unlikely, it takes months before cash flow begins.

Although the hows of freelance writing could fill an entire book, here are some basic tips:

◆ **Set a daily writing goal.** Treat it like a business, working regular hours. Invest in all the materials needed to put out a professional-looking product. As a minimum you'll need a word processor with letter-quality printer, business stationery, and a dependable address. If you can manage telephone or other communication service (answering service or electronic mailbox), so much the better.

◆ **Buy a copy of *Writer's Market*,** which is published annually by Writer's Digest Books. Study it to learn what markets are most suitable for the kinds of material you write.

◆ **Write consistently and persistently.** This means turning out finished writings, as well as sending out regular proposals and query letters in search of assignments. By being a part of the literary marketplace day in and day out, even if all your efforts are rejected, you'll learn the writing business in ways that cannot be taught in any course, writers' conference, or seminar.

◆ **Find your own niche.** Editors are eager for pieces from writers who know their subject inside out, and you'll stand taller in a crowded marketplace if you can focus on a speciality. A food writer, for example, might be an expert in wines or, even more narrowly, in Napa Valley vintages. Travel writers might specialize in RV travel, but will do even better by specializing further in RV skiing, RV travel with children, environmentally sound travel, or SCUBA diving. Outdoor writers can gain special notice as experts in ecology, whitetail rabbit hunting, bass fishing, or acid rain. Fiction writers might specialize in short stories, mysteries, formula romance, religious books, children's literature, and so on.

Photography

Almost everything said above about freelance writing can also apply to freelance photography. Invest in good equipment (cameras, lenses, lighting, the best film) and presentation tools (slide sleeves, labels, mounts). Work hard. Specialize. Market aggressively.

Because you live on the go, you'll be less able to get bread-and-butter work such as weddings or industrial brochures, but you'll be free to travel, grow, and snap anything that catches your eye.

As a freelance photographer, you can sell your work by mail to magazines, calendar or postcard manufacturers, and greeting card companies. Or send all your work to a stock agency. If you can find an agency to accept your work, all you have to do is take the pictures and send them in. They'll do all the marketing and send you regular checks. While literary commissions run ten to fifteen percent, stock agencies take a larger cut; however, they may sell the same photo over and over, sending you a check for each placement. If you prefer to sell directly to the public, have your best shots made into prints. Then package them attractively, matted or framed, and offer them at arts and crafts shows.

Photographer's Market, another Writers Digest Books publication, is an excellent guide to the how, where, ethics, and business practices of selling your pictures.

Publishing

At least two fulltimer couples publish travel newsletters on the go. If you have a specialty, you can make even more money by publishing a newsletter in a narrow field. It needn't be related to RVs or even to travel. It could be anything from diesel engine repair to pet psychology to vegetarian cooking. A Florida woman founded a newsletter about exotic tropical edibles. A Maine housewife began publishing a tightwad's newsletter, telling how she and her husband raise six kids on a shoestring. She was featured on the "Phil Donahue Show," and subscriptions poured in.

The better your credentials and the narrower the focus, the more money you can charge for the fewer pages of truly meaty material. Subscribers pay as much as $100 to $300 per year for insider newsletters written by experts. If you go on line, selling through a database, you can eliminate printing and mailing completely.

Newsletters usually don't carry ads—all the income derives from subscriptions—although many newsletter publishers increase their profits by offering extra services or products. A microwave newsletter publisher, for example, also offers hard-to-find microwave cookware. A newsletter about Chinese cooking sells hard-to-find ingredients.

professions

If you do sell a product through your newsletter, you don't have to warehouse, pack, and ship the merchandise. Find a supplier who will drop-ship. You process the orders, subtracting your cut from the check you send the shipper.

Temping

Usually, in exchange for temporary employment, fulltimers settle for lower wages, few or no benefits, and little chance of advancement. Most are underemployed. The former plant manager might accept work as weekend manager of a small campground; a one-time executive secretary as a typist or receptionist; a former nursing supervisor as an on-call R.N. Yet everyone wins—the fulltimer, because he or she is free to move on with no hard feelings when the season ends, and the employer, because no long-term commitment had to be made.

Nationwide temporary help agencies, such as Kelly and Manpower, or medical agencies, such as Medical Personnel Pool, can allow you to pursue your profession and still stay on the go. We once knew a couple who worked for the same nationwide chain for years, staying in one place only long enough to build up their savings and then moving on until it was time to feed the kitty again.

The best feature of temping is that it is just that—temporary. You can work a couple of days here, a few weeks there, and move on without getting branded a "job hopper." The employer loves the no-future, no-promises arrangement as much as you do.

Meanwhile, you're building up a fine work record, and in some cases seniority and other benefits (such as group health insurance), with a national firm that can put you to work in dozens of cities. Your record is faxed from one branch to the next, so no time is wasted with repeated applications and checking of references.

If you have an easily marketed skill such as word processing, medical or legal clerking, inventory-taking, computers, or accounting, look into opportunities in temping.

Put Your RV to Work

Through the years, we've met countless couples who lived on boats fulltime before moving ashore and becoming RV fulltimers. Rose and Harry Willington were in the business of yacht chartering for twenty-five years before they went ashore at Pompano Beach, bought a thirty-four-foot motorhome, and began chartering it as a land yacht.

The Willingtons charter only by day. They pick up customers, serve breakfast and lunch on the go, and deliver guests to their destination. If the trip is for more than one day, they take the passengers to a hotel each night. It's a service popular with business travelers, entertainers, and groups of couples who want a carefree golfing or tennis weekend with a designated driver.

If you want to use your RV for hire, make sure your insurance coverage allows for whatever business you're in, and get a chauffeur's license if it's required by the state or municipality.

Another way to use your RV as a working vehicle is to lead RV caravans. Or use it as a demonstrator/showroom for a camping-related product, such as awnings.

Your RV might also be turned to some specialty use. A photographer who specializes in shooting yacht races, for instance, put a complete photo lab aboard his RV and develops his photos on the spot. An accomplished kayaker guides whitewater trips by day and retires to his RV at night. A veterinarian makes house calls in her RV; so does a visiting nurse.

Work-at-Home Resources

To be listed free in a registry that matches employers with home-based workers who have special skills, send a stamped, self-addressed envelope to HOMEbase, Box 1461, Manassas, Virginia 22110.

A book you may find helpful is *The Work-at-Home Sourcebook*, by Lynie Arden. It's available in book stores or from New Careers Inc., Box 339, Boulder, Colorado 80306.

You may come across newspaper classified ads for various kinds of work-at-home plans; shun those that sound too good to be true. Many are pyramid schemes or chain letter–type operations, in which the only way to make money is to enlist others to fall for the same scheme.

18

The Mysteries of Mobile Medicine

In the lives of all of us who wander, the possibility of being sick and friendless in a strange town is a haunting threat that sometimes becomes a reality. In a lifestyle filled with wonders and rewards, illness is one unpleasantness that must be planned for.

During our ten homeless years, we had the usual routine care plus one hospital emergency and a couple of painful, pressing ailments such as swimmer's ear and root canal. The important point is that we survived them all, even though we were in places where we didn't know anyone, and we emerged each time with a heightened sense of affection, gratitude, and respect for our countrymen.

In 1988 Paul Terhorst published a book with the eye-catching title, *Cashing In on the American Dream; How to Retire at Thirty-five* (Bantam Books). It makes instructive and inspiring reading, and we recommend it for any young person who is considering fulltiming. Although much of the book does not apply to RV living, Terhorst presents invaluable advice on planning toward early retirement.

The one topic Terhorst didn't address, however, was the soaring costs of health care, and we wrote him about it. He replied, "Your comment about health insurance made me rethink the issue. I wouldn't be surprised if health insurance turns out to be *the* issue of very early retirement."

As we write this, the American health care system is in turmoil and transition, but it's our guess that medical care will continue to be a financial problem for fulltimers, no matter what politicians do about it. So our first recommendation is to get health insurance now and hang onto it. If you develop a chronic problem, such as diabetes or high blood pressure, it will be impossible to get coverage later.

You have two other choices, unless you're old enough for Medicare:

◆ Self insure. Either pay medical costs out of your pocket or compromise by taking a very high deductible policy, say $2,500 or $5,000, in which case you are insured against minor ills, yet protected, at minimum price, against being wiped out by a catastrophic health problem.

◆ Have no assets; throw yourself on the welfare system if you become ill—an alternative many of us would not find acceptable.

Before You Go

Once you're on the go fulltime, you'll be responsible for your own health care in ways you probably never thought of before. When you have regular checkups from the same doctors, you can depend on them to note trends, dates of operations and treatments, names of drugs, allergies, worrisome changes, gains, and losses. However, when your yearly checkup is done by a different physician each time, only *you* can tell whether your blood pressure is up, your weight down, or your mole larger.

Before leaving your hometown, make sure your shots, including a tetanus shot, are up to date, and get a written record to keep with you always. World Health Organization shot record cards are recognized worldwide and are a good way to keep track, especially if you will be traveling outside North America.

Your physician might also recommend that you get elective surgery out of the way and have some baseline tests, such as a blood profile or mammogram. We carry these records with us, plus the names of our prescription drugs. Know the generic and brand names, and dosage. Every doctor you see in the future will want to know.

When having a prescription filled, we always ask the pharmacist for the "Patient Information" sheet, which usually isn't put into the package unless you request it. Laymen don't always understand all the language in a P.I., but it's an invaluable record. During subsequent treatment for this illness, or even years in the future, this information can be vital.

Keep a medical diary so you'll have all available information in one place. Note ailments, dates, symptoms, insurance policy numbers, and the names, addresses, and telephone numbers of doctors, clinics, and hospitals where you've been treated.

Have a living will made, listing your wishes concerning heroic measures, and keep a copy handy. Send other copies to next of kin. If you do not want to be kept alive by artificial means, you and your family will need all the legal ammunition you can muster, because the laws vary state by state.

The more you know about what's happening to you, and what is being done to you by health care professionals who are strangers to you, the better. Many fulltimers invest in medical reference books such as the *Merck Manual* or the *Physicians Desk Reference*. One excellent guide is *The Ship's Medical Chest and First Aid at Se*a. Because it is written for medical offices aboard ships that have no doctors on board, it covers more serious first aid than books written for people who are only minutes from the nearest hospital. Order it from the U.S. Government Printing Office, Washington, D.C. 20402; (202) 783-3238. There also are U.S.G.P.O. bookstores in some major cities; check the local telephone book to see if there's one nearby.

Ask your doctor's help in putting together a complete first-aid kit. Learn the Heimlich maneuver and take a CPR course. As you travel, keep an eye peeled for free medical services in malls and hospitals. You might find free screenings for diabetes and blood pressure, mammograms, some eye tests, and even condom giveaways.

Finding a Doctor

Because some physicians accept no new patients, or charge a huge premium for taking the medical history of a first-time patient, the fulltimer can have difficulty in finding care. One answer is to get on the CB radio and ask the location of the nearest walk-in medical facility. These freestanding clinics are ideal for minor emergencies or a one-time visit.

If the community has a doctor referral service, call it and explain your special needs, including your transportation situation. If you're driving a large motorhome, you need a doctor whose office offers suitable parking. Big-city offices in downtown skyscrapers aren't your cup of tea.

Although life on the go sets up certain problems in medical care, it also has advantages. If you need a specialist, simply drive your entire household to the Mayo Clinic, or Houston, or Memphis, or wherever you can get the best care.

Special Insurance

If it's important to you to be transported to your hometown for medical treatment, insurance is available. A company called NEAR Services offers single policies for $150 and family policies for $220 yearly. Its services include emergency transportation home from anywhere in the United States via first-class air transportation, on a stretcher and with an attendant if necessary. The list of benefits includes lost/stolen credit card insurance, lost/stolen airline ticket replacement, international message service, lost-and-found key and baggage service, and much more. International service is also available at extra cost. Write them at 450 Prairie Ave., Calumet City, Illinois 60409, or call (800) 654-6700 for full details.

Another air evac insurance policy is offered by Medical Air Services Association. You're covered anywhere in the United States, Canada, Mexico, and the Caribbean for an emergency flight home if you're injured or taken ill. Ask about group coverage, which may be available through a camping group. Some insurance companies also arrange to drive your RV for you if you and your spouse have to be rushed home by air. Call (800) 643-9023 for information.

Fitness and the Fulltimer

One of the biggest frustrations in fulltiming is that there isn't room to swing a cat, let alone fling yourself around in a strenuous exercise program. One of the best exercises is brisk walking, but if you prefer a more serious program, you can:

◆ Seek out campgrounds that have fitness directors, programs, and/or exercise equipment. Many camping resorts and destination campgrounds do.

◆ Join a YW/YMCA. As a member of one Y, you will often be welcome to use the services of another one at discounted prices. Look into short-term programs too. Aerobics and other fitness classes often are available to non-members at reasonable prices.

◆ Join a large, nationwide health club that has locations in many cities, then plan your travels so you'll always be near one. The advantage of national membership is that each of the club's individual facilities will share the same philosophy and type of equipment, so you'll get continuity of training no matter where you are.

Dental Care

Prevention and education are the keys to carefree fulltiming, at least as far as your mouth is concerned.

Get your dental house in order at least six months before you set out fulltiming, advises Dale D. Batten, D.M.D., who practices in Deland, Florida. If you've neglected your teeth, consult a dentist as early as possible, as much as a year before your target getaway date, because you may need extensive work not just on your teeth but also on your gums, which may require a long-term course of action, Dr. Batten warns.

"This is a tourist area, so I often see one-time patients who are just passing through town, as well as fulltimers who arrange to come to Deland for their regular checkups," he says. "If you've been an active patient, the only extra steps I'd take before you leave would be to take care of those teeth I'd been watching—those with minor fracture lines, for example. And I'd recommend that any teeth with large restorations or cracks receive full coverage cast restoration to add strength. Once you're on the road, you want to avoid trouble before it starts."

During your last visit to your hometown dentist, ask for a duplicate set of X-rays and a written report indicating what care you've been receiving and any special quirks or trouble spots. Ask your dentist what first-aid supplies are recommended, such as an over-the-counter, topical anesthetic gel to ease the discomfort of ulcers or other soft-tissue lesions.

If you use any special implements for oral cleaning and care, or require adaptive equipment because you are handicapped, get extras before you go because it may be difficult to find replacements later.

Dr. Batten also recommends stocking up on any prescription mouth rinses or fluoride gels you are using. "It takes up very little space to carry a year's supply, so buy before you go, because sometimes prescriptions aren't honored across state lines," he recommends.

You might also ask your dentist to show you how to fix your dislocated jaw if you're subject to recurrent dislocations. It's a simple first-aid technique that could come in handy when you're far from professional help.

Once you're on the road, continue with regular checkups, usually every six months unless you require more frequent cleanings or checks. Batten suggests two ways to find the best dentists when you're in a new area.

One way is to call several specialists—orthodontists, endodontists, periodontists—and ask who they recommend for general dentistry. Each will probably give you three names, and when the same name pops up more than once, you'll know you've found a dentist who is well respected in the profession. Or, call the Academy of General Dentistry, (312) 440-4300, and ask for Membership Services. They'll give you the names of three member dentists in the area you're visiting. Their address is 211 E. Chicago Ave., Chicago, Illinois 60611.

To qualify for A.G.D. membership, dentists have to be not just state licensed but involved in ongoing education. To qualify as a Fellow of the Academy, a dentist must have logged 500 hours of continuing education and passed a tough, all-day exam. A Master of the Academy has logged an additional 600 hours.

What about advertising in the Yellow Pages, or the referral services advertised on television? Some "referral" services are simply an advertising co-op paid for by dentists who are trying to drum up business. Referrals are made only to dentists who have paid to be listed. You may get a better profile by calling a county dental society. Some use a comprehensive database to find exactly the dentist you want according to education, years in practice, location, and even marital status. If there is a dental school in the area, you might try asking there for a recommendation too. While university dental schools do capable, highly supervised work at bargain prices, it's very slow going. Also, universities prefer to work on local people whose dental history they can track for a sustained period.

Each time you see a dentist during your travels, ask for duplicates of X-rays and a memo outlining what care was given and any other information the dentist might like to convey to the colleague who will see you next. Although some dentists charge extra for this added service or for a first-time visit, we found that most—especially in tourist areas—are understanding of the fulltimer's situation and don't take advantage of it.

Dental First Aid

Dentistry is not a do-it-yourself skill, but there are some things you should know, do, and avoid. "If a crown falls off, the first thing you want to do is to retrieve it," Dr. Batten says. "Second, replace it temporarily with denture adhesive or petroleum jelly. Don't use an over-the-counter dental adhesive, because it's probable that you'll seal the crown incorrectly. That makes it harder for the dentist to get it off again to do a proper repair, and it can lead to other problems, such as jaw pain."

When a tooth is heat or altitude sensitive, Batten says, the nerve is probably involved, and you should seek professional help as soon as possible because it can become very painful very quickly. Cold sensitivity should be checked out, but it probably isn't as immediate a problem. You might also carry a wax-type repair to place over a broken tooth, or a tooth that has lost its filling, just to protect the jagged edge until you can get to a dentist.

Some such products contain a medication that helps soothe pain. "The object is to keep the air out and to keep sharp edges from cutting your cheek or tongue," says Batten. "But just because it feels better, don't delay getting help. A permanent repair must be made before bigger problems result. Keep fillings, crowns, or tooth fragments if possible. The dentist may want to see or repair them."

What not to do? Don't press an aspirin into the painful area. That's an old-fashioned remedy that can cause severe burns to the surrounding soft issue. Remember that aspirin is a strong acid, not meant to be used in concentration.

Some additional tips on preventive care and dental first aid:

◆ Always wear a seat belt. When playing sports, wear suitable protective safety gear.

◆ If you wear braces, carry orthodontic wax to place over any rough or broken wires to protect the cheeks and tongue until a repair can be made. If you don't have wax, try a cotton ball.

◆ If a tooth is knocked out, pick it up by the crown, not the roots, rinse it very gently and replace it in the socket. Get help as soon as possible. In a young child who might swallow the tooth, take it with you in milk, water, or a damp towel. The quicker you get help, the better the chance that the tooth can be saved. If you can get to a dentist in a half hour or less, there's a ninety percent chance it can be re-implanted successfully.

◆ If a tooth breaks, save the parts and get to a dentist as soon as possible.

◆ If the jaw is broken, immobilize it with a bandana or gauze and get to a hospital emergency room. You know it's broken if there is pain and you can't move it, or if your teeth won't mesh right.

If You Wear Dentures

Sundru Moodley, president of All Denture Clinic in Denver, Colorado, suggests additional equipment to carry if all or some of your teeth are false. "Any do-it-yourself denture repair work is only a temporary measure," he says, "but there are steps you can take to resolve an immediate problem."

Moodley suggests carrying baking soda and a soft toothbrush for cleaning, a fast-setting glue, paste, or powdered denture adhesive, an emery board, and a second set of dentures, either duplicates or your old set.

"Bones change shape and structure with time," says Moodley, so your dentures may not fit as comfortably as they once did. Use denture adhesives to create a more comfortable fit in loose dentures.

If a tooth breaks off the denture, replace it using the glue according to the manufacturer's directions. Don't put the plate back into your mouth until the glue is completely dry.

A broken denture can be repaired by applying the glue to one surface and putting the pieces together. After the glue dries, use an emery board to remove rough edges that could irritate the mouth. If you have to replace a broken denture, and you wear both upper and lower plates, replace both. "Dentures are made as a set," Moodley says, "and it's best to keep them together."

CHAPTER NINETEEN

Housecleaning
on Wheels

Your rolling home looks like a home, feels like a home, *is* your home. Yet you can't clean it like a house, because RV construction differs from that of house construction in important ways. One reason is economic, to give you the most living space for the money. Another is that, to save weight on the road, manufacturers use lightweight plastics and composites that won't stand up like the hardwoods and bricks that are put into a house.

Information: Your Primary Cleaning Aid

The most important aid in caring for your RV is the owner's manual packet. You should have received multiple manuals covering the vehicle, each system, and every appliance. Read them carefully. They're full of surprises about things to do, avoid, add, and omit.

If any manuals are missing, keep nagging the dealer or manufacturer until you get every document due you, including warranties for the RV itself and for each separate item that is guaranteed. If possible, also get the manufacturer to give you use and care information for the carpeting, upholstery, surfacings, and other original equipment.

If you bought a used RV, track down as many instruction books and owner's manuals as possible. Write the factory itself, the chassis manufacturer, makers and suppliers for systems and appliances (stove, refrigerator), and perhaps the original dealer. A club for owners of your brand of RV might be a useful resource. As a last resort, write to the "Letters to the Editor" sections of RV magazines, requesting input from owners of RVs like yours.

This sounds like a lot of work, but the earlier you gather this information, the better. As companies and components come and go, it becomes harder and harder to find cleaning recommendations—not to mention replacement parts, part numbers, repair information for older units, and routine maintenance needs such as gaskets or o-rings.

RV Cleaning Products

While they may cost a bit more than their household counterparts, RV products are almost always the wisest choice because they are uniquely formulated for RV materials, soils, uses, and abuses.

Before using any cleaner, make sure it's safe to use in or around an RV. Household window cleaners could harm non-glass RV windows; household cleansers can ruin the RV's plastic surfaces; and ordinary cleaners and coatings don't usually contain the ultraviolet filters that are put into RV products to protect against sun damage. Put the wrong chemicals in your RV toilet, and you can wreck an entire campground's septic system.

Among the strict no-no's are drain cleaners (which could damage valves and umbilical hoses), powdered sink cleanser (which can abrade away a gel coat or plastic surface in seconds), and flammables (you probably have an open flame burning in the gas refrigerator or hot-water heater).

One exception is the very harsh detergent sold for use in dishwashers. It's not suitable for hand dishwashing, but carry some aboard anyway. A soak in very hot water and dishwasher detergent is the best way to get stains and odors out of (dishwasher-safe) galley plastics.

Product Tips

◆ Start with the mildest cleaner possible, then get tougher as necessary.

◆ For overhead cleaning, try a waterless hand cleaner. It will cling, rather than dripping back in your face, and it's gentle enough for the most tender surface (including your skin). It's especially effective in cleaning around the exhaust hood over the stove. Rub it in with your hands until grease dissolves. These cleaners are formulated to work at body temperature.

◆ In the galley and head, clean with baking soda. It's a food-quality abrasive, safe to use on the cutting board and other galley surfaces. It deodorizes, neutralizes, and sanitizes without leaving a dangerous, gritty residue.

◆ When you're on short water rations and can't spare the gallons of running water it takes to flush away soaps and cleansers, be very sparing with cleaning products. The chemical residues they leave could be more dangerous than the dirt they displaced.

◆ Black streaks are a special problem for RVers. Exposed to road film, bugs, tar, wind-driven dirt and sand, and then drenched with rain that reacts with both the pollutants and the RV's finish, the RV becomes streaked with insoluble mineral stains that can't be removed by ordinary cleaners. Star brite makes a product that works by chelation, removing these deposits without using acids or abrasives. It's safe to use on fiberglass, paint, and metal RV surfaces.

Plumbing

RV plumbing is very different from the septic or sewer system you had at home. "RVs are not houses. They are constructed of vastly different materials and are generally exposed to much more extreme external exposure," says Jeff Tieger, whose Star brite cleaning and maintenance products are formulated for the specific needs of the rolling home.

"Typically, formaldehyde-based holding tank chemicals are used to treat waste," Tieger says, "but they are poisoning, staining, and unfriendly to the environment. Many dump stations will not accept formaldehyde-treated waste because of these problems. Star brite utilizes much better technology in its Instant Fresh Toilet Treatment. This product contains quaternary ammonium compounds that are very effective at breaking down waste, preventing gassing, and stopping odors. Yet they are non-staining and biodegradable."

Read your owner's manual. Some RV toilets need no chemicals at all; biological breakdown occurs normally, and odors are carried away through a correctly installed vent system. If you have an odor problem, it could be a leaky seal, inadequate venting, or odors from the campground sewer, and no chemical additions can improve matters.

Carpeting

Carpeting is a major cleaning problem because it takes so much wear and abuse. And if your galley area is carpeted, that abuse ranges to the absurd. Once when we forget to lock the refrigerator door, we lurched around a corner and watched a dozen eggs fall out and break on the galley carpet. Another time, it was a pot of beef stew.

In any such accident, you must first scrape gently to lift as much goo as possible from the surface. The more you rub, the more you work the mess into the fiber. And if you add water, you dilute and spread the stain. After picking up as much as possible, press at the stain with thick bunches of paper towel. The more stain you can wick up into clean paper towel, the less you'll be scrubbing back into the carpet. If the spill is very wet, such as milk or juice, weight down layers of paper towel with stacks of books, and then give the natural wicking process time to work, replacing the paper towel often.

Once cleaning begins, don't overwet the carpeting. Dry it as quickly and thoroughly as possible. Most RV flooring is interior plywood, which can rot or delaminate if soaked.

Vacuum as often as possible, using a real vacuum cleaner, preferably one with a beater bar. Underpowered car vacs aren't strong enough. Once or twice a year, have the carpet professionally cleaned and treated with Scotchguard.

Baking soda is an effective natural carpet deodorizer. Sprinkle it on the carpet and let it stand about thirty minutes; then vacuum.

Closets and Their Contents

About once a year, during housecleaning, turn everything out of your clothes stowage locker and clean the locker itself with a strong mildewcide bathroom cleaner. Then dry it thoroughly with the hair dryer before refilling it with clean, well-aired clothes again. If it's

This unique tubular device plugs into 120-volt power and wafts a gentle flow of heat through your closets and other stuffy areas, preventing mildew. The 12-inch unit draws 8 watts; other models include a 36-inch unit that dehumidifies up to 500 cubic feet and draws 25 watts. Prices are in the $35 to $45 range. Call (800) 451-6979 for information. (GoldenRod)

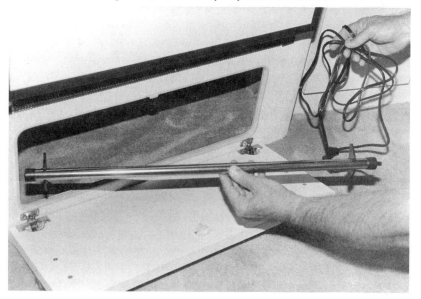

cedar lined, skip the scrubbing but give the walls, ceiling, and floor a good vacuuming.

Storing Out-of-Season Clothes

It's important that fabric items be clean before they are stored. Soil and stains, even those that are virtually invisible before you pack clothes away, can take on a life of their own in storage. Once set, they're almost impossible to remove.

Rotate all clothing and linens as much as possible. If there are some items that are never used, but are kept on hand for emergencies, take them out for a sunny airing and a good inspection every few months. We've found mold on leather shoes and boots, mildew on a dress suit that hadn't been worn in some months, and moth damage on a wool coat.

When we wear any item, even for a short time, we wash or dry clean it before banishing it again to long-term storage. Manmade materials seem to have a special affinity for soil and need frequent washing. I'd never pack away anything that had been worn against the skin for even a few minutes.

Before storing swimsuits, rinse them in several changes of water, then dry thoroughly. If you swim in salt water, hang the suit on the line until it feels dry, and then put it away, salt crystals that remain in the fabric will draw moisture out of the air and keep the fabric and everything around it damp. The same goes for beach towels or anything else that has been in or near salt water. Chlorine left in swimsuits can continue to degrade the fabric too.

Rain gear should be put away completely dry or it will rot. If we do have to bring a wet umbrella or raincoat inside, it goes back outside for a complete rinsing, drying, and airing as soon as the sun comes out.

Shops and catalogs that specialize in closet accessories sell a variety of cedar shavings, closet linings, and sachets. If your RV didn't come with a cedar-lined closet, as many do, it's easy to add this lining yourself. In a home improvement store we found thin cedar planks that can be cut to fit and used to line any closet or locker. Packaged for easy take-home, they are a fragrant way to protect woolens and to sweeten shoe lockers.

We've found that if we treat leather shoes with a natural wax, they become moldy faster. We've had better luck with silicone protectants, which also waterproof shoes and boots.

We store off-season clothes in as many separate modules as possible, even though these in turn may all be crammed into the same big locker. This way, it's easier to retrieve just the ski jackets, or only our wetsuits, without pawing through the entire jumbled bin.

By putting things in their own boxes or bags, we're also able to give them whatever special treatment is best—woolens are sealed into bags with cedar, summer lingerie is sealed in a bag with sachet, leather shoes or hiking boots are given a coat of leather protector, swim fins or rubber boots are given a generous dusting of talcum before they're put away.

Our few dressy outfits are not banished to some deep locker, but are put in their own clothes bags in the closet. They hang there ready and wrinkle free, but protected from everyday handling and jostling in the closet.

Do you have special table linens aboard that are used only a few times a year? After they are washed and dried, starched and ironed, warm them in the oven at about 120 degrees Fahrenheit, then seal in plastic bags while they're still warm. They'll stay sweet and dry until the next time you need them.

Laundry

We'll assume here that you'll be doing most of your laundry yourself, in coin-operated machines. Another choice is to do the wash by hand, which we've done when in remote areas, using an inflatable swimming pool and a toilet plunger. Many RVers also put the laundry, water, and soap into a plastic garbage can with a lock-on lid, and let it slosh clean on the highway. A third choice is to use full-service commercial laundries or the wash-and-fold service offered by some laundromats.

European washer-dryer combination units are available for RV use. The best part of having your own machine is that you can wash any time, anywhere you can get water and electricity, in your own washer. On the other hand, such units can do only small loads at a time, are useless when you don't have full hookups, and don't have all the features and settings found in full-size automatics. Only you

Wash and dry in a single unit. Several brands of imported washer-dryer combinations are available in the RV marketplace. (Berg Corporation)

can decide whether the convenience will be worth the cost, space, and weight of installing one aboard.

Of all the appliances we miss most when we're on the go, the washer and dryer are at the top of the list. Yet coin laundries have their good points. You can use as many machines as needed, to do ten loads in no more time than it takes for one. Better laundromats are air conditioned, clean, spacious, cheerful, and have generous tables where the wash can be sorted and folded. They're great places to meet local folks, and the best ones have such extras as vending machines, television, and libraries.

Here are some coin laundry tips we learned the hard way.

◆ Don't put clothes into any washer or dryer without first checking the machine, with a small flashlight if necessary. We have found a long list of horrors including mess from diapers, goo from melted crayons or rubber pants, and rust spots or burrs on the metal drum that would tear clothes to shreds.

◆ If the dryer has a lint filter, clean it.

◆ Keep a generous cache of coins on hand; you may not be able to get change when you need it. Depending on the dryer, fuel, weather, and how well the washers wring out the water, it could take twice as many coins to dry the load as you expected.

◆ Never wash an expensive piece in a machine you haven't used before. We've encountered washers that delivered hot water when the Cold button was pressed, dryers that went directly into meltdown even on the Gentle cycle, and washers that were not capable of spin-drying a heavy item such as a blanket or bedspread.

◆ Bring a clean rag or paper toweling, so you can clean the table you'll use to fold your clean clothes.

◆ Don't leave clothes unattended. An impatient customer waiting for a machine could empty the washer or dryer and pile your things heaven-knows-where. A well-meaning friend could put them in the dryer, but at the wrong setting. At worst, they could be stolen.

Few RVs have clothes hampers, so be sure to allot a large, well-ventilated space to laundry storage as you move aboard. We sort clothes as we discard them, using separate laundry bags for whites, colors, and items that will need special treatment (heavy-duty cycle, hand washable, stain treatment, etc.).

Buy laundry bags, or make your own from sturdy muslin or light

The Mending Basket

If you're an accomplished seamstress, you've probably already planned the fully equipped sewing department for your rolling home. If not, visit the notions department in a good variety store.

In addition to the basic supplies you'll need for emergency mending jobs, you'll find shirt buttons that install without sewing, and a large selection of heat-fusible materials to be used for mending and patching. They include iron-on jeans patches, sock patches, cut-your-own patches in all colors, knee patches, and even iron-in replacement pants pockets. To repair a hem, place a strip of heat-fusible tape in the fold and iron until it melts.

Speaking of ironing, we carry a Black & Decker travel iron with a folding handle and a built-in water reservoir for steam ironing. Although small ironing boards are available, we do all our touch-up ironing on the galley counter, on a folded bath towel.

canvas. Before leaving for the laundry, measure detergent, and powdered bleach if needed, into each bag. Dump the contents into the washer, then throw in the bag. After drying and folding, use the clean bags to carry the wash back to the RV.

Prevention

To help keep sand and mud out of the RV, add as many dirt-stoppers as possible. You might, for example, glue a layer of plastic turf doormat material to the RV steps. If you need an additional outside step, use an upturned milk crate, which will allow dirt to fall through. Carry one or two doormats to place outside the RV, on the slab. Better still, try living Japanese style, leaving shoes at the door.

Carpeting, upholstery, and other interior surfaces should be protected from sun fading. You might want to add solar-insulated curtains or a professionally installed solar coating on the windows. Avoid do-it-yourself solar films, which can cloud, bubble, and peel.

Inside the RV as well as outside, keep fighting against dirt, chafe,

Sun is one of the most persistent destroyers of your RV's skin and upholstery. You can make a simple windshield cover from medium-weight canvas or sailcloth. (G. Groene)

corrosion, crazing, and rust, using the best cleaners, coatings, and protectants. The payback will be longer wear and a better price at resale time.

CHAPTER TWENTY

Tools for the Fulltimer

The RV vacationer can often wait until he gets home to his workshop, floor jack, and big toolbox to do routine maintenance, upgrades, additions, and all but emergency repairs. The fulltimer, by contrast, has to deal with maintenance day by day, with tools that must be carried, hired, or borrowed.

Even if you are a savvy mechanic and can do all your own repairs, you simply can't carry all the tools you'd like to have. Tools are bulky and heavy; you have to be realistic about space and weight.

Yet even if you can't or won't do your own work, you should carry *some* tools, because it's likely that your rig requires some unique or little-used implements that not every mechanic or RV shop will have. We put together a basic kit in a plastic fishing tackle box, so the tools we need most often are handy and portable. It weighs less than ten pounds and is easy to carry around the RV for every job from tightening battery cables to fixing door locks.

Here's what our basic tool kit includes:

◆ Blade and Phillips screwdrivers, as well as whatever drivers you need to fit clinch-head screws and any other oddball screws in your RV. Screwdrivers also double as pry bars.

◆ Pliers. We prefer Channellocks because they serve as both pliers and pipe wrench; also needle-nose pliers.

Multipurpose tools like the Driver 21 save weight and space aboard an RV. (Disstim Corporation)

Don't forget drivers to fit any oddball screw heads found in your RV. (The Woodworkers' Store)

- A side cutter

- An eight-inch crescent wrench

- A small brad hammer

- Various punches and nail sets

- Three grades of rat-tail files

- A couple of bastard files

- The smaller sizes from an open end/box wrench set

While it would be nice to have additional tools to fix everything from burned engine bearings to the kitchen sink, it usually isn't practical. So let's start with the possible.

Plumbing. For plastic plumbing you'll need a hacksaw, file, or sharp knife for deburring, a can of PVC cement, and a grasping tool (such as the Channellocks) for work on threaded PVC fittings. A short-handled plumber's helper is light to carry, and will solve most sink blockage problems. For copper and brass plumbing, carry a tub-

To make up a basic tool kit, focus on multipurpose tools. A hacksaw will cut metal, wood, or plastic. An adjustable wrench, while not as good as an entire set of open-end wrenches, is light and versatile. Needle-nose pliers usually have a wire cutter, which doubles as a side cutter. Water-pump pliers are as good as regular pliers, but also function as a pipe wrench; Vise Grips can be used as a wrench on odd-shaped items, and as a clamp. (G. Groene)

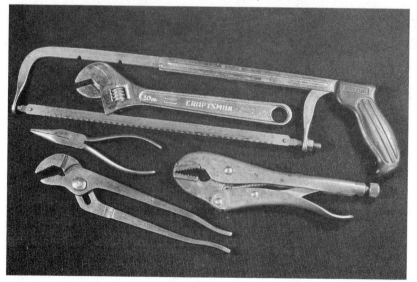

ing cutter, a flaring tool, and a selection of connectors in the sizes you're most likely to need.

Carpentry. If you'll be doing any remodeling, you'll need more than these basic woodworking tools, but for basic repairs and replacement jobs, start with a hacksaw. It's the lightest and most versatile saw. If you need something faster, add a keyhole saw or saber saw. An electric or eggbeater hand drill with a selection of bits up to ¼ inch will be useful. So will an adjustable hole saw. For smoothing equipment, include a plane, files, and sandpaper.

A pint of two-part epoxy glue can mend almost anything. We carry a couple of stamped metal, spring-loaded, clothespin-type clamps. Of all the clamps available, these weigh the least and yet exert a steady force for glue jobs.

Sewing. In addition to the usual mending supplies, bring heavy-duty needles and thread and an upholstery needle for first aid to cushion covers, curtains, and awnings.

Electrical. Take a wire cutter/stripper, crimping tool, crimp terminals and connectors, and test equipment such as a multimeter. A pen-

A compact propane torch handles soldering and other repair jobs without electricity. (CooperTools)

cil-type soldering iron weighs only a few ounces and is handy for small electrical repairs.

Engine and drive train. First, read through all the manuals that came with your RV to see if any special tools are recommended. Almost every rig needs something odd, such as a special wrench to remove wheel hub nuts, or a unique tool to remove an injector from a diesel engine. Even if you don't know how to use such tools, it's wise to have them aboard because a hired mechanic may not have them. A nut splitter is handy for exhaust work, and we also carry a pulley puller.

You probably also need a special tool for adjusting ignition timing. For oil changes, carry a strap wrench to use in removing the old oil filter.

Somewhere, you should also have the larger half (up to one inch) of the open end/box wrench set mentioned above and a spark plug wrench and/or injector tool. If you have to do a major engine job, you can usually buy an inexpensive piston ring expander and valve turning tools as needed, rather than carrying them around. Work on our RV often requires a torque wrench, so we find it worthwhile to carry one.

Tools for an automatic transmission are too specialized for most of us to carry, but with the tools already listed you can change the transmission oil and adjust the bands. If yours is a manual transmission, check to see if you need special wrenches for the oil plugs.

You can change your universal joints with basic tools, but to grease universals you'll need a special non-high-pressure grease gun. Don't let anyone grease yours with a gas station–type pressure gun—it'll blow out the seals.

Wheels and tires. It's likely that the equipment for wheel changing came with your RV, but you may prefer to invest in a heavier duty, better quality jack. A good hydraulic jack weighs more, but it's worth every ounce.

Try to remove a lug nut with the lug wrench provided by your RV manufacturer. If it bends, throw it away and buy a heavy-duty, commercial grade, X-style lug wrench. If you'll be overhauling your brakes, the tools already named will do the job. For drum-type brakes it's handy to have the special spring remover/installer sold in auto-parts stores.

If you carry a compact portable compressor aboard you can top off your tires, fill the air mattress and inflatable boat, and use compressed air for many cleaning/drying jobs. (Sears)

Spare Parts Are Important Too

To keep up and running you need not just tools, but spare parts. Again, you have to make painful decisions about what to take and what to leave behind. But keep in mind that the more offbeat your RV and its equipment, the harder and more expensive it becomes to find replacement parts in an emergency.

First on the list of spares you *must* have, even if you can't install them yourself, are fan belts. We once drove a friend all over town, trying to find a fan belt to fit one of the most common cars in the country. Double check the fan belt sizes you need and get one in each size.

If any non-standard equipment was installed when your RV was customized, you may need sizes other than those listed in the original owner's manual.

Here are some other items to consider carrying:

For the engine. Take spare radiator hoses, especially if yours are an unusual molded design. They'll keep a long time if you keep them clean and in a dark place, so the investment made today will pay off tomorrow. Carry a few extra hose clamps in appropriate sizes. We think it's well worth it to buy the best all-stainless clamps. (Beware: Some stainless steel hose clamps have steel screws.)

Many of the new fuel pumps aren't made to be repaired, but if you have an older pump that requires periodic overhauls, carry an overhaul kit. We also like to carry an extra fuel filter element or two. If we pick up a bad load of fuel and clog one filter, we have a second filter to snare the next slug of crud that comes through the line.

If your vehicle has electronic ignition, carry a spare ignition module. These "little black boxes" give no advance warning of failure, but when one goes, you're dead in the water. This is another item you can buy at a discount autoparts store for about half what you'd pay for a dealer-installed part. So, since Groene's Law states that the more desperate you are, the more difficult it will be to find the right size module, this is one spare part to have aboard at all times.

Carry at least enough of your brand of oil to do routine topping-up, and preferably enough for an oil change. When you see oil filters on sale, put one in stock. Have at least one spare spark plug; they can fail or break. If your engine is a diesel, it's good insurance to have a spare injector on board. One other spare to consider carrying is a universal joint, since you'll be stranded without one. They're fairly easy to change.

Chassis and drive. In hot climates, brake fluid is lost through evaporation, so carry an extra pint so you can top off the reservoir with a trusted brand. Our lives depend on our brakes. That's why we'd rather add fluid from our own clean, sealed can than from the derelict pail of fluid found sloshing around the gas station.

Living quarters. Unless you want to go to a motel every time something is out of whack, it's wise to have enough spares to keep your "house" up and running too. Carry some spare washers if your faucets use them, brass B-nuts for the plumbing (they crack), and an extra sewage valve. If you need a spare, it might be hard to find one in your size when you need it.

We buy light bulbs by the case, not just for economy but also because the box provides the safest way to pack them. You'll soon know what bulbs you need most often. In our case, it's clearance and reading light bulbs.

Also carry fuses in every size needed for both your 12-volt and "house" systems, spare key(s)—somewhere where you can get at them in a pinch—and a spare cartridge for the water filter. It's bulky, but it weighs very little.

One of the best things about fulltiming is a feeling of independence on an endless highway. But you'll be independent only as long as the RV remains mobile. Broken down, both your home and your wheels are at the mercy of whatever help you can get. With the right tools and spares, you'll have a better chance of coming through a breakdown with a faster getaway and a fatter wallet.

Your RV's Engine and Drive Train

When things break down after so-many miles, make a note to expect the same failure after the same interval. If you were wrong and the initial breakdown was just a fluke, fine. But stresses are stresses, and components are components. The better you know your RV, the more you can predict and prevent problems.

The Engine

Probably the most expensive single item in your rolling home is the engine. Whether the engine is in the tow car, pickup truck, or motorhome, you want to protect this investment and ensure the utmost dependability. A breakdown on the road, besides being dangerous and troublesome, is extraordinarily expensive in an RV because towing charges are high *and* you have to pay lodging bills if your RV becomes uninhabitable.

Your most important aids are your driver's manual, any workshop manuals you can obtain from the chassis manufacturer, and perhaps other commercial manuals, such as those published by Clymer or Chilton, for your make of power plant. The more oddball your vehicle, the more important these manuals become, because even if you don't do your own maintenance, a professional mechanic will need them for reference.

Most breakdowns forecast their approach loud and clear, if only you know what to look and listen for. Often, if you pay attention, you can head off the posse at the pass.

Make replacements as soon as you notice a problem, because then you can call the shots. Pick your own time and a suitable spot to work. Pick up replacement parts at the discount store. Shop around. If you don't act now, you'll pay dearly on the road, not just because you'll experience an inconvenient delay in your travels, but because you'll pay for a tow, then pay scalper prices for supplies and labor—all for neglecting to replace, say, an inexpensive hose in time.

A word of caution: When working with flammables, never forget that your RV has many sources of ignition, including burners or pilot lights in the water heater, refrigerator, stove, and oven.

Cooling System

Most failures here give ample warning: rusted and weakening hose clamps, deteriorated or soft hoses, slight leakage at connections, unusual noise, or weeping around the water pump. All these signs point to future problems, none of which go away or heal themselves.

A modern pressurized cooling system with overflow tanks should need little, if any, added fluid for as long as a year. Water in the coolant mixture can't boil away because it condenses in the overflow reservoir. Consider any change in the amount of loss an advance warning that problems are brewing.

Perhaps all you have to do to stop this loss is to tighten hose clamps—a good thing to do periodically anyway. If you can't see any leaks, try observing all connections with the engine just started from cold, because this is when leaks usually occur. While pressure is starting to build, and before various parts expand from heat, you may be able to spot where you're losing coolant.

Any sign of air bubbles in your overflow tank is an indication of head gasket leakage. The trouble must be found and fixed immediately because, if antifreeze gets into the oil, bearings seize very quickly.

Spares for your cooling system should include at least one complete set of radiator hoses and a spare water pump, especially if you'll be in areas where you can't buy them readily as needed. (Heater hoses and any other straight pieces of hose usually can be found anywhere, so you don't need a supply of those.)

Be faithful about changing permanent antifreeze at least every second year, because rust and corrosion inhibitors wear out in time. Usually the system needs a good flush by then anyway to wash away abrasive particles that have broken loose.

With the engine cold, open all drains. Usually there are several on the block and one on the bottom of the radiator. While the old coolant is draining (into a suitable container for whatever waste disposal or recycling is practiced in your area), remove and clean the overflow tank if there's any sign of sludge or scale. Then stick a water hose into the radiator opening and let the water flow through freely for several minutes.

Now, with the water flow adjusted so it just keeps the system full (you may have to close one or two of the drains to maintain the water level), start the engine and let it idle for ten minutes while fresh water flows through it.

Watch to make sure water flow continues to be adequate. Finally, turn off the engine, turn off the water, drain thoroughly, and let the engine cool. You don't want to shock a hot engine by filling it with cold coolant.

Then close all the drains and pour in a fifty-fifty mix of water and the coolant recommended by your engine manufacturer. If the local water has a high mineral or chlorine content, use distilled water to cut down on sediment and corrosion in the future.

Carry a complete set of fan belts. Even if you can't change them yourself, you'll always have the proper size with you. If one breaks on the road, you can soon be up and running—even if a mechanic has to come out to do the work. Otherwise you have to be towed in and pay top dollar for the fan belt—if the garage *has* the right size belt—as well as the asking price for towing and labor.

Oil

Oil, like coolant, is a critical protector for your expensive engine. Many manufacturers now specify long periods between oil changes—perhaps as long as 6,000 miles. It's not just a matter of cost and convenience. Oil disposal has become a problem; lubricants have become better and longer lasting. In the old days, engines were engines and oil was oil. However, to get maximum protection and oil effectiveness today, it's important to select the right, manufacturer-recommended oil for *your* engine.

When you drive for long periods at a time, impurities and condensation are cooked out of the oil, making it more effective longer. If, however, your RV stands idle a lot and is used only for short hops, consider changing the oil and filter more often—especially if it's equipped with a turbocharger, because the bearings are very sensitive to contaminants in the oil.

Because most RVs won't fit on a standard gas station lift and must be taken to a special garage for service, consider doing your own oil changes. Savings are several. First, you buy the oil at a discount store or at sale prices, instead of paying what the garage charges. Filters too can be bought at discount stores. While you're there, pick up a strap-type wrench if you don't have one. You will save time, too, because you can do the job when and where you choose. And you may save on cleanup, because if oil must be added inside your motorhome's cab, you may be more fastidious than a stranger would be.

When you change oil, do it at the end of a long day's drive, while the oil is hot and contaminants are in suspension. It isn't enough just to start the engine and warm it up. The more impurities you can flush out with the oil, the better. Be sure to dispose of used oil in accordance with state and federal laws.

If you change your own oil and other fluids it's important to collect and dispose of waste products properly. (G. Groene)

After the oil has drained, replace the drain plug and refill the system with oil. Now start the engine, which is still warm, to get the new oil circulating through the engine and the new filter. If you wait until the next morning when everything is cold, oil won't start circulating as readily.

Whatever oil you choose, try to use the same brand consistently. When you're a fulltime rover, it's best to start with a brand that is sold internationally (Shell, Castrol) so you'll be able to get it throughout the United States, Canada, Mexico, and other countries you may visit.

Gear oil and automatic transmission oil are also available in discount auto-supply stores, so you may as well start changing them yourself too. Your driver's manual will tell you what grade to buy.

Exhaust Manifold

Only a few years ago, you could whip off the interstate into a rest stop, snap off the engine without a thought, and rush off to make a phone call. However, today's exhaust manifolds are usually made out of a low-quality iron that expands and contracts at a rate different from the high-quality iron or aluminum cylinder heads they're bolted to.

If you're running red-hot and turn off the engine abruptly, engine parts cool at different rates, placing undue stress on the manifold. It's just a matter of time until a weak spot in the casting fails. A cooldown period before shutoff is a safety precaution (for turbocharged engines it's essential). If you do have to replace the manifold, look into high-quality, jointed (i.e., less likely to crack) manifolds sold in the aftermarket.

Engine Gauges

Although today's cockpits house sophisticated panels filled with gauges and indicator lights, here are additional gauges we consider important. We suggest adding any that you don't already have.

Coolant temperature gauge. A warning light can tell you only when the coolant overheats. A gauge, on the other hand, shows if the coolant is too hot or too cold (which usually means the thermostat has failed).

Oil pressure gauge. An idiot light tells you you've lost oil pressure and must shut down immediately or die. However, earlier warning of falling pressure gives you more time to get out of traffic and into a safe area before shutting down.

Battery condition. You may have a stock ammeter, but a battery voltage gauge will tell you more about the general condition of your electrical system and voltage regulator. This information is especially important when your "house" is operating on battery power.

Transmission oil temperature. When transmission oil gets too hot, its lubricating abilities diminish rapidly. With a gauge, you always know when to ease up on the load. If overheat is chronic, you know you need more transmission cooling capacity.

The Drive Train

Wheels

When things come in sets, suspect the entire set if one part fails. Our RV's rear wheels crack radially about every 30,000 miles. When the first one cracked, we guessed that its twins would probably crack soon too. We replaced them all at once and were proved right. When we replaced them the second time, two had already started to fracture.

Bearings

Wheel bearings need regular service, which is an easy, straight-forward job (on non-drive wheels) requiring only a few tools, the proper size cotter pins, and, in most cases, new dust seals. Drive wheels get more complicated, so refer to a manual before opening them. We've had excellent luck with Lubriplate's waterproof wheel bearing grease.

It's especially important to keep close tabs on trailer wheel bearings, because often they aren't the best quality and they may wear quickly. If bearings themselves show any signs of wearing or scoring, replace them with one of the better brands such as Federal-Mogul or Timken.

To adjust any type of wheel bearing that uses a cotter pin, tighten the nut by hand until all play is gone and the wheel rotates freely. Then back the nut up to the next hole. On infinitely adjustable axle

If you have an equipment failure, such as a cracked wheel, assume the worst—that similar failures will happen again at the same mileage. If you were wrong, the extra vigilance cost you little time; if you were right, you may have prevented an expensive and potentially life-threatening breakdown. (G. Groene)

nuts, tighten down snugly and then back off just until the wheel rotates freely with no discernible play in the bearings.

To repack bearings, first clean them thoroughly and give them a final rinse in clear kerosene or diesel fuel. Never dry a bearing by rotating it with compressed air, which could magnetize it. Bearings can best be packed by hand. Just put a glob of grease in the palm of one hand and scrape at it with the edge of the bearing cage, forcing grease up between the rollers until the bearing is completely full. This is usually all the grease that is needed unless manufacturer directions call for a specific amount in the hub.

After packing inside bearings, you'll have to replace dust seals. Be sure the new seals are seated squarely in their grooves, with the lip facing the bearing. As you finish the job, be sure the dust cap fits snugly. A wheel should never be operated with a missing dust cap because even the slightest bit of grit in a roller bearing can cause failure. In a pinch, make a temporary cap out of a tin can. Keep a special eye on boots on constant-velocity joints. The joints are expensive and

The easiest way to pack wheel bearings is by hand. Fill one palm with a good wheel-bearing grease and scoop the grease into the bearing cage. (G. Groene)

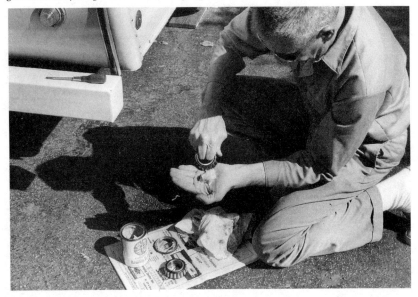

can quickly be ruined if dirt or water gets to them.

One more point: Never replace just part of a bearing. Drive or press out the old outer race and put in a new one.

Greasing the RV

Few vehicles today have grease fittings. If yours does, you're lucky—using them faithfully over the long run will assure longer wear than you'll get with the so-called permanently packed joints. Your owner's manual will tell you where these fittings are and how often they should be greased.

A few years ago, a popular coach manufacturer neglected to mention in its owner's manual that inner drive axle bearings were to be lubricated every 24,000 miles. When failures started to occur, owners found themselves facing garage bills in the $4,000 range. To protect yourself from this type of disaster, know your RV and its needs as thoroughly as possible and keep talking to owners of similar rigs and reading RV magazines for reports of a pattern of failures in units like yours.

The only thing you need to do the job yourself is a grease gun,

A faithful rust-proofing program will ensure years more wear and more trouble-free miles on the highway. (G. Groene)

preferably the cartridge type, and grease cartridges. Use a high-pressure, lithium-type grease for chassis fittings and universal joints unless the manufacturer directs otherwise.

Take two precautions. First, any suspension parts that carry the weight of the vehicle should be unloaded before greasing, if possible. (This doesn't include tie-rods.) Second, universal joints should be filled very slowly so that seals aren't forced out.

While you're lubricating, put a drop of oil on all hinges including the service doors, entry doors, carburetor linkage, and emergency brake linkage. We always keep handy an oil can filled with engine oil, and for lighter duty a household-type, multipurpose oil.

Tires

One of the most important elements in tire care is to maintain the right pressure. As a bonus, you'll get better fuel mileage and safer handling.

Your owner's manual will tell you what pressures are optimum for your tires. Keep in mind that this is a reference; some fine-tuning should be made to accommodate your load and driving habits.

Tire pressure should always be checked when tires are cold. Correct pressure is essential to tire wear and handling safety. (G. Groene)

Pressure should always be checked when the tires are cold. After about a mile of driving, pressures start increasing and you won't get an accurate reading.

For best wear, duals should always be within a pound of each other. An old truck driver's trick for checking duals is to "sound" them with a billy club. You'll soon learn to tell by the sound if one tire is at a lower pressure than its mate. This is the cleanest, most dependable way to check hot duals.

If the tread is wearing around the edges, you're underinflating. Cupping usually means that the wheels are out of balance or the shock absorbers are wearing out. Uneven wear on the front tires indicates misalignment. Because RV tires can be very expensive, you'll save greatly by watching for early wear and correcting it at once.

When you're not on the road, RV tires continue to take a licking from the sun. Try to keep yours shaded; if the RV doesn't have covers or awnings for this purpose, have some made. A good spray-on coating, such as Star brite's Protector, which has ultraviolet absorbers, will help shield tires.

It's vital to have a spare tire and, if your tires are not all alike, one in each size. If tires match, rotate them once in a while to keep the wear the same. Just as it's important to keep working tires out of the sun, the spare should be covered at all times. We found that plastic covers disintegrated after a year or so, so we had a sturdier one made from waterproof canvas sewn with heavy-duty Dacron (not cotton) thread. It costs more but wears years longer.

Brakes

Unless you have a complete set of tools and equipment for brake work, it's best to leave overhauls to a specialist. What you can do is to check the hydraulic-fluid reservoirs regularly and change the fluid as recommended by the vehicle manufacturer, inspect brake hoses for signs of deterioration and cuts, and keep tabs on the thickness of brake linings.

If your brakes are not self-adjusting, adjustment is covered in your owner's manual. Any time brake drums are removed, be sure to clean all dust and rust out of them to ensure smoother operation. If you have an older vehicle, this debris may be asbestos, so don't breathe or handle it. Always take care that no oily substances get near brake linings.

A Word to the Fumblefingered

"I'm sixty-three, about to retire, and a woman alone," wrote one of our readers. "Fulltiming has been my dream, and I'm about to take off, but I've heard a lot of horror stories about mechanics cheating and overcharging women. Do you have any advice?"

This woman's dilemma applies not just to singles, women, or senior citizens. Any of us is fair game when we get into today's technology over our heads. You may be able to fix anything electronic, but be taken for a ride in a clothing shop. The sharpest mechanic could get burned when buying a computer. The plumber could be bamboozled by a TV repairman, and the woman who can run a million-dollar aircraft company can be beguiled by a smooth pitch for overpriced cosmetics.

The one defense we all have against techno-scam is to know as much as possible about our RVs, how they work, what harms them, and what sort of service they need when. It's a tall order, to be taken seriously, not as a sometime sideline when you run out of other things to do.

First, we'll make a Pollyanna observation. We find most of our countrymen to be honest, fair, and hard working. Sure, there are service station attendants who sell you oil you don't need, or who will slash a tire so you'll have to buy a new one. There are also those who give a break to the elderly, the helpless, and the handicapped. Moreover, the customer is not always right. Sometimes he's demanding, cheap, tipsy, or unwilling to admit that the breakdown was his own fault. She may be late for workshop appointments. He may think he knows more than the mechanic does.

Assuming that you're an honest and considerate customer, here are some defense strategies.

Begin by studying all the manuals that came with the RV, even if you don't understand half of what is being said. Even if you're sure you already know how to put a tape in the stereo, adjust the furnace, light the oven, or check the oil, read these books until you know them forward and backward. Most of the time you can solve a problem just by going through the troubleshooting guide.

Talk to others in campgrounds, especially to people who have RVs like yours, but don't take one person's advice as gospel. The less you know about RVs, and the more intimidated you are by technobabble, the more advice you'll get from veteran campers—many of whom really aren't qualified to make suggestions, let alone cram advice down your throat.

Try to get a consensus from people who have similar vehicles, loads, mileage, and driving habits about such things as whether you really need new shock absorbers after 45,000 miles, or how long brake pads should last in your unit, or how your tire wear compares. Keep notes and soon you'll have a good feel for how long things should last, and how they feel or sound or look when they're nearing the end.

Among those components you can *see* nearing Boot Hill are vee belts, hoses, tires, shock absorbers (you can tell when they start leaking oil), and oil seals. Those you might *hear* as they start to fail include vee belts, tires, universal joints, wheel bearings, windshield wiper motors, and the exhaust system. Your *nose* is a good tool in sensing leakage in fuel, oils, or sewage; transmission overheat; electrical problems; or dragging brakes.

In short, learn to look, listen, and sniff for abnormalities. The best mechanic in the world can't have the ear for your engine that you'll have. By keeping attuned to the everyday look, sound, and feel of your own rig, you'll become your own best diagnostician. Even if you don't know what's wrong or what to do about it, you'll at least know to have it investigated.

Mechanical troubles almost never recover by themselves, so any early warnings can clue you that you need preventive maintenance well in advance of a highway breakdown. This in turn allows you to shop around for the right price, time, and place to have work done. Keep careful records and soon you'll see a pattern developing, alerting you to maintenance tasks every so-many months or so-many miles.

Unless you're handicapped, never hand your credit card out the window and let a service station attendant fill your tanks. It's during such times that most horror stories occur. A dishonest person may slit a hose, drop oil under a shock absorber so you'll think you need new ones, or stick an ice pick into a tire.

Get out of the driver's seat and stay alert so the attendant doesn't forget your filler cap, overlook a soft tire, or run off extra copies of your credit card. Check and fill your own tires, oil, cooling system, batteries, drinking water, and automatic transmission oil. Even if you're not filling propane tanks yourself, you can observe that the meter and scale are set properly.

Anyone can do these tasks. In doing them yourself you save money, make sure they're done right (even an honest mechanic could do the wrong thing for your particular RV), and avoid a chance of being cheated.

No outsider can know as much as you do about your driving habits, your maintenance history, and your needs. Armed with common sense, regular reviews of your RV's manuals, and an ever-increasing knowledge that builds like a snowball, you will be a better mechanic than you ever dreamed possible.

For the want of a shoe, a horse was lost. For the want of a horse, the battle was lost. Your battle against highway breakdown, equipment failure, and accelerated wear begins with preventive maintenance—most of it simple to do, at your leisure, with minimal equipment.

The Circle Check

Every time you start up, no matter whether you've spent a month at a campsite or two minutes in a roadside phone booth, take a walk all the way around the RV. This kind of routine is a religion with truckers and other professional drivers. Aside from helping you nip problems in the bud, it will give you peace of mind. You'll know for sure that you remembered to lock the bumper, that you didn't leave loose lashings that would allow a rooftop tarp to flap in the wind while everything else got drenched in the rain, that you did pick up the cooler from under the picnic table. . . .

Here's what to look for.

◆ Inspect all tires to see if they've softened, been cut, or picked up nails.

◆ Check under the rig for leakage of fuel, oil, or water.

◆ Make sure you've shut all windows that should be closed when you're underway.

◆ Check every accessory door to make sure it's securely fastened, and the fuel cap to make sure it's screwed on tight.

◆ Check the roof rack, tiedowns, bike racks, and hitches.

◆ At night, make sure all the lights are working. Occasionally have someone check the backup and brake lights for you.

◆ Mentally list everything you took out of the RV. Did you bring it all back aboard?

◆ Is the way clear ahead? Behind? Overhead? (You should know your rig's highest point in exact feet and inches.) Pay special attention to curb drop-off angles, choosing your route so your overhang won't scrape on the slope.

◆ As a last step before takeoff, you may want to record in a logbook such information as the name of the service station, the mile number of the rest stop, and the telephone number of the booth where you made a call. If you find later that you forgot something, or got cheated, or otherwise need to retrace your steps, this information may prove invaluable.

As you circle the RV, use the time not only to look for trouble spots, but also to psych yourself up for the responsibility of taking the wheel and giving all your attention to the road. Some drivers use this time for meditation or a short prayer.

Now, confident that the way is clear, relax and enjoy the view.

CHAPTER TWENTY-TWO

Maintaining Your RV's Utility Systems

Here's a sobering thought: All the utilities you took for granted while living in a house are now yours to provide, fuel, maintain, and regulate. It's a tall order even for the most accomplished, longtime campers.

The owner's manuals that came with your RV should provide all the information you need for your systems. You can also order a basic primer about hookups by sending a stamped, self-addressed envelope to RVIA, Box 2999, Reston, Virginia 22090 and requesting the "Lifestyle Publications Catalogue." It lists a number of generic how-to manuals.

Each of your utilities is supplied in two or more ways, which means your maintenance duties are doubled but so are your conveniences and backups.

In a full-hookup campsite, you get water through a hose and electricity through a heavy-duty extension cord. Waste water goes directly into your campsite's sewer outlet, via a hose you supply. In fancier campgrounds, you may also have telephone and cable TV hookups too. It sounds simple, and except for a few caveats, it is.

Away from the campground, things get more complicated. Your electricity is supplied by generator, battery, and/or alternator. You have water in your own tanks, but you have to supply the water pres-

Umbilicals should be the best, heaviest, most waterproof and bugproof available. Shown here are electrical, telephone, and cable-TV umbilicals. (G. Groene)

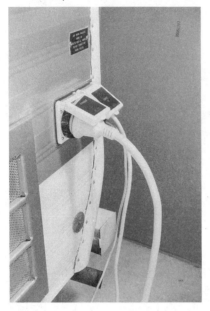
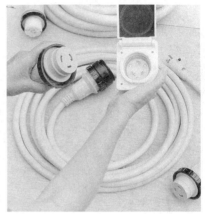

sure and keep track of your reserves so you don't run out in the middle of a soapy shower.

Waste water accumulates in two tanks, one for "black" water (sewage) and the other "gray" water (sink and shower drains), which you'll have to empty eventually. And the propane you use at all times to run the stove now also cools the refrigerator.

The Water System

When you're using campground umbilicals, you have only a couple of things to worry about. First, the water may have an unpleasant taste, or you may be concerned about its safety. A light-duty filter can be added to sieve out particulated matter at the point of entry into the RV. You may also want to plumb in a heavy-duty filter at the kitchen sink.

The more serious filtration, treatment, or reverse osmosis systems have their own faucet; you filter or treat only water to be used for drinking and cooking. Otherwise, you'll spend a fortune on replacement media.

Your second concern is "city" water pressure, which varies wildly from campground to campground. If you hook into a system whose pressure is too high, your RV's plumbing can be damaged. Invest in a pressure regulator valve for the hose, and never hook up without it, even if pressure reads in the safe range. We've seen pressure shoot up, off and on, at the whim of the campground's water system.

On the road, when you are supplying your own water, your concerns include monitoring water level so you'll have adequate reserves, pump maintenance (read the manual; water pumps are fairly care free), and taking care of the water gauges. Most Class A motorhomes have a control panel in the galley area, showing tank levels.

Some older RVs have no water pump but use an air pump to build air pressure in the water tank, forcing water to the faucets. If you have such a system, and if it hasn't already rusted out, replace it anyway. You can carry more water in less space and weight by getting a new, lightweight plastic tank and water pump. (An air pressure system can't be used with a thin-walled tank.)

One problem with many RV water pressure systems is that the pump runs on demand, even if you are drawing only a teaspoon of water for a recipe. The more jerks and starts, the more wear to the pump. To even things out, many systems are equipped with an accumulator tank, which maintains a reserve head of air. The larger the accumulator tank, the less often the pump has to run.

If your water pump zzzzts off and on every few seconds, see an RV serviceman who specializes in plumbing. He'll know how and where to plumb in an accumulator. And, if you also have a problem with pipes rattling when a washing machine or a dishwasher shuts off abruptly, an RV plumbing specialist can add what is called a water hammer eliminator.

Always turn off the water pump before leaving the RV. If you don't have a separate switch, use the circuit breaker. If the pump is on and a pipe or hose breaks, water will continue to pump until your tanks are empty or the battery is dead, flooding the RV.

Among the equipment we recommend: a white drinking water–quality hose that won't impart an unpleasant taste to the water; a Y fitting in case you have to share a water outlet with another camper; and

The hot-water tank should be drained regularly to float away accumulated scale and debris. (G. Groene)

quick-release fittings, described below. You also will find it handy to add a simple, inexpensive water shut-off valve to the hose so you can have off-and-on water control in your hand rather than having to go back to the faucet when you're working with the hose.

Two types of hot-water systems are commonly used in RVs. One is a gas unit, a miniature version of a household gas water heater. The other is an all-electric system. Both systems sometimes incorporate a heat exchanger that captures engine heat. On the road, engine-heated water is stored in the hot-water tank. At rest, a gas flame or 110-volt heating element is used. Don't buy a cheap or jury-rigged system. The best ones are expensive, using the finest materials to eliminate any danger of getting antifreeze into your drinking water or drinking water into your coolant.

All hot-water tanks are equipped with a drain valve and should be flushed every few weeks. Even if you use a particle filter on your hose, some sand and scale gets through and settles. If you see any signs of soot on the tank or on the RV, you know the gas flame isn't adjusted properly. It could be running rich because the air shutter jiggled closed, or bugs got into it. Clean and readjust it.

maintenance

Waste Water

Your owner's manual tells you how to flush sewer tanks and hoses. It's a nasty job, but some steps can make it less onerous. First, add a shut-off valve and a quick-release fitting to your hose, and matching quick-release fittings where the hose connects to the RV and on an adjustable, trigger-type nozzle. You can now flick the hose off the RV, hook up a nozzle, and adjust water spray and pressure for whatever cleanup tasks are at hand.

If your RV doesn't have a built-in flush system that allows you to blast water through pipes and into the black-water tank, add one or have an RV plumber do it for you. It's a fairly simple matter of tapping into a vent pipe from the outside of the RV, allowing you to stick the hose into an exterior fitting. Water flows through the pipes and tank and out the sewer hose, giving everything a thorough washdown.

Home centers and RV suppliers carry do-it-yourself plumbing fittings that allow even the most inexperienced plumbers to customize or expand plastic and copper plumbing. Brand names include Genova's

Using a few dollars' worth of plastic plumbing supplies, you can tee into the sewer line. These are the parts you'll need: adhesive for plastic pipe; a threaded adapter and screw cap for the outside of the RV; an elbow and a 45° fitting to tap into the vent pipe.

Locate a suitable spot outside the RV that is handy to the holding-tank vent pipe. (Because the vent pipe is probably inside a closet or cabinet, your additions won't show.) For the best flushing action, locate the fitting as high as possible on the side of the RV.

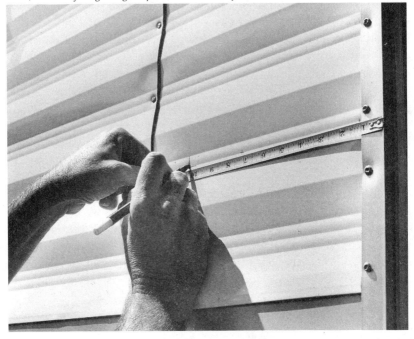

Make a wood spacer block to fit between the inner and outer panels. Cut a hole to make a snug fit around the elbow and threaded adapter. The outer skin of the RV is flared into the wood block and sealed with silicone. If the outer skin of your RV is fiberglass, seal it with epoxy. (G. Groene)

New plumbing fittings are designed for do-it-yourself installation on plastic or metal pipes. (Genova)

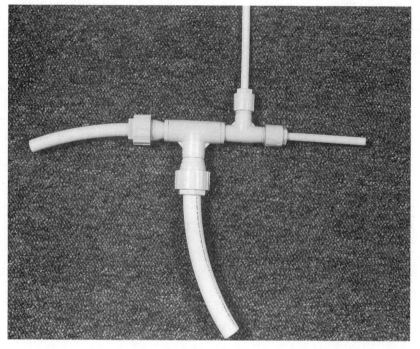

Uncopper, and Flair-It. If you explain your needs to a knowledgeable salesman, he'll be able to find all the fittings needed for plastic–plastic or plastic–metal additions.

An excellent guide to plumbing with the new plastics is *Do-It-Yourself Plumbing: It's Easy with Genova* by Richard Day. For information, write Genova Products, 7034 E. Court St., Davison, Michigan 48423. Although it's written for homeowners, the book explains the different types of plastic piping and how to join the various types, and covers many plumbing basics that apply to the RV. A simpler and more basic help for the rock-bottom beginner is *The All-Thumbs Guide to Home Plumbing* by Robert Wood (TAB Books).

Lastly, leave the campsite or the dump station squeaky clean for the next resident.

It's important that the wrong things don't go into your tanks: grease, caustic chemicals that could damage your RV's system, and sewage treatment chemicals that could damage the campground's septic system.

Biodegradable toilet papers are available, but we have never used them or any chemicals, and we've never had a problem with our straight-through flush system. If you do have odors, they could be caused by improper venting, leaky seals, or a valve that doesn't seat properly. With today's high-efficiency/low-water flush toilets, you can have all the odor-free, clean-water-flush convenience of a home toilet.

Empty the tank immediately after parking, before solids have a chance to settle and compact. Periodically take a bumpy ride with nothing in the waste tanks but a few gallons of water and a cup of baking soda. Then hook up immediately and flush out the tanks.

Don't flush tampons, disposable diapers, baby wipes, waste paper, or facial tissues, not because they'd hurt the tank but because they may not even get that far. Most RV toilets aren't designed to swallow things that swirl easily down a household john. When yours chokes up, repairs can be a nightmare.

When you have guests aboard who are not campers, make sure they know the rules. We posted a sign with the old sailor's saying, "Never put anything into the toilet that you haven't eaten first," and it gives everyone a smile as well as a lesson.

One more maintenance tip: If your RV manufacturer has supplied a steel storage compartment for the sewer hose, it will soon rust out from constant wetting. Replace it with a plastic one. A length of four- or five-inch-diameter PVC pipe, hung somewhere under the RV, is ideal. We left ours open on both ends for the best air flow. Ends do need some sort of clip or pin closure, though, so the hose doesn't slip out.

The Propane System

This ready, efficient, cheap, easily available fuel provides you with cooking, baking, heat, hot water, refrigeration, and perhaps an outdoor barbecue—all without the noise and stink of a generator.

The gas pipes in your home might be neglected for years, but your house doesn't move. Because your RV bounces, twists, and vibrates, a lot more vigilance is needed. Always be on the lookout for loose or leaky fittings and chafed or damaged tubing. About twice a year, inspect the fittings by painting them with a soapy solution. If it bubbles, you can see the leak.

Propane connections can weaken or fail due to vibration and fatigue. Check for leaks periodically using a liquid preparation made for the purpose. (G. Groene)

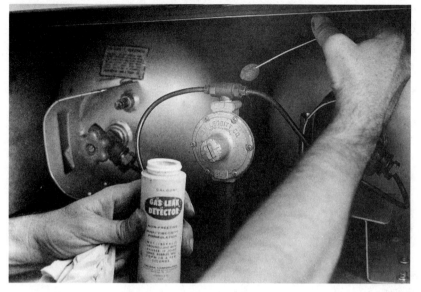

Don't allow rust to build up on your propane tanks. The more dampness and road slop they're exposed to, the quicker they'll corrode. When the tanks are empty, keep them tightly closed so air and dampness can't get inside and start rust there. In case any air did get in, purge the bottle with a little gas before recharging it. Make sure the bottles are well secured in the vehicle so they can't shift and damage nearby pipes.

Propane use on an RV also requires some common sense. Don't drive with any propane flame or pilot light lit. In a fuel station, or if you come upon a highway accident in which fuel has spilled, it could cause an explosion. Don't leave the gas stove unattended on a windy day. If the flame blows out and gas continues to flow, an explosion could result.

If your RV didn't come already equipped with a sniffer and an automatic solenoid shut-off, consider adding them.

If you ever have an opportunity to attend one of Hal and Penny Gaynor's trailer safety clinics, offered at campgrounds and RV rallies around the country, do so. Their knowledge of propane safety is invaluable.

Propane lines should be isolated against vibration and abrasion. (G. Groene)

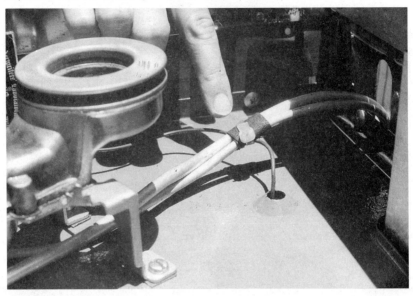

Refrigeration

Most RV refrigerators are the absorption type, not the compressor systems used in household refrigeration, so they require special treatment. For one thing, they're comparatively inefficient, able to keep foods at only forty to forty-five degrees below ambient temperatures.

When starting the refrigerator, give it eight to twelve hours to cool down and stabilize. Don't overwhelm it with too many new room-temperature foods at once, and don't load it with leftovers until they've cooled off.

Hang a refrigerator thermometer right inside the door and glance at it each time you open the door. When temperatures rise above forty degrees, foods begin to spoil more rapidly. So, keep a close eye on refrigerator temperatures, especially in hot weather.

In any RV supply house or catalog you can buy a small, battery-operated fan that will improve air circulation inside the unit. On hot days, try to keep the RV shaded so that the sun doesn't shine on the area containing the refrigerator's works and, as much as possible, improve air flow to the coils.

If you find that the refrigerator won't cool, especially after being in storage for a while, check first to see that the flame or heating element is working. If it is, and the unit still won't cool down, try driving a bumpy road. Sometimes that gets the circulation going. If that doesn't work, remove the refrigerator from the RV and turn it upside down for a day or two.

Another surprisingly common problem is that spiders love to nest in the chimney. If the refrigerator doesn't cool, check the chimney for spiders, debris, or soot. If heat can't go up the chimney to heat the boiler, no cooling is achieved. Soot, by the way, shouldn't be a problem if the flame is adjusted properly.

Lights and Wiring

Most RVs are wired for both 12-volt and 110/115-volt service. It's likely that some or all of your lights, entertainment electronics, and some other accessories such as the furnace blower and the exhaust fan over the stove, will be 12-volt only.

Most refrigerators work on 110-volt and gas. Some are three-way and work on gas, 12-volt, and 110-volt. If you have one of the latter units, be very careful about leaving it on 12-volt service after the engine is shut down because it will drain the battery fairly quickly.

Because of the danger of running down the start battery accidentally, it's best to have two separate electric systems, one to start the engine and a second to run the "house." The more you know about battery management, the more you can fine-tune the system. For example, we can gang up both systems, or use the "house" battery to start the engine in a pinch. However, it's dangerous to play this game, because if you confuse the switching arrangements, you can find yourself with two dead batteries instead of one. Again, your best guide is your RV manual.

Two new aids to your electrical management are available. One is a heavy-duty AC alternator that works off your main engine to supply as much as 5 kilowatts underway. It's the RoadPower system from Power Technology Inc., 1200 S. Sherman, Suite 100, Richardson, Texas 75081. The other is a new inverter technology that allows higher output from more compact, more efficient units.

If you have plenty of battery power in reserve and would like to be

Sophisticated new inverter/battery charger units give you full-time energy management, including 120xvolt power from 12-volt batteries, in camp and on the road. (Heart Interface)

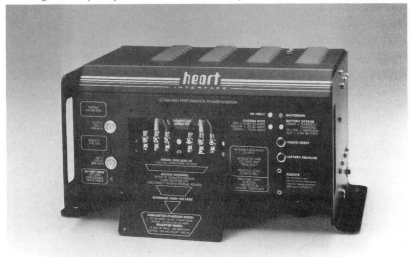

able to run a hair dryer, vacuum cleaner, heavy-duty drill, or microwave oven by converting 12-volt juice to 110/120-volt power, ask your RV supplier what's available in inverters.

Keep in mind, of course, the limitations of your batteries before putting a twenty-pound turkey into the microwave oven. A 1,200-watt hair dryer draws about 12 amps when it's in the AC plug, but running off an inverter, it draws 100 amps from the battery. Even if your inverter is 100 percent efficient (which it isn't), and even if your battery delivers its full 600-amp-hour charge from start to finish (which it won't), we're talking a fairly short time before the battery is stone cold dead.

Unless you're savvy about electricity, it's best to have repairs and troubleshooting done by a professional, especially when you're dealing with household current. You could electrocute yourself, or set up your RV for a future fire. Working with 12-volt systems is somewhat simpler, but it's still important to play by the safety rules. Very good 12-volt how-to manuals, usually designed for use on boats or cars, are available (particularly *The 12-Volt Bible for Boats* by Miner Brotherton, International Marine). Even the non-techie can find failures in the 12-

Fuses and circuit breakers come in many shapes and capacities. If you add circuits you must protect them, preferably with fuses or circuit breakers that match your original equipment so you won't have to carry many different types of spares. (G. Groene)

volt system by using a multimeter. If you have a failure in a 12-volt fan, light, or television, start checking at the item itself, and keep working backward toward the battery until you find the problem—usually an open wire, a blown fuse, or a loose connection at the battery end. When a light fails, check the bulb first, then the socket, which could be corroded.

The Generator

Because generators come in so many types and sizes, for use with diesel, gasoline, or propane, we'll concentrate here on some general guidelines. Again, the owner's manual that came with your generator is the best guide to its use and maintenance.

Just as your odometer is an essential log for engine and drive train maintenance, the generator's hour meter will tell you when routine inspections and maintenance should be done. If it doesn't have one, keep a log manually.

First, know the unit's capacity and don't try to exceed it. The generator could be damaged; so could an expensive air conditioner or appliance. The safest procedure is to note the electrical draw of each of your appliances so you'll always have an idea of what demands are being made on the generator.

Your generator is rated in watts; for example, a 4.5 KW (kilowatt) generator puts out 4,500 watts. Add up the wattage of all the 110-volt items that you might be using on generator power. You'll find them listed somewhere on each item. Don't forget the battery charger, electric water heater, or anything else that kicks in automatically when the generator goes on.

If an item is rated only in amps, as many power tools are, get watts by multiplying amps times volts. For example, 3 amps times 115 volts equals 345 watts. If the item is rated only in horsepower, figure about 750 watts per horsepower. If there are two ratings, one for starting load and one for running, list the higher one.

If you have motors that are rated only in horsepower, here are their approximate wattages:

HP	STARTING LOAD (WATTS)	RUNNING LOAD (WATTS)
¼	600	275
⅓	800	400
½	1200	500
¾	2100	500
1	2500	1200
2	3500	2200

If you have a marginally sized generator (which isn't a bad idea because you want to keep generator cost, weight, and fuel costs at a minimum), and don't have sufficient juice to run everything at once, you'll soon develop a sixth sense about generator juggling. For example, you'll turn off the air conditioner before using the heavy-duty drill; or you'll turn off the electric skillet before using the hair dryer.

Regardless of your generator's output, conservation is the key. *Every watt will cost you fuel dollars.* Don't assume that just because the generator is running anyway, all the juice is free.

Powerful, space-saving new generators allow fulltimers to have household power no matter where they are. It's important, though, to know how much juice you're generating and the power draw of all tools and appliances. Incorrect use could damage both the generator and the items it runs. (Kohler)

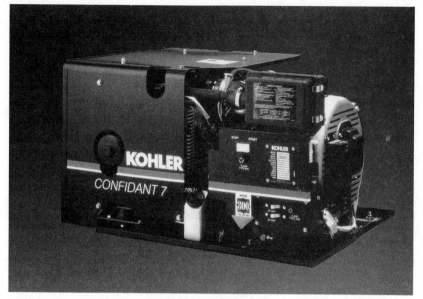

Campground Electricity

Electrical hookup can mean many things. We've been in campgrounds where the wiring was so old and flimsy, there wasn't enough juice to run the battery charger. At others, there wasn't enough power to handle the starting load of our medium-size air conditioner.

If you have a voltmeter and can see that incoming juice is not adequate, don't try to use any motorized equipment. At or below 90 volts, motors will overheat and eventually burn out. If you know the power demand of each electric item you have aboard, as described above, and know what amperage the service is (usually 15 or 30 amps), you can stagger appliance use so you don't damage anything.

You will need an adequately sized power cord. Try to keep it twenty-five feet long or less, because the longer the cord, the more electrical potential is lost. If your service cord feels warm, you know it's too light for the duty. If plugs feel hot, it means it's time to clean and brighten the contacts.

If your plug won't fit the campground's receptacle, ask at the office to borrow (usually a deposit is charged) a "pigtail." If you find yourself constantly encountering the same receptacles, buy your own pigtail in that size.

You'll also need a polarity tester, which will show whether the polarity to the two power connectors is reversed and whether there is current to the safety ground, which would mean the entire RV, including doorknobs and metal steps, could zap you with up to 110/115 volts. Always test before plugging in.

It's also a good idea to have a portable ground-fault interrupter or two. Say you're using a power tool outdoors in wet grass, and it's plugged into the receptacle on the side of the RV. If you have used a ground-fault interrupter, current cuts off the instant any shorted current is sensed.

Exterior

Your RV is a big financial investment, and because it's also your home, it's an emotional investment too. It deserves the best care you can give it.

No matter whether its skin is fiberglass, steel, or aluminum, your biggest enemy, second only to road damage, is the sun. Use the best polishes and protective coatings, which not only coat the finish but contain ultraviolet inhibitors that keep harmful rays from getting through to the paint.

Underneath the RV, rust is the chief destroyer. If you drive salted roads in winter, or drive along beach roads where you're throwing up salty sand and the wind is filled with ocean spume, wash off the salt as soon as possible. Salt is a quick, formidable destroyer.

Some RVs require annual recoating of roof seams. Your owner's manual will tell you where, why, and what to use. Since so many RVs are "stick" built, with a metal skin over a wood framework, leaks in the roof or skin should be dealt with immediately. Wood rot starts easily, spreads fast, and consumes rapidly.

maintenance

We've seen RVs with frames so completely rotted away that nothing was left but a thin shell. Kitchen cupboards fell down, and when a few screws were removed, the entire back end fell off the RV. Just the merest whiff of dry rot should send you off in search of the source of the leak. In the case of the RV mentioned above, cabinets had been hung using screws through the roof. Leakage around these screws wept through the entire structure. We once had a leak around a roof seam that led to a strip of dry rot under the carpeting.

Dry rot has no easy cure. First, the leak(s) must be found and eliminated. Second, the wood has to be exposed and dried. Softened wood must be dug out and replaced with sound new wood. Third, a constant check should be kept on seals and bedding compound at every joint, rivet, screw, or other point where water could enter. Such seals can crack, dry out, or shrink. Again, it pays to buy the best and most ultraviolet-resistant sealants for exterior use.

Heat and Air

Heating and air conditioning systems differ, so once again, the owner's manual for each unit is the most reliable guide. Among universal rules: Change filters often; restricting air flow reduces efficiency. Check over the furnace at the start of each cold season. Clean the grills, touch up rust with high-temperature paint, check the pilot light or ignition and main-burner flame, and clean the fan blades.

If manufacturer instructions call for oiling the fan motor, do it now. (Some motors are sealed and don't normally require additional oil.) An RV is a small area that can fill rapidly with carbon monoxide when things go wrong. A wise addition to any RV is a good electronic CO detector.

Inspect wiring bundles to make sure they haven't been damaged by chafe, working, or contact with stowed items. Look over the ductwork for signs of leaks, twisting, or dents. If ducting runs through storage areas, it could have taken some knocking-about.

Check exhaust and intake ports for restrictions (mud dauber nests, for example). And if you ever camp in snow, make sure these ports are kept free of blockage.

CHAPTER TWENTY-THREE

Safety and Security

You can drive away from a tiresome job, loudmouth neighbors, and city pollution, but there is no escape from crime, highway hazards, and everyday household dangers.

Buckle Up

Seat belts are still the most important defense against being killed or injured on the highway. Even if you have air bags, they must be used in concert with the time-tested seat belt. If you don't believe buckling up is important, here are a few things to consider.

◆ Your fears of being burned alive are not justified. Fire occurs in only one crash in ten. If your vehicle does burn, you are more likely to be able to extricate yourself and your loved ones if you were protected by a seat belt from being knocked out in the crash.

◆ The same goes for drowning in a vehicle that drops off a bank or a bridge. In Holland, a land laced with canals, special courses in driver safety emphasize the importance of wearing a seat belt. You're less likely to be injured on impact; more likely to be able to get yourself out of a submerged vehicle.

◆ Many drivers feel they are protected by the wheel, but the worst injuries of all are sustained by the driver who is impaled on the steering column before being thrown against the windshield. As the captain of this land yacht, your primary duty is to stay at your station and in control of the vehicle until it comes to a stop. If you're thrown out of the driver's seat by an impact, whatever control you might have exercised has been snatched from you. The driver needs a seat belt as much as anyone.

◆ Seat belts are required by law in many states—and those laws are getting stiffer. States that formerly required seat belts but did not cite violators unless they were stopped for some other reason are now writing tickets for seat belt non-compliance as a primary offense.

Do you still feel that seat belts are wimpy? Pilots, professional race car drivers, and thousands of highway crash survivors do not agree.

Firearms

Should you carry a gun aboard to ensure personal safety? It's a very personal decision, one that we can't discourage or encourage. The one difference between keeping a gun in your home and carrying one in your RV is that your RV usually comes under laws covering vehicles, not domiciles. Even in states where it's legal to have a gun in your house, you can be arrested for having one in your rolling home, even if you are merely passing through and have no intention of making so much as a fuel stop.

For information on firearm safety and how to comply with the tangled maze of state laws having to do with guns and vehicles, write the National Rifle Association, 1600 Rhode Island Ave. N.W., Washington, DC 20036.

Other Personal Safety Tips

◆ Paint a huge number or symbol on the roof of your RV. It will help rescuers find you if you radio for help in an emergency and aid officials in finding the RV if it's stolen.

◆ Guard against being hit at the roadside when you're stopped for a tire change or other breakdown. Get everyone out of the RV and to a safe spot well off the road. You might make an occasional announcement on the CB, alerting drivers that there is a stopped vehicle at Mile Marker so-and-so.

◆ Set flares, or better still, xenon strobe lights. Such strobes are available through dive shops, marine stores, and emergency supply houses. Firemen use them for marking a route through smoke-filled buildings; SCUBA divers use the waterproof versions in cave and wreck diving.

◆ As folksy and friendly as it seems to be, it's not wise to hang a sign on your RV announcing your name. A stranger who wants to catch you unawares in the wee hours can pound on your door, calling your name. Assuming it's a campground neighbor, or the manager bringing you an emergency message, you open the door and. . . .

Theftproofing

You have three primary weapons in this battle: vigilance, locks, and electronic security devices.

Some of the simplest steps are the most effective. One is simply to close the curtains securely when you're not aboard. If you don't, a

For valuables you keep on board, install a safe permanently in the wall or floor. (Sentry)

For camping in some areas, it's best to protect fuel and water tanks with heavy-duty locks. (Jerry Martin Company)

thief can easily see your television, cameras, radios, purse, and other valuables, size up the situation, smash a window, grab something, and run.

We installed extra light switches over the bed, so we can maintain darkness inside and yet turn on bright outdoor lights around the RV if we hear anything suspicious outside. You might also want to be able to use the loudhailer, a siren/strobe, or the CB radio from your bed.

When you leave the RV, close and lock all doors and windows. For ventilation, open only overheads. If your RV has no locks on its service doors, buy and install them (except on propane doors, which should not be locked). If your original service door locks were the cheap, flimsy type that soon corrode away, get new, rustproof locks. Padlock the spare tire and, for travel in high-crime areas, get a locking fuel cap. Various types of tongue locks are available to secure travel trailers.

Various locks are available to hinder trailer theft. This Safe-T-Hitch also prevents accidental unhitching underway. (Flushette Manufacturing Company)

If you're ordering a new RV, ask what security features are provided as standard equipment or as optional extras. By planning such devices early in the construction of an RV, you can assure the best installation, the least wiring, the most convenience and concealment, and the components most compatible with the RV and its systems.

So many alarm systems are available in the automotive, household, and marine market, it's just a matter of shopping for the one(s) that best suit your needs. It all depends on how much money you want to spend and how much electronic gamesmanship you are willing to play. Specialists in RV security systems include ECCO, Box 7246, Boise, Idaho 83707; Fat Socks USA, Box 2972, Hemet, California 92543; INTAC Corporation, Box 1209, Cottage Grove, Oregon 97424; Trekmate Security, 5085 Caesena Way, Oceanside, California 92056; and Yarnell Security Systems, 24 Hellers Church Rd., Leola, Pennyslvania 17540.

Warning Devices

Sometimes the greatest dangers come from within. They include carbon monoxide, gasoline fumes, propane, overheat, and smoke. One or two smoke alarms are a must, but keep in mind that they can't "see" other dangerous fumes. For those, you'll need other sniffers.

This sniffer is a sophisticated safety device that automatically starts a blower if it detects gasoline fumes in the generator compartment. (Fireboy)

You might put a gasoline sniffer in the engine compartment, a high-temperature alarm in the generator compartment, and another temperature alarm, set to a low temperature, to warn you if the refrigerator or the freezer warms up above food-safe temperatures. We also have a small, battery-operated water alarm the size of a deck of cards. Placed on the bathroom floor, it buzzes if it gets damp, giving ample warning that water is leaking or the toilet flooding.

Fire Safety

For a free pamphlet, write Alexander & Alexander, 600 Fisher Bldg., Detroit, Michigan 48202 and ask for "In the Know About RV Fire Safety." Among fire safety suggestions we recommend are:

◆ Know how your emergency exits work. Discuss alternate escape routes, including escape means if you're involved in an accident in which the RV lands on its roof or sides.

◆ Test the smoke alarms regularly. Don't just rely on a signal light to tell you it's operating or a buzzer to tell you that a battery is getting weak.

◆ Check fire extinguishers regularly. If they are the Halon type, they must be weighed—gauges aren't reliable. If they are dry powder, drive with them on their side occasionally to keep the powder from packing down. For either type, if the gauge reads "low" or the extinguisher is out of date, have it recharged. The local fire department should be able to steer you to a fire extinguisher service station.

◆ Damp charcoal can ignite from spontaneous combustion. Carry charcoal in a sealed can.

By pulling a handle as you exit the RV you can immediately snuff engine-room fires with this safe, effective Halon system. (Fireboy)

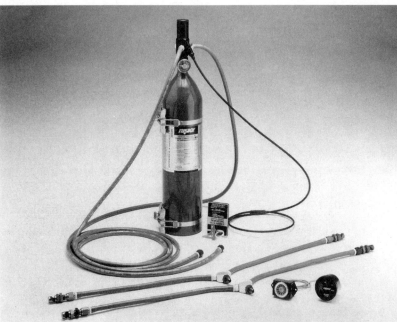

◆ Keep a box of baking soda handy for extinguishing minor flareups in the galley.

◆ With your family, have a "scramble" drill so you'll all know how to get yourselves and your RV to safety in case of a forest fire or a fire in a neighboring RV.

◆ Don't leave an open flame unattended in the RV. Keep combustibles well away from the stove.

◆ Fix fuel leaks immediately. Propane is explosive, and it settles in heavy, invisible pools where you least expect them. Gasoline evaporates quickly, but its fumes, too, sink into lethal, unseen puddles. Diesel is less explosive, but it soaks into everything and lingers there, posing a fire hazard for a long time. Any leak is dangerous.

◆ Keep battery terminals and fuse blocks clean. Corrosion creates heat creates fire.

◆ A dragging brake can start a fire in brake fluid. A dual tire that goes flat and remains unnoticed as it drags on for miles can catch fire. A stuck vee

safety

belt can ignite. A fire can also start under the chassis if you drive through high, dry weeds with a hot catalytic converter.

Long available in boats, automatic engine room fire extinguishers have finally been developed for RVs. The problem in RVs was always that, unlike the engine room in a boat, the compartment has a constant, high-volume flow of air. In a boat action is instantaneous, but if the same system were discharged in an RV at 55 mph, the snuffers would be carried away on the wind.

Developed by Fireboy, Box 152, Grand Rapids, Michigan 49501, the RV system allows you to pull to the side of the road and discharge the system as you exit the RV, using a pull cable near the door. Discharge goes on for forty seconds, quelling the fire and allowing a brief cooldown to prevent re-flash. You can install it yourself; prices start at under $650.

Bad things happen to good people, but now you're free to keep searching for the right area, the right equipment, and the right preventive measures. Maybe you can't escape crime and accidents completely, but as a fulltimer you can give them a darned good run for the money.

The End
of the Road

Every story has an end, so even if you're just beginning your full-time journey, it's not too soon to give some thought to the rest of the tale.

For some fulltimers, the roaming life ends suddenly and dramatically with death, divorce, illness, or a family crisis. For others—and you'll meet them as you travel—life just grinds to a sour stop; all the magic and motion has gone out of fulltiming, but they just don't have enough starch to do something about it.

In boating, there's a saying, "Until she leaves the dock, a boat is simply sub-standard housing." The same can be said of an RV. When it's free to fly down the highway, to rush to the next sunrise, and to nose around the next corner to see what adventures await, your rolling home is a magic carpet.

However, when it's stuck in a seedy campsite, surrounded by tall grass and short ambitions, an RV is just a house that's too small.

In a happy ending, fulltiming comes to an end because you're ready for the next adventure. As long as you and your travel partner(s) keep communicating and caring about each other, the transition out of fulltiming can be just as exciting as the move into your RV.

One of the best things about fulltiming is that it can give you a lingering look at every part of the country. Instead of making a hurried choice of a place to settle down, you can reside temporarily in one community after another. Join a church and clubs, make friends, perhaps find a job, look over the different neighborhoods in town, and get a sense of local politics. As long as you're living in your RV, you're free to move on the minute you don't like the set-up.

We spent one summer in a state that we thought would be our eventual home. For months, we made the rounds with real estate agents, looking at property. We loved the community for its symphony and good libraries, nice folks, and good shopping. The climate was perfect in summer, with warm days and cool nights.

But gradually disenchantment began to set in. With fall came north winds, bearing the stink of a pulp mill on the other side of the next mountain. Weather turned dank, and we began to have stiffness in joints we'd forgotten we had. Our statement from a local bank reflected a debit for a state tax we didn't know existed.

Then a local widow told us how she was struggling to pay her taxes. She'd owned her home jointly with her husband, and when he died, she had to pay inheritance taxes on half of her own home. We ruled out that state as a future home.

Another time, we found a beautiful piece of acreage in the pine woods of north-central Florida. With the owner's permission, we parked our RV on it for a few nights while we looked it over. One night when the wind shifted, we realized the land was just downwind of a landfill. Camping on another piece of land we were close to buying, we realized it was on a seven-year flood plain. What was now a lovely trout stream could become a raging torrent in a wet spring.

We left another state when we learned that the high sales tax also applied to food. In others, we just didn't feel comfortable with the crowding or high crime rates or climate or sleazy politics.

In some areas, we discovered that local well water was so bad we'd always have to buy our drinking water. And in one locale, to our complete amazement, there were lots for sale that had no water at all. There was no rain, no river, no well water. Every drop would have to be trucked in.

No state or climate is perfect, but when you're fulltiming, you can experience all climates, all seasons, all wind directions, and many different societies before settling down. You can live tentatively among the people who will be your permanent neighbors, read local papers, sit in on local council meetings, and learn about—or even have to pay—local and state taxes and license fees. And all the while you're investigating all this, you're living comfortably in your own rolling home, ready to move along without so much as a fare-thee-well.

When we first went fulltiming, it was a step taken over many months, with lots of praying and planning. When you decide to leave fulltiming to buy a house, enter a retirement community, resume a career, or adopt any other new lifestyle, that transition too should be taken slowly and carefully. If you wait until you're too fed up, too broke, too cold, too hot, or on the verge of divorce, it's too late to act with restraint, prudence, and economy.

It was with a sense of adventure and joy that we eased out of fulltiming, first by buying acreage and returning to it once or twice a year to camp under our trees, listen to our land, meet our neighbors. After a few years, we knew it was right, so we built a small house. Later, we added another house and more acreage. We continue to slip away, still in the same RV, knowing that we now have the courage and know-how to become fulltimers again any time we choose.

To break away was tough. To stay away was sometimes even tougher. What we gained, though, was ten years of travel that nobody can ever take away from us, no matter what the future holds.

As the saying goes, just do it.

APPENDIX 1

••••

Useful Addresses

Alaska bound? Holland America Line offers one-way passage for the RV and a luxury cruise for you. Most travelers say that driving the Alaska Highway once is enough. Drive up and cruise back, or vice versa. See a travel agent or write Holland America, 300 Elliott Ave. W., Seattle, Washington 98119.

American Association of Retired Persons. AARP, a nonprofit organization open to people age 50 and older, offers group health insurance, a discount pharmacy, and other benefits. For information write: AARP Membership Processing Center, 3200 E. Carson St., Lakewood, California, 90712.

Catalogs. For some free catalogs you'll find helpful, write Camping World, Box 90018, Bowling Green, Kentucky 42102; Cabela's, 812 13th Ave., Sidney, Nebraska 69160; L.L. Bean, Freeport, Maine 04033. Also pick up some Sears "specialogs" for camping, boating, health and handicap, big and tall sizes, RV furnishings and accessories, and other hard-to-find items. They are available free at any Sears store.

Customs service. Make sure you don't run afoul of the law when returning from another country. The pre-Columbian antique you bought in Mexico or the whalebone artifact from Canada may be confiscated at the border. Travel with pets, firearms, large amounts of cash, cigarettes and alcohol, plants, and certain souvenirs can be complicated if not illegal. Request the booklet "Know Before You Go" from the U.S. Customs Service, Department of the Treasury, 1301 Constitution Ave. N.W., Washington, DC 20229.

Disabilities. For books on all areas of travel with any type of physical limitation, write The Disability Bookshop, Box 129, Vancouver, Washington 98666.

Driver rehabilitation. If you have to learn to drive with a physical impairment, contact the Memorial Hospital Driver Education Center, 615 N. Michigan St., South Bend, Indiana 46601.

Home schooling. One of the best and most respected mail-order school systems is the Calvert School, Tuscany Rd., Baltimore, Maryland 21210; (301) 243-6030; FAX, (301) 366-0674. Courses, which are available for kindergarten through eighth grade, are designed to be administered by parents who are not professional teachers. Several credit and supplies options are available.

Recreational Vehicle Industry Association, P.O. Box 2999, 1896 Preston White Drive, Reston, Virginia 22090-0999; (800) 336-0154 or (703) 620-6003. Call or write the RVIA for information on RV rental sources, RV manufacturers (see Appendix 2), RV camping clubs, industry standards, RV publications, and much more.

Road conditions. The following states will supply highway reports, some of them all year and others just in winter. Conditions are: R1, snow tread allowed or chains required; R2, four-wheel drive allowed, others require chains; R3, chains required on all vehicles.

California (916) 581-1400	New Hampshire (603) 485-5767
Colorado (303) 639-1234	New Mexico (505) 291-6625
Idaho (208) 336-6606	New York (800) 843-7623
Maine (207) 289-2225	North Dakota (800) 472-2686
Michigan (800) 482-5300	Oregon (503) 899-3999
Minnesota (800) 542-0220	Utah (801) 964-6000
Montana (406) 444-6339	Wisconsin (800) 762-3947
Nevada (702) 793-1313	Wyoming (800) 442-7850

RV publications. For a list of books and pamphlets on RVs, write RVIA, Box 2999, Reston, Virginia 22090.

Safes for RVs. JCP Enterprises, 17671 Falkirk Ln., Huntington Beach, California 92649.

Social Security Administration. (800) SSA-1213.

Solar products. RV Solar Electric, 14415 N. 73rd St., Scottsdale, Arizona 85260, (800) 999-8520 (full range of solar products as well as a book, *The RVer's Guide to Solar and Inverter Power*); Atlantic Solar Products, 9351-J Philadelphia Rd., Baito, Maryland 21237; Energy Products, 10905 Tea Bark, Moreno Valley, California 91287; Energy Specialists Solar Electric, Box 188710, Sacramento, California 95818; Gilbert Lightner Enterprises, 23 Hampton Ct., Alameda, California 94501; Solar City, 1 Moon Mountain Rd., Quartsite, Arizona 85359; Solar Electric Specialties, 9838 Via Ct., Elk Grove, California 95624;

SolarMetrics, 140 Bouchard St., Manchester, New Hampshire 03103; Solar River RV and Marine, Box 2588, Quartsite, Arizona 85346; and The 12-Volt Catalog, 2649 N.W. 28th Terrace, Boca Raton, Florida 33434.

Superintendent of Documents. The U.S. Government Printing Office, Washington, DC 20402 publishes a long list of advisory books and pamphlets on all phases of camping, consumerism, and lifestyle.

Tax forms. Request needed forms from (800) 829-3676. The most commonly used forms are also available at post offices and libraries at tax time.

Toll-free dialing. A directory of companies that have toll-free numbers is available for $9.95 from AT&T, (800) 426-8686.

Travel supplies. A catalog devoted entirely to unusual travel items is available free from Magellan's, Box 5485, Santa Barbara, California 93150.

Truck stops. When all you want is a safe place to park and a quick night's sleep, a truck stop offers basic needs: fuel, food, plenty of parking, higher drive-throughs at the fuel pumps, and sometimes electric and water hookups. Send $6.95 for the National Truck Stop Directory from NATSO, Box 1285, Alexandria, Virginia 22313.

Window treatments. RV Privacy Window Fashions, 2805 Wilderness Pl., Boulder, Colorado 80301.

Windshield covers. Best RV, 1104 N. Marshall, El Cajon, California 92020 specializes in custom covers, awnings, and sun screens.

APPENDIX 2

●●●●

What's Available in RVs

Dozens of manufacturers and hundreds of RV retailers compete for the dollars the fulltimer will spend on his or her dream house. Visit dealers in your hometown and step aboard as many models as possible in order to get a feel for construction, size, livability, and special features. Then write to the manufacturers listed here so you can see what else is available.

Manufacturers' Product Codes

TT - Travel Trailer

PT - Park Trailer

FW - Fifth Wheel

FC - Folding Camping Trailer

MA - Motor Homes Type A

MB - Motor Homes Type B

MC - Motor Homes Type C

TC - Truck Camper

ABI Leisure Products, 726 Broad St. E., Dunnville, Ontario, CANADA N1A 2X1 (TT)

Alfa Leisure, Inc., 5163 "G" St., Chino, California 91710 (TT, FW)

American Travel Systems, 21746 Buckingham Rd., Elkhart, Indiana 46516 (TT, FW)

Amerigo, Inc., 807 S. Division St., Bristol, Indiana 46507 (FW, PT, TC)

Anaheim Industries of Texas, 2305 Bennington, Houston, Texas 77093 (TC)

Auto-Mate Rec. Prod., Inc., 150 West G St., Los Banos, California 93635 (FW, TT)

Barth, Inc., P.O. Box 768, Milford, Indiana 46542 (MC)

Beaver Coaches, Inc., 20545 Murray Rd., Bend, Oregon 97701 (MA)

Belair, Inc., 907 S. Division St., Bristol, Indiana 46507 (TT, PT, FW, TC)

Big Foot Industries Inc., 3405 43rd Ave., Vernon, B.C., CANADA V1T 8P5 (FW, MC, TC, TT)

Bill Yoder Vans, 18449 S.E. Stark, Portland, Oregon 97233 (MB)

Blue Bird Wanderlodge, P.O. Box 1259, Ft. Valley, Georgia 31030 (MA)

Bonair Leisure Products, 766 Frontenac Blvd., Black Lake, QB, CANADA G0N 1A0 (FC)

Caravan Coach, Inc., 30170 Eden Church Rd., Denham Springs, Louisiana 70726 (PT)

Carriage, Inc., #5 Industrial Park, Millersburg, Indiana 46543 (TT, FW, MC)

Casa Villa Inc., P.O. Box 567, Wakarusa, Indiana 46573 (PT)

Castle Industries, 2125 W. Wilden Ave., Goshen, Indiana 46526 (PT)

Champion Enterprises, Inc., 5573 North St., Dryden, Michigan 48428 (PT, MA, MC)

Chariot Eagle, 931 N.W. 37th Ave., Ocala, Florida 32675 (PT)

Classic Custom Coaches, Inc., Hwy. 72 E., Colbert, Georgia 30628 (MB)

Coach House, 208-D Warfield Ave., Venice, Florida 34292 (MB)

Coachmen Industries, Inc., 601 E. Beardsley Ave., Elkhart, Indiana 46514 (TT, PT, FW, FC, TC, MA, MB, MC)

Columbia Northwest, Inc., 1 Main St., Mammoth, Pennsylvania 15664 (FC)

Commodore Home Systems, Inc., S.R. 13 N., Syracuse, Indiana 46567 (PT)

Continental Coach, 419 S. Houston, Yuma, Colorado 80759 (TC, MB)

Country Coach, Inc., 135 E. First St., Junction City, Oregon 97448 (MA, MC)

Country Park, Inc., 65213 C.R. 31, Goshen, Indiana 46526 (PT)

Craft Products, Inc., 1045 N. Nappanee St., Elkhart, Indiana 46514 (MC)

Custom Camp Vans, 7575 Jurupa Ave., Riverside, California 92504 (MB)

Custom Craft Vehicles, 960 W. Armour Ave., Milwaukee, Wisconsin 53221 (TC)

D.M. Van Conversions, Ltd., 12651 West Silver Spring Dr., Butler, Wisconsin 53007 (MB)

DMR Van Conversions, Inc., 204 S. Cedar St., Monticello, Iowa 52310 (TC)

DNA Enterprises, Inc., 17091 C.R. 33, Goshen, Indiana 46526 (PT)

Damon Corporation, 52570 Paul Dr., Elkhart, Indiana 46514 (TT, PT, FW, MA, MC)

DeRose Industries, Inc., 1080 S. Main St., Chambersburg, Pennsylvania 17201 (PT)

Diamond Coach Corporation, 2300 W. 4th St., Oswego, Kansas 67356 (MC)

Dodgen Industries, Inc., Hwy. 169 North, Humboldt, Iowa 50548 (MC)

Excel Trailer Co., Inc., 11238 Peoria St., Sun Valley, California 91352 (TT, FW)

Fairmont Homes, Inc., 502 South Oakland Ave., Nappanee, Indiana 46550 (PT)

Fireside RV, 405 Kesco Dr., Bristol, Indiana 46507 (FW, PT, TT)

Fisher Corporation, Hwy. 52 S., Richfield, North Carolina 28137 (PT)

Fleetwood Enterprises, Inc., 3125 Myers St., Riverside, California 92503 (TT, PT, FW, MA, MC)

Foretravel, Inc., 1221 N.W. Stallings Dr., Nacogdoches, Texas 75961 (MA)

Four Winds International Corporation, 55667 C.R. 15, Elkhart, Indiana 46516 (MC)

Franklin Coach Co., Inc., S. Oakland Ave., Nappanee, Indiana 46550 (TT, PT, FW)

Freedom Wheels, 11055 LeRoy Dr., Northglenn, Colorado 80233 (TC)

Geneva Luxury Motor Vans/CTI, Inc., 1070 Carey St., Lake Geneva, Wisconsin 53147 (TC)

Georgie Boy Manufacturing, Inc., P.O. Drawer H, Edwardsburg, Michigan 49112 (MA)

Glendale R.V., 145 Queen St., Strathroy, Ontario, CANADA N7G 3J6 (TT, PT, FW, MC)

Go Vacations Industries, Inc., 66 Mohawk St., Brantford, Ontario, CANADA N3S 2W3 (TC, MB, MC)

Gulf Stream Coach, Inc., P.O. Box 1005, Nappanee, Indiana 46550 (TT, PT, FW, MA, MC)

Hallcraft RV Industries, Inc., 1760 Chicago Ave., Riverside, California 92507 (MA)

Hawkins Motor Coach, Inc., 1610 S. Cucamonga Ave., Ontario, California 91761 (MA)

Hi Lo Trailer Co., 145 Elm St., Butler, Ohio 44822 (TT, FW)

Holiday Rambler Corporation, 65528 State Rd. 19, Wakarusa, Indiana 46573 (TT, FW, MA, MC)

Home & Park Motorhomes, 75 Ardelt Pl., Kitchener, Ontario, CANADA N2C 2C8 (MB)

Homesteader, Inc., 1510 Cedar Ln., New Tazewell, Tennessee 37825 (TT, PT)

Honorbuilt Industries, Inc., 1200 W. 10th St., Minneapolis, Kansas 67467 (MA, MB, MC)

Horizons, Inc., 2323 N. Jackson, Junction City, Kansas 66441 (TT, FW)

Hy-Line Enterprises Inc., 21674 Beck Dr., Elkhart, Indiana 46516 (TT, PT)

International Vehicles Corp., P.O. Box 459, Bristol, Indiana 46507 (MB, MC)

Jayco, Inc., 58075 S.R. 13 S., Middlebury, Indiana 46540 (TT, FW, FC, TC, MC)

Kentron, Inc., 52897 Dexter Dr., Elkhart, Indiana 46514 (TC)

Key West Mfg., Inc., 8826 U.S. Hwy. 19, Port Richey, Florida 34668 (PT)

King of the Road, 553 Front St., Russell, Kansas 67665 (TT, PT, FW)

Kit Manufacturing Company, 412 Kit Ave., Caldwell, Idaho 83605 (TT, PT, FW)

Kropf Manufacturing Co., Inc., 58647 S.R. 15, Goshen, Indiana 46526 (TT, PT, FW)

K-Z, Inc., Sportsmen's, 9270 West U.S. 20, Shipshewana, Indiana 46565 (FW, TC, TT)

L.E.R. Industries, Inc., 19475 U.S. 12 E., Edwardsburg, Michigan 49112 (TC, MB)

Lake Capital Corp., 3701 SE Naef Rd., Milwaukie, Oregon 97267 (TT, FW)

Lance Camper Mfg. Corp., 10234 Glenoaks Blvd., Pacoima, California 91331 (FW, TC)

Lazy Daze, Inc., 4303 E. Mission Blvd., Pomona, California 91766 (MC)

Lee Enterprises Manufacturing Co., Inc., 25883 N. Park Ave., Elkhart, Indiana 46514 (PT)

Leisure Guide of America, Inc., Rt. 1, Box 1078, Royston, Georgia 30662 (TC)

Liberty Homes, Inc., 1101 Eisenhower Dr. N., Goshen, Indiana 46526 (PT)

Mallard Coach Co., Inc., 2404 E. Market St., Nappanee, Indiana 46550 (TT, PT, FW, MA, MC)

Marathon Homes Corp., 22741 Pine Creek Rd., Elkhart, Indiana 46515 (TT, FW, MC)

Mascot Homes, Inc., Hwy. 176, Gramling, South Carolina 29348 (PT)

Monaco Coach Corp., 325 E. First St., Junction City, Oregon 97448 (MA)

National RV, Inc., 3411 N. Perris Blvd., Perris, California 92370 (MA, MC)

Newmar Corporation, 355 N. Delaware St., Nappanee, Indiana 46550 (TT, PT, FW, MA, MC)

Northern Lite Mfg. Co., 7410 S.E. Johnson Creek, Portland, Oregon 97206 (PT)

Nu Wa Industries, Inc., 4002 Ross Ln., Chanute, Kansas 66720 (TT, FW)

Odessa Industries, Inc., 2208 Middlebury St., Elkhart, Indiana 46516 (MA)

Peachtree Housing, Rt. 6, Box 241C, Moultrie, Georgia 31768 (PT)

Peterson Industries, Inc., R.R. 2, Box 95, Smith Center, Kansas 66967 (TT, FW)

Play-Mor Trailers, Inc., Hwy. 63 S, Westphalia, Missouri 65085 (TT, PT, FW)

Pleasure-Way Industries Ltd., 302 Portage Ave., Saskatoon, Sk., CANADA S7J 4C6 (MB)

Quality Vans, 1457 N. Arizona Ave., Chandler, Arizona 85225 (TC)

R.C. Willett Co., Inc., 3040 Leversee Rd., Cedar Falls, Iowa 50613 (TC)

Recreational Vehicles, Inc., 2211 W. Wilden Ave., Goshen, Indiana 46526 (TT, PT, FW)

Red-E-Kamp, Inc., 3401 Etiwanda Ave., Mira Loma, California 91752 (MB, MC)

Redman Homes, Inc. 1602 Industrial Park Dr., P.O. Box SS, Plant City, Florida 33564 (PT)

Rexhall Industries, Inc., 25655 Springbrook Ave., Santa Clarita, California 91380 (MA)

Royalty Vans, Inc., 610 N.W. 2nd St., Richmond, Indiana 47374 (TC)

SCI Sport-Cam Industries, 9306 Weston Ave., Schofield, Wisconsin 54476 (TC)

Sebring Homes Corporation, 52645 Park Six Ct., Elkhart, Indiana 46514 (PT)

Serro Travel Trailer Co., 450 Arona Rd., Irwin, Pennsylvania 15642 (TT, FW)

Shadow Cruiser, Inc., 13861 C.R. 4, Bristol, Indiana 46507 (FW, TC)

Sierra Motor Corporation, 22800 Pine Creek Rd., Elkhart, Indiana 46516 (MB)

Silver Eagle Coach, Inc., P.O. Box 38, Vina, Alabama 35593 (MA)

Skamper Corporation, State Rd. 15 N., Bristol, Indiana 46507 (TT, FW, FC, TC)

Skyline Corporation, 2520 By-Pass Rd., Elkhart, Indiana 46515 (TT, PT, FW, MC)

Southern Coach, Inc., 406 Pine St., Greensboro, North Carolina 27420 (TC)

Southern Comfort Conversions, Inc., 916 Markeeta Spur Rd., Moody, Alabama 35004 (TC)

Sportsmobile, Inc., 250 Court St., Huntington, Indiana 46750 (MB)

Sportsmobile West, 5477 E. Hedges, Fresno, California 93727 (MB)

Starcraft Automotive Corporation, 2703 College Ave., Goshen, Indiana 46526 (TT, FW, FC, TC, MA, MB, MC)

Sun-Lite, Inc., P.O. Box 517, Bristol, Indiana 46507 (TC)

Sunline Coach Company, 245 S. Muddy Creek Rd., Denver, Pennsylvania 17517 (TT, FW, TC)

Teton Homes, P.O. Box 2349, Mills, Wyoming 82644 (FW)

Thor Industries, Inc., 419 W. Pike St., Jackson Center, Ohio 45334 (TT, FW, MA, MB, MC)

Tiffin Motor Homes, Inc., Golden Rd., Red Bay, Alabama 35582 (MA, MC)

Tradewinds Conversions, Inc., 2535 Bryant St., Elkhart, Indiana 46516 (TC)

Trail Wagons, Inc., 1100 E. Lincoln Ave., Yakima, Washington 98907 (MB)

TrailManor, Inc., 304 Church St., Lake City, Tennessee 37769 (TT)

Trans-Aire International Inc., 3012 Mobile Dr., Elkhart, Indiana 46515 (TC)

Travel Line Enterprises, 25876 Miner Road, Elkhart, Indiana 46514 (TT, PT)

Travel Supreme, Inc., 711 E. Waterford St., Wakarusa, Indiana 46573 (TT, PT, FW)

Triple E Canada Ltd., P.O. Box 1230, Winkler, Manitoba, CANADA R6W 4C4 (MA, MB, MC)

Trophy Homes, Inc., 52807 Co. Rd. 7 North, Elkhart, Indiana 46514 (PT)

Turtle Top, 67895 Industrial Dr., New Paris, Indiana 46553 (MB)

Van American, Inc./Cobra, 2766 E. College Ave., Goshen, Indiana 46526 (TT, FW, MA, MB, MC)

The Van House, 1801 Cushman Dr., Lincoln, Nebraska 68512 (TC)

Vanguard Industries of MI Inc., 31450 M-86-West, Colon, Michigan 49040 (FC, TC)

Vehicle Concepts, 1809 West Hively Ave., Elkhart, Indiana 46517 (MB)

Waldoch Crafts Inc., 13821 Lake Dr., Forest Lake, Minnesota 55025 (MC)

Western Recreational Veh., 3401 W. Washington Ave., Yakima, Washington 98903 (TT, FW, TC)

Winnebago Industries, Inc., P.O. Box 152, Forest City, Iowa 50436 (MA, MC)

Woodland Park, Inc., 58074 St. Rd. 13, Middlebury, Indiana 46540 (PT)

APPENDIX 3

●●●●

RVIA Standards

Established by an American National Standards Committee under the aegis of the American National Standards Institute, the American National Standard for Recreational Vehicles includes more than 500 specifications. Below are some of the main requirements manufacturers must meet.

Fire and Life Safety

◆ Minimum flamespread ratings are specified for interior walls and ceilings.

◆ Fire extinguishers are required in any vehicle equipped with fuel-burning appliances or an internal combustion engine.

◆ A minimum of two means of egress is required; alternate exits must be labeled.

◆ Generator units driven by internal combustion engines must be installed in a compartment that is vapor-tight to the interior of the vehicle.

Plumbing System Codes

◆ Approval of all fixtures, fittings, materials, and equipment by a testing agency such as the National Sanitation Foundation or the International Association of Plumbing and Mechanical Officials is required. After certification, all components must display the insignia of the approving agency.

◆ Water supply lines must be sized according to the number of fixtures to assure an adequate flow rate. Sanitizing instructions for periodic cleansing of the water system must be furnished with each vehicle.

◆ It must be possible to drain the water system by gravity with a valve, drain plug, or cap. (Drainage system requirements are intended primarily to eliminate the possibility of the entry of sewer gas into the interior atmosphere.)

♦ Water seal traps are specified in the drain line of each plumbing fixture except for approved toilets that have a mechanical seal.

♦ Drain outlets must be placed at specified locations, and each drain line must be vented to prevent the buildup of back pressure or vacuums that could overcome the water seal in the trap, or siphon off the water and defeat the purpose of the trap. Waste holding tanks must be vented to dissipate gas and odors and to enable complete, unimpeded discharge at sanitation stations.

♦ The manufacturer must test each vehicle's water supply and drainage systems to determine that it is leak-free.

Electrical Systems

While many of the requirements of the RV standard are based on the National Electrical Code governing safety principles in the home, there are some differences:

♦ All electric fixtures, appliances, equipment, and materials used in or connected to the 120-volt electric systems must carry the approval and listing of a nationally recognized testing agency such as Underwriters' Laboratory.

♦ The exterior power supply cord must be factory installed or supplied to insure that it has sufficient capacity to carry current for the RV's system.

♦ The distribution panel board must provide the equipment necessary to safely connect an outside source of power to the various branch circuits within the system. It must provide protection to circuits, appliances, and equipment by using fuses or circuit breakers to cut off power when current exceeds the circuit's capacity.

♦ The distribution panel board must provide for interconnecting an electrical grounding path from the external source of electricity to all metallic parts of the vehicle that may become energized and to all exposed metallic parts of the electric system. (Proper electrical grounding is essential as a final safeguard against electrical shock.)

♦ Receptacle outlets are required in all interior locations in sufficient quantity to handle normal needs without the use of extension cords or other multipliers. Those installed on exterior locations, in bathrooms, and within six feet of kitchen sinks require ground fault protection.

♦ Branch circuit specifications depend on the total number of lighting and receptacle outlets installed and on the total rating of the fixed appliances.

♦ The manufacturer must perform high-voltage tests on the completed electrical system to determine that it is adequately insulated and to avoid potential short circuits.

Liquid Propane Gas Systems

♦ Proper venting is required.

♦ LPG containers must be shown to withstand excessive pressure, and must be equipped with a safety relief valve designed to discharge gas whenever internal pressure becomes excessive because of extreme temperature, in conformity with American Society of Mechanical Engineers (ASME) or U.S. Department of Transportation (DOT) standards.

♦ Gas piping must be large enough to assure that gas appliances receive sufficient fuel to function properly.

♦ Unless protected by a metal conduit, gas tubing made of copper, steel, or brass cannot be installed in areas where it could be punctured by fasteners such as nails or screws.

♦ Pipe or tubing joints may not be installed in a concealed construction space inaccessible for leak testing or repair.

♦ Appliances must be certified by a nationally recognized testing lab such as the American Gas Association or Underwriters' Laboratories.

♦ Clearances between adjacent combustible surfaces and heat-producing appliances must be sufficient to prevent ignition.

♦ The manufacturer must test the complete piping system for leakage before and after appliances are connected.

♦ Except for gas ranges and ovens, all LPG appliances must be of the sealed combustion design to provide complete separation of the combustion chamber from the atmosphere of the vehicle. An LPG heater, for instance, must use only air outside the RV for combustion, and its exhaust gases must be vented to the outside.

INDEX

●●●●